THiS IS
BALANCED LITERACY

Grades K-6

THiS IS
BALANCED LITERACY

Grades K-6

Douglas Fisher
Nancy Frey
Nancy Akhavan

CORWIN
Fisher & Frey

FOR INFORMATION:

Corwin
A SAGE Company
2455 Teller Road
Thousand Oaks, California 91320
(800) 233–9936
www.corwin.com

SAGE Publications Ltd.
1 Oliver's Yard
55 City Road
London EC1Y 1SP
United Kingdom

SAGE Publications India Pvt. Ltd.
B 1/I 1 Mohan Cooperative
    Industrial Area
Mathura Road, New Delhi 110 044
India

SAGE Publications Asia-Pacific Pte. Ltd.
18 Cross Street #10–10/11/12
China Square Central
Singapore 048423

Director and Publisher, Corwin
    Classroom: Lisa Luedeke
Editorial Development
    Manager: Julie Nemer
Senior Editorial Assistant: Sharon Wu
Production Editor: Melanie Birdsall
Copy Editor: Cate Huisman
Typesetter: Integra
Proofreader: Theresa Kay
Indexer: Sheila Bodell
Cover Designer: Rose Storey
Interior Designer: Scott Van Atta
Marketing Manager: Deena Meyer

Printed in the United States of America

This book is printed on acid-free paper.

Library of Congress Cataloging-in-Publication Data

Names: Fisher, Douglas, author. | Frey, Nancy, author. | Akhavan, Nancy L., author.
Title: This is balanced literacy, grades k-6 / Douglas Fisher, Nancy Frey, Nancy Akhavan.
Description: Thousand Oaks, California : Corwin, A SAGE Company, [2020] | Includes bibliographical references and index.
Identifiers: LCCN 2019020774 | ISBN 9781544360942 (paperback)
Subjects: LCSH: Language arts (Elementary) | Literacy—Study and teaching (Elementary) | Reading—Phonetic method—Study and teaching (Elementary)
Classification: LCC LB1576 .F4465 2020 | DDC 372.6—dc23
LC record available at https://lccn.loc.gov/2019020774

19 20 21 22 23 10 9 8 7 6 5 4 3 2 1

CONTENTS

CHAPTER 1:
DEFINING BALANCE, FINDING BALANCE

CHAPTER 2:
WHOLE-CLASS READING INSTRUCTION: HIGH-LEVEL SUPPORT FOR LEARNING

CHAPTER 3:
WHOLE-CLASS WRITING INSTRUCTION: HIGH-LEVEL SUPPORT FOR LEARNING

CHAPTER 4:
COLLABORATIVE READING AND WRITING: LEARNING IN THE COMPANY OF PEERS

CHAPTER 5:
SMALL-GROUP READING INSTRUCTION: TARGETED SUPPORT THROUGH GUIDED LEARNING

CHAPTER 6:
SMALL-GROUP WRITING INSTRUCTION: TARGETED SUPPORT THROUGH GUIDED LEARNING

CHAPTER 7:
INDEPENDENT READING: PRACTICING, APPLYING, AND EXTENDING LEARNING

CHAPTER 8:
INDEPENDENT WRITING INSTRUCTION: PRACTICING, APPLYING, AND EXTENDING LEARNING

CHAPTER 9:
ASSESSMENT AND INTERVENTION IN THE BALANCED LITERACY CLASSROOM: NOTICING AND RESPONDING TO STUDENTS' NEEDS

Visit the companion website at
resources.corwin.com/thisisbalancedliteracy
to access videos and downloadable resources.

ACKNOWLEDGMENTS

Corwin gratefully acknowledges the contributions of the following reviewers:

Jane Bean-Folkes
Marist College
Poughkeepsie, NY

Melissa Black
Instruction and Culture Director
Harlem Village Academy's Progressive Education Institute
Washington, DC

Wiley Blevins
Author and Educational Consultant
New York, NY

Kate Ferguson
Resident Teacher Program Director
Hillbrook School
Los Gatos, CA

Lura A. Hanks
Supervisor for English Language Arts and Social Studies
Washington County Public Schools
Hagerstown, MD

Melanie Spence
Assistant Principal, Curriculum Coordinator, Educational Consultant
Sloan-Hendrix School District
Imboden, AR

Judy Wallis
Literacy Consultant and Author
Sugar Land, TX

LIST OF VIDEOS

Note From the Publisher: The authors have provided video and web content throughout the book that is available to you through QR (quick response) codes. To read a QR code, you must have a smartphone or tablet with a camera. We recommend that you download a QR code reader app that is made specifically for your phone or tablet brand.

Videos may also be accessed at **resources.corwin.com/thisisbalancedliteracy**

LETTER FROM THE AUTHORS

DEAR READER,

Imagine implementing literacy instruction in your classroom that is based on research and aligned to essential elements like universal design for learning (UDL), response to intervention (RTI), differentiation, and an increase in the use of devices to engage and excite learners. Your path to implementing literacy in this way is inside this book. We have written about balanced literacy because we believe it is the best way to teach reading and writing in grades K through 6. However, we have written about it in a way that doesn't ask you to depend on a program to implement balanced literacy. This book provides the plan. You can rely on your own intuition, collaboration with peers, and implementation of research-based strategies to implement high-quality instruction.

The components of balanced literacy that we lay out in this book—including the balance of skills and knowledge in phonics with meaning making, the balance of reading and writing with small- and whole-group instruction, and the balance of direct instruction with dialogic instruction—can be your guide to implementing a strong, successful balanced literacy program. This book will provide you the tools you need, including videos that show strategies in action in the classroom.

Universal design for learning (UDL) is an underlying component of the instructional practices we discuss. We focus on providing all students ways of succeeding that meet their needs, based on how they learn. This is why we show how to balance direct and dialogic instruction with small- and whole-group instruction. In a balanced literacy classroom, students will have a variety of ways of showing what they know. Through balance, we don't expect students to learn in the same ways, and we don't expect them to be successful in the same ways. By understanding our students' needs we—all of us—can appropriately plan lessons that highlight multiple ways of knowing.

As we have worked with districts nationally and internationally, we have been asked about how best to teach reading. Is it phonics or comprehension that matters more? We believe that it is the balance of instruction in systematic phonics instruction with high-quality, engaging comprehension instruction that grows readers who can make meaning of and bring meaning to text. Small-group instruction is another important component of balanced literacy. Through small-group instruction, we are able to teach students based on their needs, and through their interests in subject matter, to engage and ignite their ability and desire to read. This is one way to respond to their needs through response to intervention (RTI). We intervene during small-group reading and writing instruction.

Essentially, RTI and UDL are about differentiating instruction so that all students learn to their maximum potential. Coherent instruction, which aligns teaching to students' needs based on grade-level expectations, doesn't focus on teaching to cover material, but instead on teaching from a well-designed instructional plan that considers the instructional needs of all students through different modalities. The learning activities, instructional materials, and grouping are designed and configured to the learning needs of the students so that all students have access to content and are able to learn to their maximum potential. This is differentiated instruction.

While we may not provide every activity describing how students could be using a device to learn, we are intentional in our thinking about technology. We see technology as a tool. Implementing the use of devices and applications in your room should not simply be about student engagement. The use of technology needs to answer the question: Which tool is right for this learning situation? Students can use devices in any of the balanced literacy components and activities in this book. They can read using print or virtual text, they can write in journals or in a Google Doc. What matters is how the technology will increase their learning and be the best tool for the lesson. All of us work with teachers who have different levels of technology implemented in their classrooms; some are one-to-one with devices; others only have a few devices available. You can implement balanced literacy with technology; just focus on it as a tool, not the answer to your students' learning needs.

Our hope is that this book provides you with a road map for implementing balanced literacy or deepening the implementation of your current literacy approach. We believe balanced literacy is *the* best way students can grow as readers and writers. We also believe that through implementation and collaboration with peers you can grow as a reading and writing teacher.

Thank you for your efforts to improve students' literacy lives.

—DOUG, NANCY, AND NANCY

DEFINING BALANCE, FINDING BALANCE

CHAPTER 1

Jim West/PhotoEdit

Derek reads really well. Jovanni does not. And they are in the same first-grade classroom, along with 22 other students whose reading proficiencies vary widely. Luckily for them, their teacher Marla Christensen understands and implements a balanced literacy approach in her classroom. Her students are flexibly grouped and regrouped often, and their lessons focus on foundational skills as well as meaning making from authentic texts. She collects evidence of students' progress and makes decisions based on the data. There are whole-class shared reading and writing lessons as well as small-group, needs-based lessons. Sometimes Ms. Christensen uses a direct or deliberate instructional approach, and other times she uses a dialogic approach, depending on her students' needs. Students read and write narrative and expository texts and complete a range of tasks independently as they develop their literacy skills.

Unfortunately, this is not always the case. In fact, some students are lucky that their teachers understand balanced literacy instruction, and some are not so lucky. In some classes, students experience *hour after hour of whole-class instruction. In other classes, students hear only stories and do not have access to informational texts. In other classes, students are expected to break the code and develop an understanding of sound-symbol correspondence on their own. And in other cases, reading dominates classroom instruction, and students have few opportunities to develop as writers. These are classes that are out of balance and will probably not ensure that all students learn to read and write more or better.*

There are several factors that contribute to a balanced literacy approach. What factors come to mind when you hear the term *balanced literacy*? The term was first introduced by the California Department of Education in an attempt to end the reading wars (Honig, 1996). During the 1980s and early 1990s, there were significant disagreements about the best way to teach students to read. Some argued for a whole-language approach, while others advocated for a phonics-based approach. Whole-language advocates believe that children should select their own reading matter and that instruction should emphasize the use and recognition of words in everyday contexts. This perspective is very different from that of those who advocated for a phonics-based approach, which "breaks written language down into small and simple components. It is taught by having children use letter sounds and letter symbols. Using this technique, children identify letters with certain sounds and piece them back together—a process is called decoding" (www.ectutoring.com). Balanced literacy was an attempt to integrate these two approaches.

resources.corwin.com/
thisisbalancedliteracy

To read a QR code, you must have a smartphone or tablet with a camera. We recommend that you download a QR code reader app that is made specifically for your phone or tablet brand.

Video 1
What Is
Balanced Literacy?

Since the 1990s, the definition of balanced literacy has evolved, and there are many variations. Therefore, this book is not about the reading wars or advocating one approach over another. Instead, it focuses on the current knowledge about teaching students in kindergarten through grade 6 to read and write well. As such, there are several factors you need to consider for your instruction to be considered balanced. In the next section, we will focus on each of these considerations. Then you will have a quick review of the instructional basis for balanced literacy: the gradual release of responsibility (GRR) framework. To our thinking, balanced literacy learning requires maintaining equilibrium across the language arts domains (reading, writing, speaking, listening, and viewing), ensuring students have access to instruction in foundational skills (phonemic awareness, phonics, fluency) and meaning making (vocabulary and comprehension), and varying instructional delivery modes (direct, dialogic, and independent).

FACTORS TO CONSIDER IN A BALANCED LITERACY APPROACH

As we have noted, the original notion of balanced literacy was to ensure that students received instruction in phonics (and other foundational skills) while still providing access to meaning-making opportunities in authentic texts (texts that are not explicitly written for teaching some aspect of language, as would be the case in decodable texts or vocabulary-controlled texts). That remains an important consideration in balanced literacy today. Students should be taught the foundational skills of oral language, phonemic awareness, and phonics and fluency while also engaging in meaning making in texts as they develop vocabulary knowledge and comprehension skills. The purpose of phonics instruction is to teach children sound-spelling relationships and how to use those relationships to read words. Phonics instruction should be explicit and systematic. Systematic and early instruction in phonics leads to better reading. This is because phonics knowledge facilitates the development of word recognition. Word recognition increases fluency. Reading fluency influences reading comprehension, since children are not struggling with decoding and are able to devote their full attention to making meaning from text. The characteristics of systemic instruction in phonics are found in Figure 1.1.

The balanced literacy approach strives to provide children with systematic instruction in the graphophonic elements of written language, embedded within thematic units that build student knowledge and capitalize on their interests using both authentic and engineered texts. But that's not all it does. There are several other considerations that you can use to create a healthy, balanced literacy classroom. Figure 1.2 contains a list of considerations for balanced literacy.

Narrative and Informational Texts

In the past, it was common for students in elementary school classrooms to read mostly narratives. You likely remember that stories made up the bulk of the reading selections you experienced. And fiction was probably the dominant text type your teachers used to teach you to read. In 2000, Duke reported that first graders averaged 3.6 minutes per day with

▼ FIGURE 1.1 CHARACTERISTICS OF EXPLICIT AND SYSTEMATIC PHONICS INSTRUCTION

Explicit	Systematic

• Children are taught letter-sound relationships and build toward whole words.
 	
• Children are asked to produce sounds of letters that appear in isolation.
 	
• Children blend isolated sounds.
 	
• Children receive explicit instruction in the sound structure of oral language.
 	
• Instruction is direct and involves learner practice.
 	
• Practice materials are crafted to emphasize specific phonics concepts.
 	
• Instruction is in letter-sound relationships, and practice is in decodable text.
	• Phonics is usually taught
	
	   ○ before sight words.
	
	   ○ separately from connected reading.
	
	• Emphasis is on teaching sound values of letters.
	
	• Usually a synthetic approach is taken.
	
	• Instruction is sequenced and code driven.

Source: Mesmer, H. A. E., & Griffith, P. L. (2005). Everybody's selling it—But just what is explicit, systematic phonics instruction? *The Reading Teacher, 59,* 366–376.

informational text. Her study shined a light on the fact that students rarely had access to informational or expository texts, despite the fact that they would be required to gain a lot of information from these types of texts in middle and high school, not to mention college and careers. Further, evidence at the time was suggesting that students enjoy reading nonfiction as they explore the biological, physical, and social world around them (Leal & Moss, 1999).

As a result, one consideration in balancing literacy instruction is the recognition that students need access to both narrative and expository or informational texts.

▼ FIGURE 1.2 CONSIDERATIONS FOR BALANCED LITERACY

Narrative Texts _____	Informational Texts
Reading and Listening _____	Writing and Speaking
Skills _____	Knowledge
Direct Instruction _____	Indirect and Dialogic Instruction
Whole-Class Teaching _____	Small-Group Teaching

We know lots of adults who really love to read about the physical, biological, and social world. You may be one of those readers. Most current state standards acknowledge this need, and they include expectations that students read a variety of text types and learn text structures and common features of different genres. In planning instruction for a balanced literacy classroom, you likely design or implement units of study that allow students to access a wide variety of genres. In some cases, these units of study focus on a specific type of text, as would be the case in an investigation of opinion writing. In such a unit, your students read a number of informational texts that include opinions with reasons for those opinions and then write their own opinion piece based on research and investigation that they have done. In other cases, the unit of study focuses on a topic, theme, or question, and students read across genres to develop their understanding. For example, while learning about westward expansion, your students might read informational texts including primary source documents, personal narratives, and fiction about the time period. In this unit, students might write a report of information using some of the texts as well as a poem about the perspective of one person from the time period.

Cleve Bryant/PhotoEdit

Students need access to both narrative and informational texts.

Reading, Listening, Writing, and Speaking

Did you notice that students were expected to read, listen, write, *and* speak in the scenarios described above? This is important when it comes to balanced literacy instruction. Having said that, we recognize the testing pressure that you experience and thus the desire to spend more time on things that are assessed, specifically reading. However, we are reminded of a saying that we believe is true: Every writer can read, but not every reader can write. Think about that for a minute. You can read everything that you write. There is power in writing, not only in terms of reading, but in being able to share (and clarify) one's thinking and potentially impact the thinking of others.

In their meta-analysis, Graham et al. (2018) identified 38 studies that tested balance in terms of reading and writing and noted statistically significant results in both reading and writing achievement when the two were balanced. As they note, reading instruction can facilitate writing growth, and writing instruction can promote reading development. Some have argued that reading and writing are different sides of the same coin, meaning that you can meet the goal of literacy by focusing on both reading and writing, each building the other as the student progresses (Graham & Hebert, 2010).

In balanced literacy classrooms, we teach students to write and actually have them write every day.

Thus, in the balanced literacy classroom, we do not spend 80% or more of our instructional minutes on reading with little attention to writing. In balanced literacy classrooms, we teach students to write and actually have them write every day. They write in response to what they are reading, and they write about things that matter to them. Sometimes they write short pieces, and other times they write long pieces. We use students' writing as a source of information to plan future instruction, and students learn to respond to each other's writing.

In addition, speaking and listening are critical in the balanced literacy classroom. Students should be producing language—speaking and writing—on a regular and systematic basis. They should also be receiving language—reading and listening—daily. All four of these are important processes that combine to ensure that students progress in their literacy achievement.

Skills and Knowledge

To read and write well, students have to develop a number of skills and strategies. To our thinking, strategies are processes that readers and writers deploy with conscious awareness, whereas skills have become automatic (Fisher & Frey, 2008b). As strategies become skills, working memory is freed up to focus on other things. For example, as students' decoding and sight word recognition becomes increasingly automatic, they can focus working memory on comprehension such as predicting, summarizing, or inferring. We have argued that our goal is not to simply produce strategic readers and writers, but rather skilled readers and writers who can use what they have learned automatically, without consciously focusing on the strategies. In other words, we want to develop habits with students that they can use in a wide variety of settings.

In thinking about skills and strategies, it is useful to consider the types of skills and strategies that students need to read and write well. There are decoding and fluency skills that top out. Researchers call these the *constrained skills,* because once they have been mastered, there is no room for additional growth (Paris, 2005). Once a student knows all of the letters in the alphabet, the skill has been mastered. There are also *unconstrained skills* that continue to develop across our lifetimes, namely vocabulary and comprehension. Your vocabulary is stronger today than it was a few years ago. And your ability to make inferences or support a claim also grows and develops over time. Figure 1.3 includes a list of constrained and unconstrained skills.

▼ FIGURE 1.3 CONSTRAINED AND UNCONSTRAINED SKILLS

Constrained Skills	Unconstrained Skills
Phonemic Awareness	Vocabulary
Phonics	Comprehension
Reading Fluency	Writing Proficiency
Writing Fluency	Oral Language
Handwriting	

Both constrained and unconstrained skills are important for learning to read and write. But they are not the only focus of balanced literacy instruction. Knowledge is also important. This relates to our earlier point about reading and writing informational texts, but it's worth noting more specifically. The goal of balanced literacy instruction is to build both skills and knowledge. Accordingly, lessons should include a focus on the knowledge that students gain from the experience. And knowledge can be gained from both informational and narrative texts. Narrative texts help our students think about characters' actions and behavior. These texts often contain social and emotional learning opportunities as well. We have already discussed the value of informational texts in developing our students' knowledge base. But it is worth noting that background knowledge is among the greatest predictors of comprehension, and we have known this for several decades (e.g., Langer & Nicolich, 1981). Unfortunately, building conceptual and content knowledge is not typically seen as a valued area for literacy efforts and may even be declining in importance as school systems focus on testable skills (Duke & Block, 2012). To achieve balance, we need to consider the ways in which they are building and activating students' background knowledge. And your own experience has probably taught you what researchers have documented, namely that background knowledge is the best predictor of comprehension.

We say this because we believe that learning is cyclical. This cycle has a number of parts, as noted in Figure 1.4. You'll probably be able to remember learning something and the impact each part had on your learning. Engaging in this cycle of learning builds and modifies students' schema (Rumelhart, 1980). Although you and your students can start anywhere in the cycle, it is important to note the role of knowledge. As depicted in the figure, knowledge generates interest. In other words, what students know helps them figure out what they want to know. Interest, in turn, directs attention. We don't know of a teacher who wouldn't like his or her students to pay attention better. Wouldn't you? Attention, then, selects information worthy of that attention. And that information creates understanding, given the right conditions, which then modifies what students already know. For this cycle to work in the balanced literacy classroom, we have to focus on both skills and knowledge, because knowledge plays a vital role in students' learning.

▼ FIGURE 1.4 THE LEARNING CYCLE

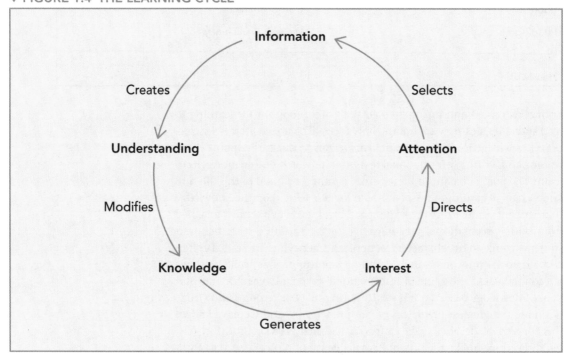

Direct and Dialogic Instruction

One of the long-standing debates in education centers on the role of direct instruction and other forms of learning. There are extremes on both sides of the debate, with some arguing that direct, explicit instruction is the answer to the achievement problems some students and schools experience. Others argue that learning should be fully experiential, constructivist, and inquiry driven. In both cases, students suffer. Balanced literacy instruction takes into account student needs and the type of learning that students need to accomplish. We recognize that some things can be learned quickly through direct instruction, and other things need more interactive, or dialogic, approaches. Some content is best developed as students struggle through ideas and concepts, whereas other information is best explained directly. For example, we see no reason why students would need to figure out the name of the letter *s* or the sounds that it makes in English. It's more efficient to use direct instruction. We also recognize that students need practice using the letter *s* and recognizing the letter in words, which will require other forms of instruction. At the same time, telling students the theme of a text robs them of the thinking process that they need to develop.

Some content is best developed as students struggle through ideas and concepts, whereas other information is best explained directly.

Direct Instruction

Complicating this area of balance is the lack of understanding about direct instruction. Unfortunately, many teachers and parents think that direct instruction is telling students specific information over and over (and that it's really boring). There are really three main components to the design and delivery of direct instruction (Marchand-Martella, Slocum, & Martella, 2004):

a. **Program design.** Skills are sequenced, and there is a focus on clear communication and evidence-based instructional formats.

b. **Organization of instruction.** Direct instruction requires flexible grouping of students, dedicated instructional time, and continuous assessment.

c. **Teacher-student interactions.** Teacher-student interactions are characterized by active student participation, unison responding, signals that cue a response, rapid pacing, teaching to mastery, error correction, and practice.

In terms of planning lessons, direct instruction typically includes these aspects:

- A clear objective
- A plan or script that includes modeling
- Student response opportunities
- Examples and guided practice
- Assessment of the student learning or performance

We explore direct, explicit instruction more fully in later chapters of this book, but suffice to say that this is more complex than some people believe. Direct instruction works especially well on constrained skills, such as phonemic awareness, phonics, and fluency. But students also need to practice those skills with others and on their own, away from their teacher. This book is not limited to direct instruction, but it recognizes the value of balancing direct and indirect as well as dialogic forms of learning.

Dialogic Instruction

Dialogic instruction requires that humans interact with others. This can be accomplished through teacher-led or peer-led discussions. Simply said, some of the learning students do in a balanced literacy classroom is better accomplished through dialogic instruction. As Britton noted, "Reading and writing float on a sea of talk" (1983, p. 11). If that is true, and we believe it is, then students need to be building their speaking and listening skills so that their reading and writing skills can also improve. We devote a chapter of this book to dialogic instruction. In general, we implement the following as part of dialogic learning:

- Students work in small groups.

- Complex texts or tasks are the focus.

- Students talk and interact with one another using academic language.

- Individual accountability is part of the task.

As with all of the other areas of balanced literacy, we have to be careful not to let one type of instruction dominate the other. But in the case of direct and dialogic instruction, we are not advocating a 50/50 split in terms of instructional minutes. We do advocate that text selections be fairly evenly balanced and that time devoted to reading and writing be generally balanced (maybe 60% reading and 40% writing), but this is not the case for direct and dialogic instruction. In part, this is because students also need time to complete tasks independently. But it's also the case that teacher-led dialogic lessons, which include teacher modeling, shared readings, and close readings, are powerful ways to develop student thinking. It is hard to recommend a specific amount of time for direct instruction, as it will vary based on the content to be learned, but generally it is used during less than 25% of the instructional minutes. Having said that, when direct instruction is used well, students learn.

Whole Class and Small Group

The last area for consideration in balanced literacy instruction is grouping. In the balanced literacy classroom, students do not experience hour after hour of whole class instruction. Instead, they are grouped and regrouped for different learning experiences. That is not to say that whole-group instruction is banned. When using a balanced literacy approach, we use whole-class instruction strategically to address needs that students have in common. We also use small-group instruction to meet the needs of students who have similar learning needs, needs that often are not shared with the whole class. Importantly, small-group, needs-based instruction focuses on students' next steps for learning and is not limited to remediation or used solely for students who perform below grade level. Students who read really well also need small-group instruction to accelerate their thinking and development.

Bob Daemmrich/PhotoEdit

Small-group, needs-based instruction focuses on students' next steps for learning.

Whole-class instruction can be used to introduce new content or skills for students, for setting the daily learning expectations, or for having a shared experience that students will draw on during other parts of the day. During whole-class instruction, you can read aloud and write aloud for students, explaining your thinking as you do so. You can also engage in shared reading or shared writing lessons with the whole class, or engage the class in a close reading experience. In these instructional arrangements, the selected text is at least grade level and requires some level of scaffolding. In addition, you can use direct instruction with the whole class. Of course, direct instruction and modeling can be done with small groups as well. But there is an economy of scale that saves instructional time when some of the learning is conducted with the whole class, especially when the teacher has compelling evidence that the majority of students have a shared need.

Most current definitions of balanced literacy center on the instructional grouping arrangements and include terms such as *write aloud, guided reading, independent writing,* and *shared reading,* to name a few. We believe that these are important considerations in balancing literacy, but not the only ones. To truly achieve balance, we believe that all of the components discussed in this chapter are important. At the same time, we acknowledge your need to plan lessons that ensure students' learning. The structure of this book centers on instructional grouping and includes appropriate instructional routines, mixing both direct and dialogic approaches. The lessons and chapters include informational and narrative texts used in both reading and writing as well as the intentional instruction of foundational skills. Before we delve into those areas, let's explore the foundation of a balanced literacy approach, which is the gradual release of responsibility.

GRADUALLY RELEASING RESPONSIBILITY HELPS BALANCE TEACHING AND LEARNING

First proposed by Pearson and Gallagher (1983), the GRR model of instruction suggests that the cognitive load should shift purposefully from teacher-as-model, to joint responsibility, to independent practice and application by the learner. This framework suggests that we intentionally and purposefully move from assuming "all the responsibility for performing a task . . . to a situation in which the students assume all of the responsibility" (Duke & Pearson, 2002, p. 211). As Graves and Fitzgerald (2003) note,

> Effective instruction often follows a progression in which teachers gradually do less of the work and students gradually assume increased responsibility for their learning. It is through this process of gradually assuming more and more responsibility for their learning that students become competent, independent learners. (p. 98)

Fisher and Frey (2008a, 2014a) published an interpretation of the GRR model that includes four major phases (see Figure 1.5). Importantly, they are not presented in a prescriptive order, and assessment information drives the decisions that teachers make as they move from one phase to another. The model is not linear and does not require us to start at any one place. There are excellent lessons that begin with an independent learning task, such as responding to a prompt in a journal writing. Other excellent lessons might begin with a collaborative task in

The gradual release of responsibility framework suggests that the cognitive load should shift purposefully from teacher-as-model, to joint responsibility, to independent practice and application by the learner.

which students discuss a shared experience before individually writing about it. Rather, these four phases can be combined, and we can start anywhere. Additionally, we can cycle through these phases several times in a given lesson. For example, you may model a cognitive strategy and then invite students to try it, either collaboratively or independently. As you observe students, you may note patterns of error and then bring the students back together as a whole class and model again.

▼ FIGURE 1.5 GRADUAL RELEASE OF RESPONSIBILITY

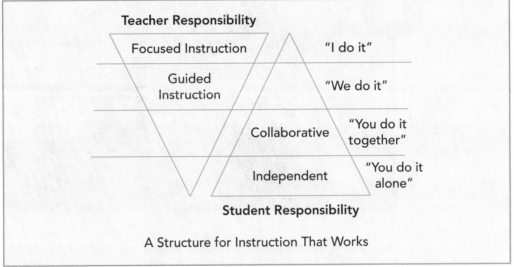

Source: Fisher, D., & Frey, N. (2014a). *Better learning through structured teaching: A framework for the gradual release of responsibility* (2nd ed.). Alexandria, VA: ASCD.

Of course, all learning should be based on clear learning intentions and success criteria. Regardless of whether the lesson is given to a whole class or small group, students should be informed about the purpose of the learning and what success looks like. We identify specific content goals based on grade-level standards and communicate the expected learning outcomes to students. Also, given the number of English language learners and standard English learners, we analyze the content to identify an appropriate language learning expectation, and communicate that to students as well. Further, we identify the social aspects of learning and communicate those expectations to students. For more information about this aspect of learning, see Fisher, Frey, Amador, and Assof (2018). The instructional components we look for in a lesson designed around the GRR framework include the following:

- **Focused instruction (modeling):** Students are provided an example of the thinking required to complete each task. We, not students, share our thinking while reading, so that students get a glimpse inside the minds of experts. As Duffy (2014) points out, "The only way to model thinking is to talk about how to do it. That is, we provide a verbal description of the thinking one does or, more accurately, an *approximation* of the thinking involved" (p. 11). We will explore modeling in more detail in Chapters 2 and 3.

resources.corwin.com/
thisisbalancedliteracy

Video 2
Learning Intentions

- **Guided instruction:** Through the strategic use of prompts, cues, and questions, we transfer some of the responsibility for learning to students. Typically, this occurs in needs-based groups of three to six students who have been purposefully selected based on formative assessment data (Avalos, Plasencia, Chavez, & Rascón, 2007/2008). Guided instruction can also occur with the whole class or with individual students as we address errors without telling students the answers. In this book, we focus on small-group, needs-based instruction in Chapters 5 and 6.

- **Collaborative learning:** Students complete collaborative learning activities designed to provide them opportunities to use language and explore the content. The tasks must be structured to build on students' knowledge and be differentiated so as to not cause stress for students who currently perform below grade level (Matthews & Kesner, 2003). As we will see in Chapter 4, some tasks include individual accountability as part of the group interaction (Johnson, Johnson, & Holubec, 2008), which allows us to check for understanding.

- **Independent learning:** As part of the gradual release of responsibility, students must apply what they have learned, especially in new situations or contexts (Harvey & Chickie-Wolf, 2007). Although independent learning is the goal of education, students are often assigned independent tasks that they do not yet have the skills to complete alone. Some tasks, such as independent reading, writing prompts, and journaling, can be completed in the classroom. Others, especially spiral review tasks, can be completed outside of the school day, either in an afterschool program or at home. Chapters 7 and 8 focus on independent learning in reading and writing.

The GRR framework can be used for a variety of learning outcomes and class grouping structures. For example, teachers can model during whole-class instruction, small-group instruction, or for an individual student. To our thinking, the implementation of balanced literacy allows for the implementation of the GRR framework. In other words, the evidence base we draw on for recommending balanced literacy builds on the work that has been done for several decades on the gradual release of responsibility.

CONCLUSION

Simply said, elementary students learn to read and write best when we balance literacy instruction. Students need high-quality learning experiences that are differentiated. When we think of differentiation, we are reminded that it is more than the product or the materials. We have to differentiate the instructional supports provided for students. We believe that this can occur in efficient and effective ways during balanced literacy instruction, especially during small-group, needs-based learning.

Balance requires that we focus on instructional materials, using both informational and narrative texts. And we need to consider the best uses of direct instruction and how to ensure that students also have opportunities for dialogic instruction. Further, we have to consider the grouping patterns that will work best to accomplish our learning aims, and we need to remember that those learning aims include a wide range of skills and knowledge, including literacy processes such as oral language, phonemic awareness, phonics, fluency, vocabulary, comprehension, and writing. Balance is our goal, and the remainder of this book provides evidence-based approaches to ensure that the goal is realized.

CHAPTER 2

WHOLE-CLASS READING INSTRUCTION

HIGH-LEVEL SUPPORT FOR LEARNING

Bob Daemmrich/PhotoEdit

The first graders in Deborah Matlovsky's class hurry to the rug, because their teacher is about to begin her interactive read-aloud. Some of the students had been working collaboratively on word study, while others had been working with Ms. Matlovsky in a small group focused on blending sounds. As they take their seats on the rug, Ms. Matlovsky reminds her students that they have been looking for details in texts during the read-alouds this week. She points to several language charts that document the details from various texts that the students have explored as part of this unit and says, "We'll create another

language chart today, after we finish our first reading of this book the librarian just gave to me. As I read it, think about the important details that help us understand the story. Are you ready?" In unison, the students respond "Yes!" Ms. Matlovsky knows that the first read of a new text is a gift that allows students to enjoy, wonder about, or question the text. Later reads focus on skills.

Ms. Matlovsky begins her read-aloud of How to Babysit a Grandpa *(Reagan, 2012). She changes her voice when the text includes dialogue and pauses periodically to share some of her thinking. For example, several pages in, Grandpa is going for a walk. The text says, "If there's a puddle or sprinkler, show him what to do" (n.p.), and Ms. Matlovsky says, "I'm going to have to take a look at the picture for this one, because the text isn't telling me what to do when you take your grandpa out and there is a puddle or sprinkler. Oh, I see. You jump in it! I'm looking at Grandpa's face, and it really does look like a lot of fun. The text also says to 'Look for lizards.' Turn to your partner and talk about what you see in the illustrations about lizards." The students turn quickly to* talk about the lizard biting Grandpa's finger. Melissa says, "I don't think Grandpa likes that one very much. He put his foot up, and his face looks like he is hurt."

Ms. Matlovsky brings the students back together and says, "These are very funny and interesting details, but I don't think that they are the key details that we're looking for. When I think about this page, I think that the key detail is that you have to have fun together when you babysit a grandpa."

When Ms. Matlovsky finishes the first read through the text, she invites students to talk with a partner about an important detail in the story. She has arranged her classroom such that students are seated next to their discussion partner for the month. As she says, "Remember, we're looking for details that are really important for us to understand the text. There are a lot of funny details in this text, but they aren't critical to our understanding of the story. Talk with your partner about the important details, and then we'll record them on our chart." The students talk for several minutes, and each pair decides on one important detail and a backup, just in case another pair shares that detail first. Some of the details include the following:

- Parents always come back.

- You have to clean up before parents come home.

- Grandpas like to have fun.

- You have to make sure that grandpas eat, walk, and nap.

Once they have completed their language chart focused on details, with Ms. Matlovsky recording all of the ideas on chart paper, the students are ready for a second reading of the book. On the second read, the students identify sight words. At this point in the year, their class word wall has over 100 sight words on it. Ms. Matlovsky projects each page using her document camera, and students come to the screen with a fly swatter with the middle cut out of it. They use the flyswatter to frame in specific sight words, such as when, he, for, him, home, I, the, fun, and as. Ms. Matlovsky also shows them the spelling of the word grandpa (and grandfather) and adds this word to a separate list of content words for the book they are reading. Students will add the content words to their own writing journals, so they can use them in their independent writing.

Ms. Matlovsky then invites students to write about their own grandparents, or another relative or care-taker, using three sentence frames:

- The first thing I would do with my _____ is _____.

- The next thing I would do is _____.

- The third thing I would do with my _____ is _____.

This whole-class experience focused on a specific standard—locating key details—and provided students practice with word recognition. Whole-class instruction is useful for developing skills and knowledge that everyone needs. The key is to keep whole-class instruction at grade level, so that students can apprentice into the type of knowledge and thinking that is appropriate for their age. Given that her young students would not be able to read the story independently, Ms. Matlovsky did not ask her students to read the text on their own. Instead, she read it to them and focused on their understanding of details and word identification. At other times during the literacy block, students are reading on their own, with their partners, and with targeted support from the teacher.

There are several appropriate instructional routines that are useful during whole-class reading instruction. In this chapter, we focus on the following:

- Interactive read-alouds

- Shared readings

- Direct and deliberate instruction

- Close readings

Each of these approaches provides students with examples of the type of thinking that they will be expected to do as they progress in their learning. In addition, each of these approaches provides students with opportunities to practice during the whole-class experience. Ms. Matlovsky did not talk the entire time the students were together. Instead, she punctuated her whole-class instruction with opportunities for students to talk with peers so that they could try on the thinking she modeled for them.

In addition to comprehension of texts, elementary students must also learn the foundational skills of phonemic awareness, phonics, and fluency. These skills require direct instruction and teaching with intention. In this chapter, we will also discuss how these crucial elements of reading are evidenced in whole-group instruction. In this chapter, we will highlight the following:

- The importance of a scope and sequence for phonemic awareness and phonics instruction

- The use of word sorts, chants, and other letter- and word-level activities to build reading foundations

There is a range of experiences students should have with text. One type, called interactive read-alouds, is what Ms. Matlovsky used. This method focuses on the development of knowledge, listening, and thinking, while removing the barrier of decoding. This practice allows us to utilize texts that are higher in complexity than our students' nascent decoding skills might otherwise allow them to read independently. Other components of the balanced literacy focus are intentionally focused on decoding and other foundational skills. We will begin with a focus on text-driven whole-group reading instruction, before turning our attention back to foundational reading skills.

> In addition to comprehension of texts, elementary students must also learn the foundational skills of phonemic awareness, phonics, and fluency.

INTERACTIVE READ-ALOUDS

Reading aloud to students is a time-honored practice in elementary schools. Almost all the adults we encounter can tell us about a book their teacher read to them. Some of these adults are quite passionate about the experience. A certified public accountant who is a friend of ours recalled, "My teacher read to us every day after lunch. We could not wait to find out what would happen next in the books she selected. I had to buy my own copy of *Where the Red Fern Grows* (Rawls, 1961), and I still have it today. It was the first story about loss that I can ever remember. I think that the author totally touched the human spirit."

Easley (2004) documented the impact of teacher actions such as read-alouds on students' future reading. She recounts seeing students in bookstores buying copies of texts that she had read aloud to them. She believed that her students came to see her as a reader because of her read-alouds, and they, in turn, wanted to read more because of those experiences. And who among us would be disappointed if our students wanted to read more because of a practice we used in our classrooms?

Reading aloud to students is a time-honored practice in elementary schools. Almost all the adults we encounter can tell us about a book their teacher read to them.

Motivation for reading is one compelling reason to read aloud. But the power of read-alouds lies in the development of listening and thinking skills. Students come to understand text structures, vocabulary, concepts, and a host of other things about reading (Beck & McKeown, 2001; Justice, Sofka, & Sofka, 2010). Read-alouds also build background knowledge that students can mobilize when they read complex texts. As Eaton (1913) noted,

> This ability to read aloud so that literature shall be lifted from the dead page of print into complete expression should be far more than it is at present a prerequisite for the teaching of English. Teachers too often fail to appreciate that all real literature is addressed to the mind through the ear, not through the eye—word-symbols are merely convenient for transmission—and that since this is so, the ear must be appealed to if the student is to understand literature aright, or to appreciate at all the sensuous beauty which is latent in it. (p. 151)

Interactive read-alouds, however, differ in two important ways from the traditional read-aloud Easley (2004) and Eaton (1913) referenced. An interactive read-aloud in a balanced literacy classroom is notable for the teacher's use of questioning to engage students in learning.

Rather than students remaining silent throughout the reading, they are pressed to consider facets of reading, including word-level and text-level work. The second distinguishing feature of an interactive read-aloud is the teacher's strategic use of modeling and think-alouds to expose expert thinking.

resources.corwin.com/
thisisbalancedliteracy

Video 3
Interactive Read-Aloud

As you discuss implementation of balanced literacy in your school or district, pay close attention to how you frame your thinking, planning, and discussions. Are teachers reporting that they "do" read aloud, or that they "do" shared reading? Maybe they report that they "do" guided reading every day. We recommend shifting that language to the following:

- I use read aloud to . . .

- I use shared reading to . . .

- I use guided reading/practice to . . .

- I use independent practice to . . .

ACHIEVE THE LEARNING GOAL!

Of course, we can still read aloud to students after lunch as our teachers did for us. Elementary students will probably find that enjoyable, not to mention a calming way to settle back into the classroom. Having said that, balanced literacy requires that we teach skills and knowledge that are then connected with tasks they do with others and on their own. There are several considerations that are useful in planning interactive read-alouds (Fisher, Flood, Lapp, & Frey, 2004).

PLANNING SUCCESSFUL INTERACTIVE READ-ALOUDS

Quality interactive read-alouds don't just happen. They are marked by a high degree of teacher intention about the purpose of the lesson and the desired outcomes as well as a plan for how students will apply the skills and concepts taught in the lesson.

Select an Appropriate Text

The text selected for a read-aloud should have several characteristics:

- **The text should provide an opportunity for us to model some aspect of reading or thinking.** What we model should be based on students' needs. If students need to develop their word-solving skills, the selected text should provide us with many opportunities to solve unknown words. If students need to develop their ability to glean information from graphs, charts, and diagrams, the text we select must have those features.

  Ted Shepard chose to read-aloud a section from the informational text *Toys: Amazing Stories Behind Some Great Inventions* (Wulffson, 2000) to introduce a unit of study that focused on explaining how an author uses reasons and evidence to support particular points in a text. His fourth graders were confused about the difference between reasons and evidence. The author of this text presents interesting information and makes a series of claims with supporting evidence. As part of the read-aloud, Mr. Shepard paused to make note of reasons and evidence, recording information on a chart for later discussion with his students.

- **The text selected should be appropriate to the content being learned, students' social and emotional development, and students' interests.** Shannon Palmer's third-grade class was dealing with bullying on the playground. She read aloud *Enemy Pie* (Munson, 2000) as the students listened intently. They asked questions about some of the words and shared stories about the problems they had had with peers in the past and how they planned to solve those problems. In this case, the read-aloud was connected with the writing students would do later that day.

- **The text should be a strong piece of literature that students may use as a mentor text when they write.** When students are exposed to a wide variety of writers and explore the ways that texts work, they begin to internalize writing structures and tools, thus improving their own writing. Use award-winning books such as Newbery or Caldecott winners, as well as those singled out by associations for their quality (e.g., the International Literacy Association's Teachers' Choice Awards, National Book Award).

Have a Clear Purpose

A second area of consideration for quality interactive read-alouds is establishing a clear purpose for the book and lesson. As we noted before, read-alouds during the literacy block are not only for pleasure; they are designed to develop students' skills and knowledge. Some lessons are designed to build students' foundational skills, and the students should know that. Others are designed to build comprehension skills, and still others focus on specific standards. For example, Will Corley read aloud a chapter of *Charlie and the Chocolate Factory* (Dahl, 1964) as his third-grade students engaged in a character analysis. Mr. Corley had different purposes for different chapters of the book, including character development, vocabulary, dialogue, and figurative language.

Preview and Practice for a Fluent Reading Experience

This should go without saying, but we're going to say it anyway. If at all possible, review and practice the selection before reading it to students. They deserve to hear a fluent reader sharing the text. Of course, we all make some errors as we read aloud. We're not looking for perfection. But previewing and practicing allows you to pause effectively and add emphasis and inflections, which are often neglected aspects of fluency instruction. We do not read aloud to show students how fast we read but rather that reading has a cadence, and there are times when we slow down, speed up, linger on a word, change our voice, and so on. Previewing the text in advance also allows you to identify stopping points to allow students opportunities for questioning. If you haven't been able to preview or practice the text, when you make errors or have to clarify your thinking, make that visible to students. But if this becomes regular practice, your students will know! And you are at risk of revealing to students that you were not fully prepared for the lesson, and some students may miss the point of the experience.

We do not read aloud to show students how fast we read but rather that reading has a cadence, and there are times when we slow down, speed up, linger on a word, change our voice, and so on.

When Ann Cole read *Sarah, Plain and Tall* (MacLachlan, 1985) to her fifth-grade students, she identified places to stop by putting sticky notes on some pages and writing her thoughts on them. She knew exactly what she would say at each place she planned to pause. Her students were reading historical narratives related to westward expansion and life in America at the time. She selected this text as an example of historical fiction and noted information from the text that she would later attempt to verify. Ms. Cole expected her students to do the same. In addition, she selected this text to highlight written dialogue, which her students would be producing during one of their independent tasks.

resources.corwin.com/
thisisbalancedliteracy

Video 4
Previewing
Narrative Text

Use Animation and Expression

In addition to fluent reading, which requires that we preview and practice the text, effective read-alouds require that we be animated and expressive. Our students should track us with their eyes as we read the text. If we move around the room while reading, our students should follow us with their eyes because they are so engrossed in what they are hearing.

Ms. Matlovsky, from the opening scenario, changed her voice for the dialogue. In addition, we can change our voices to denote the emotions of different characters and various moods the author suggests. Further, we can use movement, hand gestures, and facial expressions to build comprehension.

Importantly, it's not just narrative texts that should be read with animation and expression. Informational texts deserve this level of attention as well. And younger and older students appreciate when we demonstrate passion while reading. Barbara Flynn read the book *What's the Weather* (Scholastic, 2010) to her kindergarten students. When she came to the words *splish* and *splash,* she changed her voice. She then thought aloud about using the images in the book to predict the type of weather, saying, for example, "I see a raincoat on this boy and someone splashing in the water. I think the weather is rainy [adding emphasis to the word *rainy*]. Let's turn the page and see if I'm right. Oh, I am!" The teacher and students later shared facts about rain drawn from the text. Randall, one of her students, said, "I like to read informational books because I learn new things all the time."

David Gonzales teaches sixth grade, and his students write several reports of information over the course of the year. The sixth-grade team at his school believes that students should vote on topics to research and investigate. Once students have voted, their teachers identify texts that will help students learn about an issue and how authors frame their writing such that they can write their reports. During the second quarter, the students wanted to talk about sustainability. Their science teacher had introduced them to a range of topics, including plastics in the ocean and solar energy. To expand their thinking about sustainability and to highlight the ways that authors address issues that readers might find difficult or controversial, Mr. Gonzales selected a text from the Chapul website titled "Why I Eat Insects" (www.chapul.com). It's a short text that also includes a video that he decided to show after the students had experienced the read-aloud. Mr. Gonzales set the purpose (to identify ways that authors address sensitive issues with their audience) and started reading. He stopped after the first sentence, saying, "Wait, what? Humans think that insects are a good source of protein? NO WAY. What humans? Maybe a long time ago when they couldn't get other food, but not today. I can't believe it. I'm already doubting this author." Mr. Gonzales then returned to the text, reading the rest of the paragraph. When he finished he said, "It says 80% of the people on earth eat insects. I'm feeling left out. Why am I in the 20%? I'm totally grossed out about it right now, but it can't be all bad, right? I mean, like a lot of people seem to like eating insects." He continued reading through the rest of the text, as his students sat mesmerized in their seats.

Discuss the Text

As we have noted in each of the glimpses into classroom practice thus far, interactive read-alouds are not monologue. Students are allowed to interact with their peers at specific points in the text. This allows them to try on some of the strategies or knowledge that the text contains. It also increases engagement and interest, not to mention motivation. These discussions also provide students with opportunities to think more deeply about the text as they interact with others and their ideas. To initiate the discussions, we can ask a balance of efferent and aesthetic questions (e.g., Cox & Many, 1992) during our read-alouds. Students should understand the information and details presented in the text (efferent) and make connections between the text and their own lives (aesthetic).

For example, during a read-aloud of *The Raft* (Lamarche, 2000), Megan King provided each of her second-grade students with four index cards. One card said *Yes*, another *No*, another *Grandmother*, and another *Nicky*.

As Ms. King read the book aloud to the class, she asked questions and encouraged all of the students to hold up one of the cards for the answer. At one point, she asked a student to predict what might happen next in the story. She then asked the whole class to hold up a *Yes* card if they agreed with the prediction or a *No* card if they thought something else might happen. At another point in the story, Ms. King asked who was riding the raft. She did this because the text is a bit ambiguous, and she wanted her students to engage, move, and use their cards. Every student held up the card that read *Nicky*. At another point, she asked the class, "Can you see yourself doing this?" Still later, she asked, "Have you ever been on a raft?" One of the students who had her *Yes* card held up was called on to explain her raft trip.

Effective read-alouds require that we be animated and expressive.

Integrate the Interactive Read-Aloud Into the Literacy Block

The final consideration for interactive read-alouds is that they should connect to other learning during the literacy block. They are not commercials or simply entertainment but rather opportunities for us to model thinking for students and share information and strategies with them.

Each of the examples we have provided thus far included connections to other learning tasks, and the interactive read-aloud was part of the bigger picture of learning that students needed to do.

SHARED READINGS

Shared reading and interactive read-alouds have a lot in common. They both involve careful text selection that provides students with knowledge or examples of skills. Both involve texts that are complex and interesting for students. Both require that we be animated and expressive. And both involve discussions and should be integrated into the literacy block.

But there are some notable differences between read-alouds and shared readings. The major difference is in what the students see. In a read-aloud, we may show pages of the text like Ms. Matlovsky did, but the focus is not on students reading along as the teacher reads. As such, read-alouds are very useful in building students' listening comprehension, vocabulary, and knowledge base.

resources.corwin.com/
thisisbalancedliteracy

Video 5
Shared Reading

During a shared reading lesson, students see the entire text as we read it. Sometimes students have a copy of the text themselves, and other times the students see the text projected on a screen from a document camera or smartboard. Typically, we annotate the text during a shared reading, noting specific words or ideas. If students have their own copy of the text, they can annotate as well and then add their own notes when they discuss the text with a peer. As a result, shared readings are usually slower than a read-aloud, given that we need to be careful that students' eyes don't fall behind their ears. Tips for effective shared readings can be found in Figure 2.1.

▼ FIGURE 2.1 TIPS FOR EFFECTIVE SHARED READINGS

Choose a short piece of text.
Shared readings are most effective when they are focused and well paced. A brief shared reading, using a passage of one to four paragraphs, will have more impact than a longer reading because student interest is maintained. As well, it prevents the temptation to model too many strategies.

Let the text tell you what to do.
Plan what you want to model for students during the shared reading. Teaching points should be focused and clear to students. Read the text several times, and make notes about the comprehension and word-solving strategies you are using to understand. These will provide you with ideas for the content of your shared reading. Annotate the text, so you will have something to refer to as you read.

Keep your think-alouds authentic.
It can be a little disconcerting to say aloud what's going on in your head. Most teachers adopt a conversational tone that mirrors the informal language people use when they are thinking. An overly academic tone will sound contrived. It's better to say, "Hey—when I read this part about the penguins, right away I saw a penguin in my mind," rather than, "I am metacognitively aware and activated my visualizing strategy to formulate an image of a penguin as I read that paragraph."

Tell them what you did.
Using an authentic voice doesn't mean you can't name the strategy. Tell your students what strategy you used to help you comprehend. This allows students to begin to form schemas about reading comprehension. Underline or highlight words or phrases that helped you understand, and encourage students to do likewise, if possible.

Resist the urge to overthink.
The meaning of the passage should not be sacrificed for the sake of the shared reading. Don't insert so many examples of modeling into the reading that the intended message is lost. Fewer, well-crafted shared readings will have far more impact than a stream-of-consciousness rap that leaves the students bewildered by what just happened.

Modeling in Read-Alouds and Shared Reading

Modeling is part of both shared readings and read-alouds. We are apprenticing students into academic thinking. Remember that thinking is invisible, so we have to talk about our thinking such that students can witness how others utilize cognitive and metacognitive processes to make meaning. Modeling requires two specific behaviors from teachers:

- **"I" statements:** When modeling, use *I* rather than *we* or *you*. To demonstrate thinking, it's more effective to say, "I can visualize this in my mind" or "I can make the following prediction from the text . . ." than "When you visualize" or "We can predict the following. . . ." This is because students are listening in a different way when you use an "I" statement. But providing students with examples of the thinking required is not enough to ensure that they learn at high levels. The examples above show students what we can do, but don't show them *how* we did it.

- **Metacognition:** This is where we explain the *because, why,* or *how* of our actions. For example, a teacher might say, "I can visualize this in my mind *because* of these three words" or "I can make the following prediction from the text *because* the author told me. . . ." Both the "I" statements and the thinking behind the statement are required. There is evidence that this type of experience improves student learning (e.g., Fisher, Frey, & Lapp, 2011).

We can model a number of things during shared readings and read-alouds. Some of these are more appropriate for shared readings because students can see the print, and some work equally well in both shared readings and read-alouds. We can model the following:

- **Concepts about print:** Print (both on paper and digital) is organized in specific ways. Students learn that we read the symbols for a message, that illustrations correspond with the print, that text in English goes left to right, top to bottom, that we use a return sweep to the next line, and that texts are organized with front and back covers.

- **Graphophonics:** This is the symbol system use by readers, and it includes letter-sound or sound-spelling relationships of language. We can integrate phonemic awareness and phonics instruction into their read-alouds and shared readings. Because there are 26 letters but 44 sounds in English, there are many different ways to spell some of those sounds.

- **Fluency:** Reading rate is an important consideration as students increase their proficiency, and we can model fluent reading and talk about the strategies that they use to read fluently. In addition to rate, prosody is an important consideration in fluency and includes pauses, inflections, intonations, and phrase boundaries.

- **Language structures:** Languages are structured in specific ways. Verbs, for example, go in certain places in a sentence. Hearing a lot of language and beginning to internalize the structure helps build grammatical knowledge. Signal words such as *first, then, next,* and *finally* help cue readers by using common organizational patterns.

- **Comprehension:** Readers use cognitive strategies to make sense of the text. There is a range of comprehension strategies, such as predicting, visualizing, monitoring, making connections, inferencing, and summarizing.

During a shared reading lesson, students see the entire text as we read it.

- **Text structures:** Authors organize texts according to traditions, and some authors intentionally break those traditions. There are expository text structures such as problem/solution, cause/effect, and description, as well as narrative text structures that involve story grammar, including plot, setting, characters, actions, conflicts, and resolution.

- **Word solving:** The meanings of some words in a text can be determined because of the contextual clues provided by the author, but some texts have misdirective or nondirective clues. Readers need to learn to look for these clues and analyze them for their usefulness. In addition, many words in English contain affixes, bases, or roots, or are part of word families. Knowledge about using morphology (the smallest units of meaning) can also help readers solve unknown words. When these systems don't work, readers use resources to determine the meanings of words.

- **Text features:** Authors will sometimes add extratextual features designed to assist the reader or to provide supplementary information. The range of text features includes graphs, charts, diagrams, illustrations, captions, bold or italicized words, headings, and the like. Readers need to learn to understand these features, and learn how to integrate them into the main body of the text, if they are to fully understand the content. Importantly, text features are related to text structures. Understanding and recognizing text features, and their relationship with text structures, can deepen comprehension of the text.

> Text features are related to text structures. Understanding and recognizing text features, and their relationship with text structures, can deepen comprehension of the text.

- **Pragmatics:** This aspect of linguistics focuses on the ways in which context influences the implied meaning of a text. Pragmatics focuses on what people mean when they use language and is useful in understanding characters and dialogue. Because pragmatic knowledge is at times culturally bound, students may benefit from modeling that unpacks unfamiliar pragmatics. For instance, a student newer to English may not immediately perceive that a character's question, "Can you pass the potatoes?" is not just asking whether it is literally true (is another character physically able), but that it is an implied request to another to pass the dish across the dinner table.

- **Visual literacy:** Picture books and graphic novels convey much of their information through the use of nonlinguistic representations of information. The end pages of picture books often contain subtle information about the story within. Moebius (1986) refers to the codes of visual literacy in picture books:

  - *Codes of position* where objects and characters are on the page.

  - *Codes of perspective* that convey tension through the use of foreground and background.

- ◦ *Codes of the frame* as illustrations spread across two pages, bleed to the edge of the page, or are boxed.

- ◦ *Codes of line and capillarity* that convey excitement when they are crosshatched close together, or are drawn loosely.

- ◦ *Codes of color* to denote a bright and cheerful setting, or the dangerous and dark mood of a character.

We have already discussed the use of "I" statements and metacognition. Organize your think-alouds during an interactive read-aloud or shared reading, so children can follow a clear path of reasoning and logic (Fisher & Frey, 2014a):

1. Name the strategy, skill, or task.

2. State the purpose of the strategy, skill, or task.

3. Explain when the strategy or skill is used.

4. Use analogies to link prior knowledge to new learning.

5. Demonstrate how the skill, strategy, or task is completed.

6. Alert learners about errors to avoid.

7. Assess the use of the skill.

We don't use all of these for every piece of text that we share with students. Rather, they are considerations for planning effective shared readings and read-alouds. Figure 2.2 contains examples of each of these as they apply to a section of the text, *The Top of the World: Climbing Mt. Everest* (Jenkins, 2002).

This planning map for a think-aloud works well to build phonics knowledge, too. It is early fall in Eliana Lopez's kindergarten class, and her students are learning to associate sounds with letters in the initial position. Ms. Lopez explained that "teaching a letter of the week is something that isn't effective, although I often have to explain to parents why their children won't be experiencing the same kind of instruction they might recall from their own schooling experiences." Rather, Ms. Lopez stated that five-year-olds typically arrive in kindergarten already having some sound/letter knowledge: They are likely to know the first letter of their names, and they tend to know the sounds of letters that are aligned to the pronunciation of the letter (e.g., *O, B, X,* and *A;* Justice, Pence, & Bowles, 2006).

Ms. Lopez uses *The Book With No Pictures* (Novak, 2015), already a class favorite in the first weeks of school. At this point, her students know the story well; it encourages children to use their voices to express ideas

▼ FIGURE 2.2 SHARED READING OF *THE TOP OF THE WORLD: CLIMBING MT. EVEREST*

Example	The Top of the World
1. Name the strategy, skill, or task.	"Today I'm going to think aloud about how I monitor my understanding as I read this informational text about Mt. Everest."
2. State the purpose of the strategy, skill, or task.	"It's important to monitor, because I can get lost in an informational reading. It has lots of details in it that can get confusing. When I monitor my understanding, it helps me make sure that I notice when I lose the meaning. Then I can fix it."
3. Explain when the strategy or skill is used.	"When I read a text like this, I look at the headings. I turn the heading into a question. I read the passage below the heading; then I recheck the heading to see if I understand. I try to answer the question."
4. Use analogies to link prior knowledge to new learning.	"It's like when I recheck a new recipe while I'm cooking. It helps me stay on track so I don't miss an important ingredient."
5. Demonstrate how the skill, strategy, or task is completed.	[Read the first three passages. Formulate a question, read the passage, and make notes in the margins. In the first passage, underline facts. Circle *danger, fail,* and *some die trying,* and draw a link between these three terms. In the second passage, ask "Who or what are Sherpas?" Note that it is capitalized, so it is a proper noun. Underline facts about Sherpas, and write a summary note in margin to answer question.]
6. Alert learners to errors to avoid.	Read the third heading and say, "I'm not sure what the author means by 'Home away from home.'" After reading this passage say, "Hmm, he never uses that phrase again, and I still don't know what it means. I'm going to write my question in the margin and ask my group what they think it means. It would be a mistake to let an unanswered question go by without trying to solve it. That's what monitoring is for."
7. Assess the use of the skill.	[After finishing] "I'm reviewing my notes to see what I understand and what I still have questions about. Next, I'm going to ask others what they think the author means about 'home away from home.'"

(e.g., reading a page "with my monkey mouth in my monkey voice"). She tells her students,

I know we love this book, and there are so many different ways to understand it! Today I'm going to show you how I use what I know about the sounds of the first letters of words to have even more fun with this silly story! [*Name the strategy, skill, or task.*] Making the sound of the first letter of a word is a good way to help me figure out the word. [*State the purpose of the strategy, skill, or task.*] I look at the first letter of the word and read it from left to right every time I read a word [*Explain when the strategy or skill is used.*] It's like when I hook up the wooden train in the transportation center in the back corner of our classroom. I always start with the engine. The first letter of the word is the place I always begin. [*Use analogies to link prior knowledge to new learning.*]

Ms. Lopez begins reading this familiar book, pausing to demonstrate how she pairs a letter with a sound using words her students are ready to chant. For example, she comes to the page with BOO BOO BUTT written in large red letters (we told you it was a silly book):

Oh, I know this letter and its sound! It's a letter *b,* and it's at the beginning of all three words. The letter *b* makes the /b/ sound. I'm going to have fun with that sound. */b/-/b/-/b/-boo! /b/-/b/-/b/-boo! /b/-/b/-/b/-butt!* You can do it with me too! */b/-/b/-/b/-boo! /b/-/b/-/b/-boo. /b/-/b/-/b/-butt!* [*Demonstrate how the skill, strategy, or task is completed.*]

Their teacher continues to model and demonstrate, selecting words that are appealing and that her class is becoming familiar with. She selects words such as *no, silly sounds*, and *ba-dooongy face*, a term the class seems especially fond of, for similar treatment. As she continues to model, she says,

Sometimes I get too excited and I accidentally skip the first letter. I just hop right over it. But then I can't figure out the word. So sometimes I have to remind myself to always start with that first letter. [*Alert learners about errors to avoid.*]

Ms. Lopez's kindergarten class will use this strategy countless times as they learn to read. But her modeling of the strategy provides her students with the toehold they need to begin their reading journey.

Shared readings also provide a prime opportunity for teachers to model word solving. Sometimes the whole point of the shared reading is to provide students with experience in word solving, but more often teachers integrate word solving into the overall reading. In other words, word solving is something we regularly consider when modeling for students.

As an example, while reading an informational text about people who were native to their region to her fourth graders, the teacher paused on the words *overdone* and *underfed.* In both cases, the teacher modeled word solving using prefixes that were included on the class word wall. For *underfed*, she said, "I know the word *fed;* that is the past tense version of *feed,* like helping someone to eat. But *under* is a prefix that means too little or below. So, I think that *underfed* means that the children did not have enough to eat during the winter."

DIRECT AND DELIBERATE INSTRUCTION IN WHOLE-CLASS READING

Direct instruction (or as some now call it, "deliberate" instruction) is an approach that is useful for addressing specific skills with students. In this approach, we are straightforward and explicit in the explanation. There has been criticism of this approach, as it is highly teacher directed. Having said that, there is considerable evidence that direct instruction can be an effective approach (e.g., Hattie, 2012) when specific conditions are met. We believe that direct instruction is an important part of balanced literacy. In fact, we think that teachers have to balance direct instruction with indirect instruction to ensure students learn. *Indirect instruction* describes a constellation of other types of student-centered learning, such as experiential, dialogic, and inquiry-based methods. In addition, indirect instruction includes independent learning.

As we noted in Chapter 1, direct instruction is not simply telling students information.

resources.corwin.com/
thisisbalancedliteracy

Video 6
Direct Instruction

In a direct instruction lesson, we tell the students the concept or skill to be learned and then lead them through instructional activities designed to result in student learning. These activities tend to be based on behavioristic learning principles (e.g., getting students' attention, reinforcing correct responses, providing corrective feedback, practicing correct responses). We remain in control of the content, activities, and lesson pacing. The lesson progresses in a clear, sequential way, and there are typically multiple opportunities for students to respond to us. Often, these responses require all students to respond at the same time. Throughout the direct instruction lesson, we monitor our students' understanding and provide corrective feedback.

Shared readings provide a prime opportunity for teachers to model word solving.

Michael Newman/PhotoEdit

Rosenshine (2008) noted that the structure of a direct instruction lesson should follow a pattern that includes the following:

1. Begin a lesson with a short review of previous learning. Going from the known to the new is powerful.

2. Begin a lesson with a short statement of goals.

3. Present new material in small steps, providing practice for students after each step.

4. Give clear and detailed instructions and explanations.

5. Provide a high level of active practice for all students.

6. Ask a large number of questions, check for student understanding, and obtain responses from all students.

7. Guide students during initial practice.

8. Provide explicit instruction and practice for seatwork exercises, and monitor students during seatwork.

The kindergarten students in Vinu Manoj's classroom have had extensive daily practice to build phonemic awareness and can blend sounds well. But many have difficulty with segmenting sounds in words. Thus, Ms. Manoj is working on segmenting phonemes in consonant-vowel-consonant words.

One method for pairing manipulatives with phonemic awareness instruction is called Elkonin sound boxes (Elkonin, 1963). Elkonin sound boxes are represented as empty squares for each phoneme in a word. Several manipulatives (unifix cubes, bingo chips, or pennies) are given to the student along with a mat like the one seen in Figure 2.3. The teacher says each word slowly while students push a chip into a box for each sound they hear. Therefore, the word *dog* would need three boxes, as would the word *fish* (/sh/ is one phoneme). It is important to note that the goal is for students to hear sounds (phonemes)—spelling is not the goal.

▼ FIGURE 2.3 ELKONIN BOXES

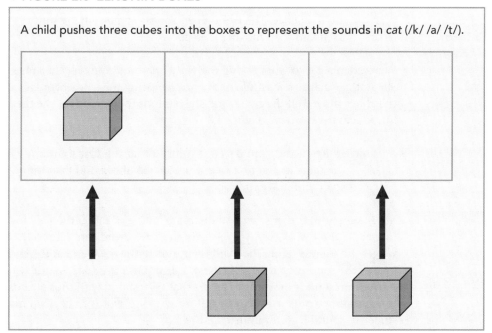

A child pushes three cubes into the boxes to represent the sounds in *cat* (/k/ /a/ /t/).

As part of her direct instruction lesson, Ms. Manoj focuses on words with three sounds and three corresponding letters. Using the document camera, she projects her copy of the sound boxes for students to see. She starts the lesson by saying,

> We've been thinking a lot about the sounds in words that we hear. Remember that we're trying to identify the specific sounds that we hear. And we're replacing some sounds with other sounds to see if they make words. Today, we're going to slow this down a

bit and move a cube for each sound we hear in a word. I'll stretch some words so that we can hear the sounds. I'll show you how I do this and then we can practice.

She says the word *cat* and then breaks the word into sound parts, moving a small cube into each box as she says the sound. As she says,

> The first sound I hear is /k/, so I move the first cube. Then I hear /a/ so I move the second cube. And then I hear /t/ and I move the last cube. And then I say the whole word again, *cat.*

Ms. Manoj continues to describe this process to her students, using several other C-V-C words before asking students to take out the cubes in the box she has placed on each table. She says,

> Now you'll practice. The word is *pat.* You should be talking softly to yourself and then moving the cubes.

Her students get to work taking the word apart and moving the cubes. She notices that several students are not repeating the whole word after they have moved all the cubes, and she reminds them to do so. She then introduces the word *pig,* saying,

> I have a new word, and it's *pig.* I noticed that the first sound in *pig* is the same as the first sound in *pat.* Go ahead and take the word apart and move the cubes.

Ms. Manoj notices that several students are saying *pit* rather than *pig* and interrupts their work, saying, "Let's listen to the word carefully so that we get the sounds right. The word is *pig,* notice the /g/ sound at the end [makes the sound of a hard *g*]. Let's try again." Over time, Ms. Manoj will move from sounds in words to letters that correspond with those words to rebuilding words with letters, still using C-V-C words to develop her students' sound-to-print understanding.

Fourth-grade teacher Andrew Busch introduced main idea and details to his students using direct instruction. As he said,

> We've been reading a lot of informational texts these past couple of weeks, and we've been talking about the ideas that are important to think about for our writing. Now we're going to use these details to identify the main idea. The main idea is what the text is mostly about. The details have to support the main idea. Let's take a few minutes to read about space junk.

Direct instruction is an important part of balanced literacy. In fact, we think that teachers have to balance direct instruction with indirect instruction to ensure students learn.

At this point, the students turn their attention to the text Mr. Busch has distributed, and they read the text to themselves. As they have been taught, they circle words and phrases they don't know and write brief margin notes to summarize and synthesize.

Bringing the class back together, Mr. Busch says,

> So, I'm going to return to my text and underline the details that I think are important. The first detail is the amount of space junk floating in the sky. See here, in the third sentence? A second detail is about the Kosmos-Iridium collision that produced over 2,000 pieces of junk. I found that in the first sentence of the second paragraph. There are some other details about this collision that are interesting, but I don't know if they are really important yet, so I am not going to underline them at this point. Another detail that I think is important is the fact that a small piece of debris can cause a lot of damage.

Mr. Busch continues reading the text, underlining details he thinks may be important. As he comes to the end of the text, he says,

> Now I have to think about the main message from this text. When I read all of the details together, I think that a main message from the author is that space debris, or junk, could cause a lot of problems for future generations. Now, let me show you how I thought about that main idea.

Mr. Busch continues his discussion of details supporting main ideas, noting that the details have to all support the main idea. He also notes that there are sometimes a few main ideas and that there are several ways to phrase the main idea. As he noted,

> There are other ways that I could have said this. This is not the one, right answer. But, there are wrong answers that are not supported by the important details. But I want you to try this. I have another piece of text, and it focuses on the reduction in smog in Los Angeles, California, over several years. I'd like you to do the same thing as before. Please read the text and use your annotations. And make sure you identify important details. Then we will come back together to identify some possible main ideas. We'll also look for tricks or distractions from the main idea, which are usually interesting bits of information that the author includes but are not really critical to understanding. Ready? Let's go.

CLOSE READINGS

Another way to engage the whole class in reading instruction is through the use of a close reading of complex text. We can use this instructional routine with small groups of students, but we also find it effective to engage the whole class at once so that we can maximize student-to-student interactions while monitoring students' responses to the text. There are a couple of characteristics that make close reading unique, which we will describe next. These may be modified for younger students, as noted in Figure 2.4.

Short Passages of Complex Texts

Like all of the other approaches discussed in this chapter, close reading works best with short passages. The texts should be at least at grade level, so they are sufficiently complex that they require revisiting and reconsidering the information contained within the text, such as was the case when Tiffany Held's first graders were reading *Earthworms* (Llewellyn, 2002). The texts also need to be short enough that students can consume them in a reasonable amount of time. There is no evidence-based answer to the question, "How short is short?" but we generally believe that a length between one paragraph and two pages will work. That doesn't mean the selection has to be stand-alone; excerpts from longer texts, strategically chosen because they are complex, also work well. Mandy Harper selected passages from *The Watsons Go to Birmingham—1963* (Curtis, 1995) for close readings but had her fifth graders reading the majority of the book with their peers. When considering length, we don't literally mean two pages, because the words may be spread out over several illustrated pages. For close reading, our experience suggests that somewhere between one hundred and one thousand words will work. Of course, this also depends on the age of the students, with younger students closely reading shorter passages than older students.

Limited Frontloading

During close reading lessons, we avoid frontloading or preteaching vocabulary. The structure of the lesson should provide students with support such that they come to understand the meaning, and implications, of the text. Sometimes we tell students the meaning of a word or two, but we do not spend a lot of time teaching vocabulary in advance of the reading. Instead of using these front-end scaffolds, which might be necessary for other instructional routines, close reading relies on distributed scaffolds that are integrated into the lesson as students encounter the text.

▼ FIGURE 2.4 COMPARING CLOSE READING IN PRIMARY AND UPPER GRADES

Close Reading in Primary Grades	Elements	Close Reading in Upper Grades
The reading level of the text is significantly higher than students' reading level.	**Text Selection**	The text complexity is slightly higher than what the student takes on during other phases of reading instruction.
The teacher is reading the text aloud to students, although they are not grasping its deeper meaning. The text may or may not be displayed.	**Initial Reading**	Students are more likely to read the text independently, although they are not fully grasping its deeper meaning.
The teacher guides annotation practices using displayed text and fosters collaboratively developed annotations.	**Annotation**	Students familiar with annotation practices are marking the text independently and adding to their annotations throughout class discussions.
The teacher reads the text aloud multiple times. Students may read along at the paragraph, sentence, phrase, or individual word level. A few students may read the text independently in subsequent readings due to practice effects.	**Repeated Readings**	Students are rereading independently or with minimal support. Students may also have access to audio supports (a poet reading her poem, a teacher reading dialogue, a peer reading a key sentence).
Text-Based Discussions		
Students engage in extended discussion, which is driven by text-dependent questions and dialogic teaching. Students deepen their understanding through analysis of the literal, structural, and inferential dimensions of the text.		
Students draw and write collaboratively and independently, with adult support and guidance. They engage in shared investigations and debate compelling questions.	**Responding to Texts**	Students write collaboratively and independently. They investigate and research, and debate compelling questions.

Source: Fisher, D., & Frey, N. (2014b). Closely reading informational texts in the primary grades. *The Reading Teacher, 68,* 222–227. Used with permission.

Rereading

As part of the close reading experience, students read and reread the text or specific parts of the text. In the primary grades, students can identify parts of the text that they want us to reread, but older students should be rereading the text themselves. We are aware that there are students who do not like to reread. Rather than simply telling them to reread, we suggest that you change the purpose, ask an interesting question, or require evidence in their responses. These three actions seem to increase the likelihood that students will reread the text. For example, when the second graders in Harvey Tilden's class were reading Edna St. Vincent Millay's poem "Afternoon on a Hill," they were invited to first read the poem for the flow and then, on the second read, to annotate.

Annotations

Marking a text allows the reader to slow down and pay attention to specific aspects of the text. Annotations also allow readers to rapidly find information in a text that they can use in conversations and in their writing. There are a number of annotation systems, but we have found that just a few of them used with a whole class are useful. We like to teach students three foundational annotations:

1. Underlining key ideas so that they learn the difference between supporting details and important messages

2. Circling words and phrases that are confusing so that they learn to monitor their own understanding

3. Creating margin notes in writing or sketching in which they restate information or ideas in their own words so that they learn to synthesize and summarize

Students may choose to use other annotations, but we've found these three valuable in developing students' habits.

Text-Dependent Questions That Encourage Discussion

During a close reading lesson, we always ask questions that draw on evidence from the text. We start with literal questions and move to structural questions and then to inferential questions as students demonstrate deeper and deeper understanding. The point of text-dependent questioning is twofold. First, these questions foster discussion between and among students as they share their thinking with each other. Second, the questions serve as a primary scaffold for understanding as they become increasingly complex and less focused on "right there" information. Figure 2.5 includes text-dependent questions from two texts. One of the texts is an Aesop's Fable for primary grades, and the other is the text that Mr. Gonzalez used with his sixth graders for a read-aloud, but in this case it is presented as a close reading.

The students in Janelle Houston's first-grade class have been examining stories that challenge gender norms. They have previously read *The Paper*

Rather than simply telling students to reread, we suggest that you change the purpose, ask an interesting question, or require evidence in their responses.

▼ FIGURE 2.5 SAMPLE TEXT-DEPENDENT QUESTIONS

	Wolf in Sheep's Clothing (Aesop's Fables)	*Why Eat Insects?* (Informational Text)
What does the text say? **LITERAL** (General understanding and key detail questions)	• What does *prowl* mean? • Reread the moral. What are the key details in the story that support the moral? • What does it mean: "made a meal of him"? • Why did the wolf need to cover his fur?	• Does the author view eating insects favorably or unfavorably? How do you know? • What evidence does the author furnish that insects are a good source of protein? • The author makes three major arguments in favor of eating insects. What are they?
How does the text work? **STRUCTURAL** (Vocabulary, text structure, and author's craft and purpose questions)	• Why does Aesop ask a question and then immediately answer it? • What words and phrases does Aesop use to show that the wolf is clever? • Who tells the story? Wolf, shepherd, sheep, or narrator?	• What words and phrases does the author use to persuade the reader? • The author uses loaded language to persuade. Cross those words out and have someone in your group read the text aloud again. What is the effect?
What does the text mean? **INFERENTIAL** (Making inferences and comparing meaning across multiple texts)	• Aesop says, "The wolf was able to get a sheep whenever he pleased." What does that sentence reveal about the wolf? • How does this fable compare with "The Tortoise and the Hare"? • The wolf is literally caught. How else might someone who is pretending be caught?	• What does the author imply with the use of the word *we*? What is its relationship to the word *revolution*? • The text comes from a company that sells food products made from cricket protein. Read the two statements from their website. How do these additional texts help you to further understand the first? What are your critical questions now?

Bag Princess (Munsch, 1980) and *Sleeping Bobby* (Osborne & Osborne, 2005) as interactive shared readings. Both books confront expectations about princesses and princes in fairy tales. Today's text for close reading is a short story titled "George and the Dragon," a traditional tale of St. George, the patron saint of England, and the story of his rescue of a princess from a dragon. "The story is told from a conventional point of view, namely that the knight rescues the damsel in distress," Ms. Houston said. "I'm hoping to push their thinking and creativity a bit, using text-dependent questions that are going to require them to think critically."

During a close reading lesson, we always ask questions that draw on evidence from the text. We start with literal questions and move to structural questions and then to inferential questions as students demonstrate deeper and deeper understanding.

The passage is 300 words long, and Ms. Houston doesn't expect her first graders to be able to read it independently. However, it is spring, and her students are making gains in their reading progress. "I'm apprenticing them into reading more complex texts," she said. "In second grade, they'll be taking on close reading at increasingly independent levels. Our goal is for them to fully take on close reading in third grade. So it's a process, getting them to that point."

Ms. Houston begins by introducing the reading briefly to her students, saying "Today we're going to read and discuss a story about a knight named George, a princess, and a dragon. The first time, I'll be the one to read it, and you're listening. Then I'll give each of you a printed copy, and I'll read it again a few more times. I've got some great questions to ask you, too."

Ms. Houston's first rendition is a read-aloud, conducted without interruption. When finished, she distributes a printed version and asks her students to number the paragraphs. "This time, as I read it, you follow along with your eyes." Again, she reads without interruption, and then asks them to underline the words *George, princess,* and *dragon.* "These are words that represent the main characters. As I read it a third time, I want you to think about what you know about each of them."

After the third reading, Ms. Houston asked questions about the main idea ("the dragon was hurting the people in the village, and George killed the dragon," said Tate) and key details. (The children spent several minutes trying to figure out why the king sent the princess to meet the dragon.) Ms. Houston then created a list of character traits for each of the three. "Let's talk about words and phrases that describe each," she said. Martine said the knight was "brave" and Albert said the dragon was "terrible." Together, the class located these words in the text and circled them. "How else can we describe them, this time using our own words?" Ms. Houston asked.

The children readily noted that George would be "strong" and "fearless," and the dragon would be "scary" and "fire-breathing." Ms. Houston wrote these, and then asked the children, "What's missing from our list?"

"We don't have anything written down about the princess," said Kelsey. "You're right," said Ms. Houston. "So what does that tell us about what our author thinks about the princess?" she asked.

Kelsey paused for a moment, and then remarked, "She's not important."

The first round of questions on the literal meaning of the story, followed by structural questions about the vocabulary and author's craft, had set the stage for their inferential thinking about the story itself.

Next, Ms. Houston said, "I'm going to read it again while you follow. You can read any parts you want to aloud with me. This time, let's think about the princess in the story." As she read, students read along silently or aloud. When she finished, she asked, "If Elizabeth [the main character in *The Paper Bag Princess*] could talk to our princess, what might she say? Talk at your tables about what that conversation might sound like."

After several minutes, Ms. Houston invited volunteers to act out the conversation. Gabriela and Kelsey's exchange was typical: "Are you crazy?" said the Paper Bag Princess, "Tell your dad the king that you're not going without a sword, a horse, and armor to wear!" To which the princess in this story replied, "You're right! I'm going to ask him why I should go instead of him!"

FOUNDATIONAL SKILLS IN WHOLE-GROUP READING INSTRUCTION

The foundational skills of reading are concepts of print, phonemic awareness, phonics, and fluency, and each is crucial in the development of young readers. Without a solid grasp of these skills, readers flounder, and the gap between those making expected progress and those who are not widens with each year of schooling. While we have embedded examples of foundational skills instruction throughout this chapter, we believe it is necessary to discuss specific aspects of this facet of the reading curriculum. These foundational skills are introduced through whole-class instruction and further deepened through small-group instruction, collaborative learning, and independent learning.

Phonemic and Phonological Awareness

Knowledge of the sounds of a language is essential for reading the language. Phonemes are the smallest units of sound; they include sounds usually associated with a single letter (/t/ for *t*), but also sounds such as those that appear in words such as *wage* (/j/ sound for g) and *of* (f voiced as a /v/ sound). There are 44 phonemes in English; estimates vary among scholars, but the number of phonemes used in the world's 7,000 languages is over 100. A broader term—*phonological awareness*—includes not only manipulation of the 44 phonemes but also syllables, rimes, and perceiving the pauses between words.

Emergent readers, as well as older readers who are new to English, must master the ability to perceive and manipulate the sounds of language.

Knowledge of the sounds of a language is essential for reading the language.

Adams (1990) describes five levels of phonological awareness. While the first four levels are in place by the end of first grade for typically developing readers, the fifth level is more advanced, and its development can extend through third or even fourth grade:

- **Level 1:** Hearing rhymes and alliteration (e.g., "Jack and Jill went up the hill. . . .")

- **Level 2:** Oddity tasks, such as figuring out which word in a string does not rhyme (e.g., *bait, gate, make*, and *weight*)

- **Level 3:** Blending words and splitting syllables (e.g., listen to the sounds of /h/ and /and/ to say *hand*; recognizing that *handshake* consists of two syllables)

- **Level 4:** Orally segmenting words is the opposite of blending words. For instance, upon hearing the word *rain*, the child can isolate the three phonemes (/rān/).

- **Level 5:** Manipulation tasks require the ability to delete, substitute, add, and reverse phonemes. An example of a phoneme reversal is *much* and *chum*.

Songs and chants are a common way of developing Level 1 phonemic awareness, especially reciting nursery rhymes and poems and singing songs.

Many of these skills are acquired through word play during whole-class instruction. Songs and chants are a common way of developing Level 1 phonemic awareness, especially reciting nursery rhymes and poems and singing songs. These can be paired with finger play and hand-clapping games that offer students a chance to identify syllables and words. ("Let's clap the words in the sentence we just heard Sophie say.") Oddity task skills are promoted through games, asking students, "Which of these doesn't belong?" and then reciting a list of rhyming words that includes one outlier. Students learn to blend, segment, delete, and substitute through word play, such as sorting pictures of objects that represent specific phonemes, replacing sounds to make new words, and deleting sounds to figure out the resulting word. Kindergarteners are introduced to these phonemes in the initial position (/b/ as in <u>b</u>at, <u>b</u>ear, <u>b</u>ug), and are soon challenged to locate sounds at the final position (/k/ as in ra<u>ke</u>, ba<u>ck</u>, spea<u>k</u>). Medial sounds are the most challenging (/ē/ as in m<u>ea</u>t, r<u>ee</u>d, wh<u>ee</u>l). Teachers in primary grades often incorporate phonemic awareness instruction during opening class routines.

Phonics

The sounds of the language are developed simultaneously with the letters of the language to apprentice school-aged students into reading. The process of bolting the sounds of the language to letters and letter combinations takes years and is foundational to reading. This begins with letter-sound knowledge, a familiar practice in primary classrooms. Children learn the names of the letters and their associated sounds, often through games and songs. Introduction to alphabetics (the representation of spoken sounds by letters) promotes visual discrimination skills, such as being able to distinguish between upper- and lowercase letters and to determine the differences in print between *d, p, b, q,* and *g.*

resources.corwin.com/
thisisbalancedliteracy

Video 7
Phonics Instruction

The graphophonic relationship between the sounds and letters of the language becomes increasingly complex. Some letters have a single sound (e.g., /b/ and /p/). Other letters represent more than one sound (e.g., long and short vowel sounds, the letter *g*). Digraphs (*wh* and *sh* are two examples), diphthongs or gliding vowels (e.g., *oi* and *ow*), blends (*fr* and *st* are two of many), trigraphs (e.g., *nth, squ*), and *r*-controlled vowels (e.g., *or* in *porch, ar* in *arm,* and *ur* in *curb*) must be mastered by young readers in order to accurately decode unfamiliar words and to build a bank of phonetically regular and irregular words that they can recognize on sight.

Phonics foundational skills should be taught using a clear scope and sequence. A well-founded criticism of literature-based approaches to reading instruction was that phonics instruction was left to chance, dependent on when a word cluster was encountered, rather than taught in a planned sequence. Most contemporary comprehensive reading and language arts curricula include a specific skills sequence. It is advisable that you become familiar with it so that you can capitalize on opportunities to reinforce the skills being taught across the school day, and not only within the language arts block.

Phonics instruction is composed of three approaches that together help students acquire the skills they need to accurately decode and recognize words. These approaches are synthetic phonics, analytic phonics, and analogy-based phonics. Synthetic phonics capitalize on a part-to-whole approach, as students learn sound-symbol connections between letters and letter combinations. Analytic phonics are taught at the word level.

The word is first identified, with phonics analysis following. For example, the teacher writes a series of words—*cup, but, sun*—and reads the words aloud before providing instruction about the short *u* in consonant-vowel-consonant (CVC) words. Analogy-based phonics require students to use known words to get to unknown words. As an example, the teacher begins with *ick* in order to build new words such as *stick, kick, pick*, and *sick*.

Analytic phonics is taught at the word level.

Bill Aron/PhotoEdit

Word sorts reinforce pattern recognition, which is vital to phonics development. Word sorts foster attention to the critical features of words, including their sounds, constructions, and meaning. In whole-class reading instruction, the words are displayed on large cards so that all the students can see them, and the teacher invites students to assign words to categories. The categories can include initial, medial, or final patterns, onset and rime, or conceptual relationships. But word sorts cannot simply become an independent activity in moving word cards. The real learning occurs with the discussion after the sort. The discussion that follows the sort is when deeper learning occurs. For example, you can ask students, "What did you notice about these spelling patterns?" or "What did you learn about words with these spellings?" Just moving cards into piles doesn't cut it.

▼ FIGURE 2.6 CONSIDERATIONS FOR TEACHING PHONICS

Practice	Considerations
Teach students to recognize and write single letter-sound correspondences.	Introduce letters that are very dissimilar in sound and appearance (e.g., /a/ and /t/) and gradually narrow the contrast in sound and appearance (e.g., /b/ and /d/).
Introduce short vowels and long vowels early so that students can form simple words.	Consonant-vowel-consonant (CVC), CVCC, and CVC-e words (silent e) compose most of the words in decodable and vocabulary-controlled texts.
Teach students to recognize and write blends, vowel and consonant digraphs, and more complex letter combinations in words.	Begin by introducing easier combinations such as /sh/ and /th/, progressing through vowel digraphs such as /ea/ and trigraphs such as /ght/ and /thr/.
Use explicit instruction of phonics to ensure all students are progressing at expected levels.	Use modeling with think-alouds and direct instruction to introduce skills. Use repetition, deliberative practice, and application through oral and written language to build automaticity.
Use synthetic, analytic, and analogy-based approaches to phonics instruction.	Young children benefit from each of these approaches, as each show students how words are decoded.
Integrate phonics skills and knowledge into connected texts.	Deepen phonics knowledge by highlighting its use to decode familiar and unknown words in reading materials.
Teach to automaticity.	Students must develop automaticity in decoding in order to gain the cognitive space needed to comprehend and make meaning.

Third-grade teacher Micah Pederson uses word sorts as part of his whole-group instruction to introduce his students to affixes. "We're on the prefixes *sub-*, *com-*, *en-*, and *pro-*," explained Mr. Pederson. "I introduce the meaning of these prefixes, and then I have the students sort and decode these with me." His students have words printed on small slips of paper, and they categorize each by similarity, and then re-sort them according to conceptual relationships. "So first they are putting words together like *subway*, *submarine*, and *subset*," said Mr. Pederson. "Then we re-sort them to look for words that hang together in meaning, like *promote* and *encourage* are related in terms of meaning," he said. "Then I have my students discuss the spelling patterns they notice."

Phonics instruction is an important facet of a balanced literacy approach to reading. Students need regular experiences with texts, as profiled in the first half of this chapter. But they also need systematic instruction in the sounds and letters that compose written language. Without this instruction, some children are left vulnerable to developing reading gaps that deepen with each grade level. Figure 2.6 is a summary of considerations for phonics instruction that moves children forward in their reading.

CONCLUSION

We use whole-class instruction in reading to introduce new skills and concepts to students and to address instructional needs that exist for the entire class. Whole-class instruction can be a meaningful experience for students, provided that they have opportunities to try things on and practice. But whole-class instruction cannot consume the entire literacy block. Students also need time to apply what they are learning with others and alone. And they need time with us in small-group, needs-based instruction to address areas of growth and build on strengths. There are some very effective instructional routines useful in whole-class instruction, including read-alouds, shared readings, direct and deliberate instruction, and close readings. Importantly, phonics instruction must include increased amounts of application to authentic reading and writing during the phonics lesson for it to have impact in the balanced literacy classroom. Students need practice with these concepts if they are going to apply their knowledge in their own reading and writing.

WHOLE-CLASS WRITING INSTRUCTION

HIGH-LEVEL SUPPORT FOR LEARNING

As part of his whole-class instruction, fifth-grade teacher Brandon Yee uses a technique called a write-aloud for his students to observe him as he writes a summary. Some people call these lessons shared writing, and some prefer write-alouds. We will use the term write-aloud, as it tends to convey the idea that writing will happen out loud, which may seem strange given that writing is often seen as solitary and personal. One of the many instructional strategies we will profile in this chapter, write-alouds are an excellent way to engage students in learning to write (Holmes, 2003).

Mr. Yee composes live in front of his students and shares his thinking as he does so. As with read-alouds and shared readings, these lessons cannot go on and on, but they do provide students with examples of the thinking that they will be expected to do later in the lesson. Mr. Yee has shared the first couple of paragraphs of a two-page article from The Week (www.theweek.com) about the composition of human tears and the various reasons that humans cry. After reading the introductory information, he says to the class, "There is a lot of interesting information in these few paragraphs. I'm going to go back and underline

Christina Kennedy/PhotoEdit

the things that I think are really important." He does so, sharing each with his students and telling them why. This is much more like a shared reading at this point. He then says, "Before I write, I have to think about my purpose as an author. Remember that we know several purposes for writing, including these:

- "My purpose is to share a sequence of events that led to. . . .

- "My purpose is to describe. . . .

- "My purpose is to compare. . . .

- "My purpose is to discuss a problem and several solutions.

"For my writing about tears, I think that my purpose is to describe the differences in human tears." Then, he opens up his laptop and says to the class,

> So, I think that I need to include the number of types of tears and the fact that the chemical composition of human tears depends on the reason that the person is crying. That seems to be the most important information. So, I think I'll write: Humans cry for different reasons, and the chemicals in the types are different. I'm going to reread that and see what I think. Humans cry for different reasons. Well, that's true, but I know how many, so I think I should revise my summary sentence to say: Humans tears come in three types, and the chemicals in each of the types are different. I think that might be better because then I can remember the three kinds of tears. I don't think that I need to know all of the chemicals in each type of tear, because I can always go back to the original.

Mr. Yee continues through the text, rereading and summarizing aloud for his students. Along the way, he provides a rationale for his actions and shares his thinking with students, in terms of content as well as composition. As with modeling during reading, modeling our thinking as we compose provides students with a window into the kinds of decision making they will need to engage in as they write. When students are allowed to observe and emulate the thinking that their teachers do, their writing improves.

- -

Here's what a write-aloud looks like in second grade. Christine Weaver is working with her students on writing about their opinions. Her analysis of her students' writing suggests that they have formed opinions, yet their reasons do not always support their opinions.

After bringing the class together, she says, "I have an opinion about the best sandwich. I think egg salad is the best. I'm going to write a paragraph with my opinion and the reasons for my opinion." Using the document camera, she starts to write. Her first sentence is: Egg salad makes the best sandwich. As she finishes writing it, she says,

> I like to start my paragraph with the opinion. I think that helps the reader know what to expect. And the reader can disagree. But the reader will think about my opinion and see if I offer good reasons. And you have all seen me with my egg salad sandwich at lunch, right?

[The children nod.] Now, I have to share my opinion about why I think egg salad is best. I have some ideas. For example, I like yellow. But I don't think that would be a good reason to say egg salad is best. I think saying a food is best should be because of the taste. I like mustard, so that could be a good reason. I also like pickles, and egg salad lets me have pickles and mustard. I think that would be a good sentence. I think I'll write: This sandwich lets me have two of my favorite flavors, pickles and mustard. I like that reason and I think it supports my opinion.

I have another reason and that is that egg salad is healthy. I really like ice cream, but that would not be a healthy choice for lunch. So, I think my next sentence will say: Egg salad is a healthy choice for lunch. I can have several reasons. When you write, you can have three or four reasons. Today, you get to write about your favorite sandwich and why. It has to be a type of sandwich and not something like pizza or burritos. Later, we will write about the best lunch ever, but today it's about sandwiches. Okay? Ready to write? You can use my opening sentence as a model and put in your type.

Over the next week, the students in Ms. Weaver's class will move from writing based on their personal opinions to writing with evidence from texts. She plans to write aloud for her students each day as she scaffolds their understanding about the role that reasons play in their writing. She will also monitor her students' writing to determine whether or not the instruction is sticking. If it is, the reasons they provide should logically support their opinions.

BUILD WRITING HABITS AND SKILLS WITH WHOLE-CLASS INSTRUCTIONAL ROUTINES

The act of writing is the product of a constellation of habits and skills that place high cognitive and metacognitive demands on students. Writers must formulate a message, regulate its structure, and physically compose on paper or screen. Operating in the background are the monitoring, editing, and revising processes needed as they compose. Importantly, these processes are occurring at the letter, word, sentence, and paragraph levels. The amount of self-regulation needed—rereading, persisting, considerations of audience and purpose—stretches young students who are still learning how to enact these habits and skills.

As with reading, writing must be taught with intention. It is not sufficient to simply *cause* writing and then hope for the best. A prompt may be a starting point, but it doesn't instruct. Our youngest writers need instruction on the physical act of writing. In addition, they need experiences that build their fluency through encoding, as well as regular practice in rapidly transferring ideas to the page. The structure of written thought is essential for them to master, as syntactical and structural errors otherwise undermine the message. Therefore, they need to experiment with how structures are used to convey a message. Finally, they must be apprenticed into the processes all writers rely upon. Fluency, structure, and processes form the core of writing instruction in a balanced literacy classroom.

Like the write-alouds used at the beginning of the chapter, the instructional routines we profile in this chapter can be used to great effect with different grade levels to teach students how to write in a range of genres and how to address a variety of writing issues and challenges. We have already discussed writing aloud, and will now feature additional whole-class approaches, including direct instruction, interactive writing, and writing fluency development. In addition, we focus attention on grammar instruction and generating sentences. We conclude the chapter with a discussion of writing traits and writing processes.

DIRECT INSTRUCTION IN WRITING

Direct instruction requires that teachers handle almost all of the tricky parts, providing manageable bits of information that students can use. As we noted in the reading chapter, direct instruction includes opportunities for students to practice and for teachers to check for understanding.

Importantly, direct instruction in writing is not limited to teachers telling students how to write. As Goeke (2008) noted, "Students must be encouraged to provide the second, complementary half of the transaction: active engagement. An optimal explicit instruction lesson involves an effective, dynamic teacher and an active, engaged learner" (p. 37). Figure 3.1 contains a list of characteristics of explicit, direct instruction in writing and compares them to what direct instruction is *not*.

As an example, Matt Hargrove was introducing paragraph writing to his third-grade students. He said,

> I'm going to teach you how to write a good paragraph. That's our learning target today. First I'll tell you what to do. Second I'll show you how to do it. Third, we will look at some examples, and I'll identify which parts of each of them are good and which could be better. Then I'll ask you to write based on a topic I will give you.

He then proceeded to explain the process of paragraph writing to his students.

There are any number of things that we can teach using a direct instruction approach. In writing, direct instruction is often used to teach students how to form letters, how to write in cursive, and to introduce basic writing skills such as capitalization and punctuation, sentence and paragraph generation, expressive writing, keyboarding, and reasoning in writing. Regardless of the content of the lessons, direct instruction in writing lessons typically includes the following components:

1. **Setting the stage for learning,** which can include a hook and should include a learning intention or objective

2. **Clear explanation of what to do,** which requires that we understand the various parts of the skill and can focus on the part that needs to be learned

Direct instruction includes opportunities for students to practice and for teachers to check for understanding.

3. **Modeling the process** and showing students how another person (we) might do it

4. **Guided practice** in which we support students as they try what we modeled

5. **Independent practice** in which students apply what they have learned

6. **Assessment** to determine if the students have met the learning target

7. **Closure,** which can include a recap of the learning intention or objective and some transition to the next task or activity

▼ FIGURE 3.1 DEFINING EXPLICIT, DIRECT INSTRUCTION

What Explicit, Direct Instruction *Is*	What Explicit, Direct Instruction *Is Not*
Explicit Instruction is skill based, but students are active participants in the learning process. They practice what has been taught.	Explicit Instruction is not skill and drill.
Explicit Instruction is holistic. For example, teachers can use Explicit Instruction to teach everything that is included in "literacy" (i.e., decoding, comprehension, spelling, and the writing process).	Explicit Instruction is not just used to teach isolated facts and procedures.
Explicit Instruction integrates smaller learning units into meaningful wholes.	Explicit Instruction does not teach basic skills in isolation from meaningful contexts.
Explicit Instruction is developmentally appropriate. Instruction is tailored specifically to students' learning and instructional needs.	Explicit Instruction is not "one size fits all."
The teacher constantly monitors understanding to make sure students are deriving meaning from instruction.	Explicit Instruction is not rote.
Explicit Instruction is used in diverse contexts and curricular areas.	Explicit Instruction is not basic skills only.
Students like it because they are learning!	Explicit Instruction is not boring and alienating.
Students are cognitively engaged throughout the learning encounter. They have opportunities throughout the lesson to self-monitor and direct their own learning and participation.	Explicit Instruction is not all teacher directed.

Source: Goeke, J. L. (2008). *Explicit instruction: A framework for meaningful direct teaching.* Upper Saddle River, NJ: Pearson. p. 10. Reprinted by permission of Pearson Education, Inc., New York.

Handwriting

We recognize that handwriting instruction is not currently popular, which is problematic because the evidence suggests that teaching handwriting is important for students' writing achievement. In their meta-analysis of handwriting instruction, Santangelo and Graham (2015) noted that impacts of handwriting instruction were impressive. A meta-analysis is a statistical tool that combines the results from several studies and generates an effect size (ES), which is a measure of the magnitude of the impact. As Hattie (2012) noted, an effect size over 0.40 is above the average for impact on student learning and likely results in a year or more of learning for a year of schooling. In the meta-analysis they conducted, Santangelo and Graham found 80 different experiments that compared student performance when they did or did not receive handwriting instruction. Importantly, the students who received handwriting instruction had greater writing legibility (ES = 0.59) and fluency (ES = 0.63).

resources.corwin.com/
thisisbalancedliteracy

Video 8
Handwriting Lesson

When teachers teach students handwriting, the number of words they write and the readability or legibility of the writing is improved. In addition, the overall length of student writing increased (ES = 1.33) as did the overall quality of their writing (ES = 0.84). Without consistent exposure to handwriting instruction, there is evidence that students will experience difficulty in certain processes required for success in reading and writing, including (Saperstein Associates, 2012):

- Retrieving letters from memory

- Reproducing letters on paper

- Spelling accurately

- Extracting meaning from a text or lecture

- Interpreting the context of words and phrases

The majority of the kindergarten students in Tiffany Barker's class could name all of the upper- and lowercase letters but had difficulty writing some of them when it came time to do so independently. They confused *b*, *d*, and *p* on a regular basis. So Ms. Barker decided that she needed to provide her students with direct instruction to address their needs. She started her lesson by gaining students' attention and alerting them to the learning target, which involved correctly writing letters that have both circles and lines in them.

Marjorie Cotera/Bob Daemmrich Photography, Inc.

Teaching handwriting is important for students' writing achievement.

She then explained,

> Today we get to learn about writing letters that seem to have a circle and a line, or, as some people tell me, they have a ball and a stick. The circle or ball can stay in the same place, but where you put the stick makes a different letter. And if you have the stick in the wrong place, your reader might not know which word you mean. So it's really important that we get this right. I'm going to show you how I remember this. When the line is before the circle, like this [she writes the lowercase letter *b*], I can remember it's the letter *b* because of the word *before*. *Before*. The line comes before the circle for *b*. But if the line is after the circle, then it is the letter *d*. Sometimes I say to myself, yo dude, the line is after the circle in the *d*, dude.

But then we have the really tricky one. The letter *p*. The line is before the circle but it's lower. See how I did that [writing the letter *p*]? I say to myself, letter *p* you just want to pop up on the line, but you have to stay down there to be right.

Let's try to make some letters. I'll say them randomly and you can write on your dry erase boards. Then we can check. And then, when we're ready, we'll write some words. Are you ready to practice?

Notice that the direct, explicit instruction was brief, and it included some information for students to use when they tried. You may have other ways for describing how the letters work or look or sound, but Ms. Barker provided her students with something to think about so that they might get it right when they attempted it.

Keyboarding

Students also need to develop skills in keyboarding in order to be effective writers. Research shows that student writing will improve once they have learned the keyboard (Balajthy, 1987) and on the flip side, that if students fail to learn to use the keyboard effectively, their writing will be slow, and the computer may actually impede their learning (Barack, 2005). When students consciously work on keyboarding skills, not leaving keyboarding to chance, they are learning a life skill that is going to help them develop into strong writers as students and develop the skills they will need as they grow older. Having keyboarding skills generally means that a student can type at the speed of thought.

It is recommended that students have explicit instruction in keyboarding so that they develop automaticity correctly and accurately. Keyboarding instruction is not simply focusing on skill and drill; it can be most effective when we engage students in meaningful activities that require keyboarding (Education World, 2017). For students who have been taught the basics of keyboarding, or for students in later grades who have already been introduced to keyboarding, try having them

- Publish their writing using a word processing program so that they type in their finished pieces and add clip art to decorate their writing

- Practice composing on devices. Make sure they are familiar with the QWERTY keyboard and have both hands on the keyboard, so they are working to hit the correct key for each letter and not hunting and pecking

Keyboarding skills generally means that a student can type at the speed of thought.

- Write short answers to constructed responses items on the device to encourage keyboarding

- Write and use a keyboard in a fun way. Web-based apps like Padlet and Explain Everything require students to write to respond. In Padlet, students can create news items, newsletters, informational articles, and stories by typing in their writing, or composing while typing, and then add pictures and print out the finished product.

Gina Morello uses a direct instruction approach to introduce keyboarding to her second graders. The keys on their laptops have been color coded to indicate which finger should be used to type a specific letter. This is an overlay for the keyboards that is designed to support students' keyboarding acquisition. On the first day of keyboarding, Ms. Morello says,

> Today, we're going to learn about finger placement on the keyboard. We've all typed with just our index fingers [she holds up her two index fingers]. This is called hunt and peck. We're going to learn how to type and not just hunt. I've displayed my keyboard on the projector, and I'm going to show you where the fingers are supposed to rest. See how my pinky on the left starts at *A*? And then I rest the other fingers over the keys *S, D,* and *F.* I skip two letters, *G* and *H,* and start my right hand on *J.* See what I'm doing? So then my pinky finger on the left is over the semicolon. That's our home row.

Ms. Morello continues with the lesson having students type *f* and *j* several times. She calls out a letter randomly and students type it. She then moves to *d* and *k* for practice. She knows that this will take several weeks to master and that her students will need more instruction and individual practice. However, she also knows that their writing will improve once they have learned the keyboard, and because they are developing proficiency with keyboarding, the computer will be a tool for them to use creatively and intuitively and will not hinder their learning.

Interactive writing is a teacher-facilitated instructional routine that moves students from idea generation to composition.

INTERACTIVE WRITING

Interactive writing is a teacher-facilitated instructional routine that moves students from idea generation to composition. Its most distinguishable feature is the practice of sharing the pen with children, who write letters and spell words on a large chart paper that all can see. Lessons are typically 10–15 minutes in length. Key goals of the lesson include coconstruction and cocreation of the agreed-upon message (McCarrier, Pinnell, & Fountas, 2000).

Given the developmental constraints of young children in terms of the physical act of writing, the messages themselves are short—usually one or two sentences. So much more is accomplished in the richness of the discussion and decision making that occurs during the lesson. The lesson is structured, although the learners ultimately influence the direction it takes. Lesson elements include the following:

1. A shared experience to write about

2. Planning and composing the message

3. Constructing the message

4. Rereading the message

During interactive writing, students write so all can see.

Michael Newman/PhotoEdit

A Shared Experience

An interactive writing lesson actually begins hours or days before the students sit down with us to write. A shared experience provides the fodder for discussion and the purpose for composing the message. Activation of prior knowledge is an important part of writing processes, and shared experiences make it possible. A field trip to a fire station might prompt the need for a thank-you note from the class. The announcement of a grade-level event might necessitate an invitation to the classroom across the hall. But most shared experiences begin with a text the students have previously read.

The students in Olivia Ruiz's first-grade class have been reading *Last Stop on Market Street* (De la Peña, 2015). This book describes the journey CJ and his grandmother take on the bus and includes descriptions about the people they meet along the way. Her students have had a number of discussions about the book, including discussions about CJ's mood change and how the author uses interesting verbs to describe the situations.

Planning and Composing the Message

The interactive writing lesson begins with planning the message. Students and the teacher generate ideas for the content of the message. The students in Ms. Ruiz's class decide to recommend the book to another first-grade class. They jointly compose a message, while the teacher assists in organizing their ideas and honing the sentence. The final message that Ms. Ruiz's students agree upon is this:

> We hope you will read the book we sent you. The characters are very interesting, and we like the verbs. Write back after you read the book. Room 35

The teacher continually restates and refines the message. During this phase, students can propose changes to the message and refine word choices. This repetition is essential in writing, as the act of composition requires continuous mental rehearsal of the sentence. Writing is an iterative practice, as the writer must monitor what has been written and what will be written next. We accomplish all of this through dialogic instruction, as we ask thought-provoking questions to spur students' thinking. This portion of the lesson usually takes about five minutes.

Constructing the Message

When the group reaches consensus on the message, the teacher shifts attention to getting ready to write. Ms. Ruiz thinks aloud for her students, counting the number of words each sentence contains. The act of writing the message requires planning how much room the words will need on the chart paper or smartboard, and counting the number of words needed assists young writers in considering the physical layout of the sentence. Ms. Ruiz also reviews the rules of construction, such as print conventions, letter formations, and spacing. Because students will be the ones writing each letter and word, these reminders help them consolidate the knowledge and many skills needed to be successful. A black bullet-tipped marker works well for students, as the size of the barrel of the pen works well in small hands.

She approaches each word individually, with students encouraged to sound out some words, and use lists of sight words and the word wall as needed. Ms. Ruiz coaches and scaffolds each child's contributions, and she alternates with other prompts and solicitations to the group to keep them engaged. Because individual children need varying levels of support depending on their current abilities, this stage of the interactive lesson is marked by differentiated instruction. Errors occur, of course, and these are handled by using white paper tape for students to write over. Crossing out errors can leave the finished message looking scrambled, so paper tape corrections preserve the integrity of the written message. There's another subtle message conveyed, and that is that when writers make errors, they fix them and keep going. With each word written, the group restates the entire sentence to recall what word will be needed next. Because sentence construction can be time consuming for emergent writers, this portion of the lesson may take seven to eight minutes to complete.

resources.corwin.com/
thisisbalancedliteracy

Video 9
Word Study

As individual students write on the chart paper, Ms. Ruiz engages the rest of the class in a range of learning activities. For example, when Mario was writing the word *book*, Ms. Ruiz asked the other students in the class to write a word that rhymed with *book* on their personal dry erase boards. Mario wrote *boke* instead of *book,* and Ms. Ruiz asked the students in the class to hold up their rhyming words and said, "Mario, take a look at the words that rhyme with *book,* and see if you can find a spelling pattern that works."

Before Andrea was called on to write the word *sent*, Ms. Ruiz said, "How exciting. *Sent* is a homophone. Remember, we talked about words that sound the same but are spelled differently and have different meanings? Can you all try to write the homophone for *sent*?" The students start to do so, and Ms. Ruiz invites Andrea to the board. Ms. Ruiz believes that Andrea knows the correct version, as she has used the word in her independent writing. The lesson continues with Ms. Ruiz integrating spelling, word study, and composition ideas into the discussion as her students write the message they have agreed upon.

Rereading the Message

The last stage of the interactive writing lesson is rereading the message to ensure meaning. All writers reread what they have written to ensure it is accurate and comprehensible. Ms. Ruiz uses this time as an opportunity to revisit the purpose of the message and its intended audience, ensuring that her students consider these elements as well in their critique of the finished message. The group can make decisions about what needs to be added to the message in the next lesson, such as providing details through additional sentences.

Interactive Writing for Older Students

Many of the same principles that make interactive writing useful for primary students apply to support for older elementary writers, with some important differences. Roth and Dabrowski (2014) suggest four key shifts when writing interactively with students in grades 2–5:

- **Fluid and dynamic lesson flow:** Older students are more skilled and are capable of producing more text in a setting, often a paragraph or more. Therefore, the teacher cycles through the planning, composing, and constructing portions of the lesson more than once, as multisentence compositions require that writers revisit and reshape their message as it develops.

- **Modifications to pace, discussion, and medium:** The pace is accelerated, as older writers are able to write entire words and complete sentences; they don't need the letter-by-letter approach that is useful for beginning writers. Discussion of difficult words and reminders about conventions may occur only once, at the beginning of the lesson. The medium itself may shift from composing on chart paper to composing in a projected digital format.

- **Lesson frequency and duration:** While primary students benefit from interactive writing lessons delivered several times a week, older writers don't require the same frequency. The lessons themselves may be a bit longer due to increased attention and self-regulation skills. However, older students need the same high levels of engagement. Otherwise, they can quickly drift to a passive role as others write.

Fluency building is often a neglected aspect of writing instruction. Too often, students stare off into space, saying "I'm thinking" when they are given a writing task.

- **Expand and extend around genres:** Older students can benefit from interactive writing lessons that explore new genres, such as informational or opinion writing. You can explore specific features, such as the format for writing science lab reports, friendly letters, and poetry forms through joint composition. Students can then use the interactive text as a model for their own independent writing.

Interactive writing empowers the youngest writers with the ability to put their thoughts in print, even as they are learning the formative skills of composition. There's no reason to wait until these skills are in place. Writing should begin right from the start, and interactive writing is the right place to begin.

WRITING FLUENCY

Fluency in writing, the ability to quickly create a cohesive message, should be a goal of our writing instruction. As students develop writing fluency, their word choice and phrasing should become more sophisticated. They should be adding expression and depth to their writing. And they should be able to write longer pieces in shorter amounts of time. However, fluency building is often a neglected aspect of writing instruction. Too often, students stare off into space, saying "I'm thinking" when they are given a writing task. Some amount of thinking is appropriate, but eventually they need to begin putting ideas down on paper. You can think without writing but not write without thinking. After all, it's hard to do anything but think about what you are writing when you are writing. Try it. Try to write about something and think about something else. Impossible. Students need to experience the power of thinking on paper (or computer) and then revising their work.

Importantly, focusing on writing fluency can improve writing performance and achievement (Kasper-Ferguson & Moxley, 2002). There are norms for reading fluency, but there are not norms for writing fluency (or speaking fluency for that matter). Having said that, the fourth graders in the Kasper-Ferguson and Moxley study averaged 25 words written per minute, with one student consistently writing 60 words per minute. Interestingly, as they implemented daily writing fluency tasks and graphed their success, student writing fluency continued to increase over the course of the year. The fastest writer in the study began in October writing an average of 20 words per minute and could sustain 59 words per minute in May. Importantly, these researchers note, "Ceiling effects in writing did not appear" (p. 249). In other words, students continued to make progress, and given enough time, there was no telling how many words per minute they could have written. But it is important to keep in mind that fluency is not an end in itself. As with the other skills we have discussed here, fluency is a means to an end. Its purpose is to help students become comfortable with getting their thoughts on paper, so that they have content to edit and revise. And, teachers use student writing to identify instructional needs that they can address in the whole class, with a small group, or individually.

Daily Power Writing

Daily power writing is an instructional tool designed to eliminate the common pitfall of "writer's block" during initial stages of the writing process (Fearn & Farnan, 2001). Students may lack writing fluency for a number of reasons: few opportunities to write, fear that what they write may be judged as incorrect, or a lack of metacognitive awareness about how to begin. The main goal of power writing is to build stamina and confidence in writing. Over time, students will improve in writing speed, ease, and automaticity. As Shanahan (1977) noted in his discussion of "writing marathons," the idea of uninterrupted writing sessions that build fluency and stamina are not new, but may have to be "rediscovered."

To begin, we provide a prompt and direct students to "*write as much as you can as well as you can.*" The prompt can be just about anything related to the classroom content. For example, the students in Rachelle Sampson's fourth-grade class have just finished *Finding Winnie: The True Story of the World's Most Famous Bear* (Mattick, 2015), which tells the story of the real Christopher Robin, a boy who meets a bear that had been rescued by a veterinarian, Harry Colebourn, which inspires the Winnie-the-Pooh stories. The first power writing task Ms. Sampson provides for her students is for them to write about *animals.*

Daily power writing is an instructional tool designed to eliminate the common pitfall of "writer's block" during initial stages of the writing process (Fearn & Farnan, 2001).

Students write for one minute, and when the timer rings, they count the number of words they have written. This process is repeated two additional times, with different prompts. Ms. Sampson uses single words as her prompts, such as *endangered* and *responsibility,* which are themes from *Finding Winnie*, but other teachers use phrases, sentences, and questions.

After the third cycle, students graph the highest number of words written on their individual graphs. These charts, which are developed on graph paper and dated, chronicle the progress students are making in their writing fluency. They are invaluable during writing conferences, as the student and teacher can view the student's gains and set goals. As they count the number of words each time, students also circle spelling and grammatical errors that they notice in their own writing. Errors that they don't notice inform us about future instructional needs, which can be another focus of a writing conference.

We may vary the amount of time for each power writing session as students' confidence and writing fluency increases. The time spent on power writing can be modified from 30 seconds to 60 seconds to 120 seconds, so students don't become accustomed to writing for one specified amount of time.

Power writing is an instructional routine that is easy to get started and one we can use on a daily basis for writing instruction with the whole class. Some tips for power writing include these:

- Provide students with a vocabulary term being used in the content to spur their thinking, and write it on the board.

- Instruct students to "write as much as they can, as well as they can" for 60 seconds.

- At the end of 60 seconds, tell them "pencils up," and ask them to count the overall number of words and tally them in the margin. We also ask students to circle errors they noticed while rereading.

- Repeat two more times.

- We ask them to write their entries in a notebook, rather than on loose paper, so that their entries are always available. Each week, we invite them to choose a previously written entry to revise, extend, and submit for review.

Dictation teaches students how to transfer reading skills to writing and solidifies the speech-to-print connection.

Dictation

Another way to build fluency is dictation. During dictation, you ask students to write letters, words, or sentences that are controlled based on the learning that has occurred thus far. As Blevins (2000) noted, dictation combined with explicit phonics instruction and reading controlled texts resulted in better learning outcomes for students. In other words, dictation teaches students how to transfer reading skills to writing and solidifies the speech-to-print connection.

Christina Torres uses dictation with her kindergarten students, asking them to write the letter for the sounds she shares. For example, she says, "Let's take out our writing notebooks and open to our dictation page. Remember this is the page that starts with the picture of the microphone on it. Ready? Please write the letter for the sound I say. /l/ /s/ /m/ And now, as a bonus, write the word with the following sounds: /p/ /i/ /g/."

Todd Gallagher uses dictation with his first-grade students, inviting them to write sentences with longer words that they have been studying. For example, during whole-class instruction following their power writing, Mr. Gallagher asked his students to write the following sentences: *The string was strung across the street. The stripe hid the streak of dirt.* In doing so, Mr. Gallagher's students had to listen, identify the sounds and words, and then encode them. In doing so, they begin to push words and ideas out of their pencils, building their writing fluency and listening comprehension skills.

By second grade these sentences should include a few multisyllabic words, and the teacher should provide strategies to help students spell these words. For example, Marci Higgins had her students write: *The character was cheating but got caught.*

SPELLING INSTRUCTION

English is known to be a confusing language. However, English is more consistent that most people realize. As Bear, Invernizzi, Templeton, and Johnston (2011) note, English requires an understanding of three systems to spell correctly: alphabet, pattern, and meaning. First, regarding alphabet, English is based, at least in part, on the sound-symbol relationship. Students have to learn to read or voice the sounds from left to right, accurately matching sounds to symbols. This approach will work for a significant portion of the words in English. However, as Moats (1995) noted, understanding basic syllable-based spelling patterns can help (see Figure 3.2).

▼ FIGURE 3.2 SIX BASIC SYLLABLE SPELLING PATTERNS

1. **Closed:** These syllables end in a consonant. The vowel sound is generally short (EXAMPLES: *rab bit, nap kin*).

2. **Open:** These syllables end in a vowel. The vowel sound is generally long (EXAMPLES: *tiger, pilot*).

3. **R-controlled:** When a vowel is followed by *r*, the letter *r* affects the sound of the vowel. The vowel and the *r* appear in the same syllable (EXAMPLES: *bird, turtle*).

4. **Vowel team:** Many vowel sounds are spelled with vowel digraphs such as *ai, ay, ea, ee, oa, ow, oo, oi, oy, ou, ie,* and *ei*. The vowel digraphs appear in the same syllable (EXAMPLES: *boat, explain*).

5. **Vowel–silent e:** These syllables generally represent long-vowel sounds (EXAMPLES: *compete, decide*).

6. **Consonant + *le*:** Usually when *le* appears at the end of a word and is preceded by a consonant, the consonant + *le* form the final syllable (EXAMPLES: *table, little*).

Source: Blevins, W. (2006). *Phonics from A to Z: A practical guide.* New York: Scholastic.

The second system that has to be mastered to spell correctly in English is the pattern. Our brain works like a pattern detector. This layer requires that readers extend beyond a single letter to understand the sound that should be produced. One pattern that guides our understanding is the

CVCe, found in words such as *bake, flake,* and *make.* Learning the pattern provides the reader with a transportable skill for decoding and encoding. It also helps students spell more complex words. If you know that *excellent* ends in *ent,* then you can spell *excellence* (*-ence*) and not worry if it should be *-ence* or *-ance.* The same is true for *different/difference, fragrant/fragrance,* and so on. Patterns help in big ways.

The alphabet and patterns are not all that are required. English also relies on meaning for some spellings (Templeton, 2011). This third layer provides readers a clue for words with sounds that do not necessarily match their spelling. For example, *clinic* and *clinician* or *physics* and *physicist* rely on the meaning level for spelling, as the individual words are pronounced differently. This is also evidenced in homographs, which are words that are spelled alike but differ in meaning and sometimes sound. Consider the following:

- Sally will <u>present</u> the <u>present</u> to the birthday girl.

- The state now <u>permits</u> <u>permits</u> for fishing and hunting.

- "I <u>object</u>!" shouted the prosecutor when the <u>object</u> was shown to the jury.

Taking into account these three systems that operate in English, teachers must focus their instruction accordingly. Early in a student's spelling career, the focus will remain on the alphabet. As students become more sophisticated in their spelling development, teachers add the patterns and meaning levels. Obviously, these systems have implications not only for instruction but also for the choice of words that compose the spelling curriculum.

Spelling Development Is Predictable

There is considerable research that suggests children progress through predictable patterns as they learn to spell. Understanding students' current developmental level allows instruction to be targeted and tailored to individual needs. As Read (1975) writes, "One sees clearly that different children chose the same phonetically motivated spellings to a degree that can hardly be explained as resulting from random choice or the influence of adults" (p. 32). Figure 3.3 contains names of common stages of spelling development as well as characteristics of each stage. Whole-class spelling lessons should challenge students, and small-group lessons should guide their understanding of the patterns they are learning.

▼ FIGURE 3.3 STAGES OF SPELLING DEVELOPMENT

Developmental Spelling Stages	Characteristics of Each Stage
Preliterate or Emergent	• Attempts toward writing • Marks include strings of scribbles, drawings, and letter-like symbols • Marks may be written in any direction or space across the page • Typical of 3- to 5-year-olds
Letter Name— Alphabetic	• Beginning to read and use inventive spelling • Rely on names of letters; prominent sounds represented, along with beginning and ending consonants and some vowels • Many sight words memorized • Typical of 5–7 years of age
Within Word Pattern	• Inventive spellings, but short and long vowels honored • Blends frequently represented • Most sight words spelled correctly • Approximations represent what "looks right" • Understandings develop in regard to vowel-consonant-e patterns, *r*-controlled patterns, long and abstract vowels, and more complex consonant patterns • An awareness of homophones and exploration with meaning • Typical of 7- to 9-year-olds
Syllable Juncture	• Frequent errors in spelling unstressed vowels (the schwa) in multisyllabic words and also in consonant doubling • Doubling and e-drop with inflectional endings (*-s, -es, -ed, -ing*) • Long vowel patterns (*ladle, complain*) and *r*-controlled vowels (*dreary, inspire*) in the stressed syllable • Consonant assimilation (*ir + relevant = irrelevant*) • Prefixes and suffixes (known as affixes) • Typical of 9–11 years of age

(continued)

(*continued*)

Developmental Spelling Stages	Characteristics of Each Stage
Derivational Constancy	• Relationships between spelling and meaning (morphology) • Morphemes are preserved even when pronunciations change (*condemn/condemnation; discuss/discussion*) • Silent and sounded consonants (*haste, hasten*) • Consonant and vowel changes or alternations (*express/expression; compose/composition*) • Greek and Latin roots and affixes • Typical of 11-year-olds through adults

Source: Created by Wendy Sheets Reed, based on Bear, D. R., Invernizzi, M., Templeton, S., & Johnston, F. (2000). *Words their way: Word study for phonics, vocabulary, and spelling instruction* (2nd ed.). Upper Saddle River, NJ: Prentice-Hall; Ganske, K. (2000). *Word journeys: Assessment-guided phonics, spelling, and vocabulary instruction.* New York: The Guilford Press; Henderson, E. H. (1985). *Teaching spelling.* Boston: Houghton Mifflin; and Sheets, W. (2013). *Developmental spelling stages* (handout for 2014 National Reading Recovery & K–6 Classroom Literacy Conference). Columbus: Literacy Collaborative, The Ohio State University.

Learning From What Doesn't Work in Spelling

There are at least three common approaches to spelling instruction that are ineffective, or even harmful, to the development of spellers who can use words correctly in their reading and writing. We cannot neglect spelling, test students on lists on Fridays, or tell them to write the word many times over.

Neglect: It's almost embarrassing to write about, but ignoring spelling instruction will not provide students the support they need to spell as they write or read independently. Unfortunately, it is still too common for teachers to believe that spelling will just develop naturally as students read. Simply reading and absorbing patterns, as Bosman and Van Orden (1997) note, "is not the most effective way to learn to spell" (p. 188). Perfetti (1997) is more explicit: "Practice at spelling should help reading more than practice at reading helps spelling" (p. 31).

The Monday-to-Friday routine: Giving students a list of words on Monday, asking them to practice the words at home during the week, and then testing their knowledge on Friday is also an insufficient route to spelling knowledge. While common, the evidence for this approach is lacking (e.g., Templeton, 2011). In contrast with this tradition of "giving the words and then the test," teachers can focus instruction on the weekly spelling words on a regular basis. Students correct their own tests, not just on Friday, but every day (e.g., Fearn & Farnan, 2001).

Writing the words 10 times (or 100 times for that matter):
Writing words as a list is also an ineffective way to improve spelling performance (Ganske, 2000). We all know students who write each letter in a column ten times until the word appears ten times. Not only is this ineffective, but it wastes time—time that students could use to learn how to spell.

Implementing What Works in Spelling

What does work? Whole-class, daily spelling tests and time to practice words that students need to learn. That may seem like a strange answer, but holding students accountable on a regular basis works. The most significant way to ensure that students learn to spell is through self-corrected tests—tests that the students correct themselves to focus on where they are making mistakes (Henderson, 1990; Templeton, 2011). Once per week is simply not sufficient to provide students the practice they need in noticing where they make mistakes. Instead, students need regular, if not daily, spelling tests to learn to spell well.

The self-corrected spelling instruction and test might occur something like this. On Monday, Brandi Allen asks students to participate in a spelling test. She reads them a list of 10 words that they have not been asked to spell before. Once she has read the list through two times, she asks students to correct their papers as she reads the words and spells each one. Students circle any missing letters, added letters, or transposed letters.

She then asks students to give themselves a letter grade for *each* word (A is no errors, B is one error, and so on). When they finish this first round, she asks her students to turn their papers over, and she presents the same list again in a different order. Following the same procedure, she provides her students with time to self-correct and circle the places on the word where they make mistakes. Students then record these words in the Words to Learn section of their journal, where they write notes to themselves about confusions.

By Wednesday, over half the class has all the words correct, and they no longer need to participate in the spelling tests. By Friday, nearly every student in her class can spell the entire list correctly and use the words in their writing. The key to learning to spell this way is successive approximations (Fearn & Farnan, 2001). In other words, students are participating in an instructional event in which they are not immediately told that they have "failed the spelling test, again," but rather can see their progress slowly increase as they pay attention to the places in the words where they make mistakes.

> The most significant way to ensure that students learn to spell is through self-corrected tests—tests that the students correct themselves to focus on where they are making mistakes (Henderson, 1990; Templeton, 2011).

We don't want to imply that spelling improves only when students use these self-corrected tests, but we do think these tests are important. A look inside Ms. Allen's class suggests that spelling is part of their regular work, both collaboratively and individually. The students in Lupita's group are writing in their spelling journals. Miriam is practicing the class focus words by using a simple study technique called "Look-Cover-Say-Write-Check." Leo is using his notes to figure out the correct spelling for *suggest*, puzzled about whether it has one *g* or two. He writes it both ways and settles on the latter, and then continues with his writing. Meanwhile, Steve and Tino are working through a word sort, trying to create categories for the list of words they are learning this week. Lupita is contemplating which of the independent spelling activities she will do next. She has just completed her Words to Learn list, where she has identified the "tricky parts" of each word. At that moment, Ms. Allen checks in on the group to see how they are progressing. "I've got a new word for Stump the Teacher," says Lupita with a twinkle in her eye. "Great!" says Ms. Allen. "Bring it on—I'm ready!"

> Just say the word "grammar," and most students start to moan. Sadly, there are many students who find the careful examination of the rules of our language exceptionally boring, maybe because of the way grammar was historically taught.

GRAMMAR TEACHING AND LEARNING

Just say the word "grammar," and most students start to moan. Sadly, there are many students who find the careful examination of the rules of our language exceptionally boring. That may be because of the way grammar was historically taught—decontextualized and through rote memorization. It also may be because students don't see the utility of grammar lessons. However, as literacy educators we all know that grammar is critical in order for students to understand the language. Without agreed-upon structures and rules, speakers and writers would have a very difficult time communicating. Language is more than random words strung together. Verb tense, syntax, punctuation, pronouns, and such guide our understanding of the message. As Truss (2004) notes, there is a significant difference between "eats, shoots, and leaves" and "eats shoots and leaves." In other words, comprehension is impacted when students do not understand the rules that govern language use.

Traditionally, grammar instruction focused on morphology and syntax. Students were required to learn word structure (morphology), a branch of linguistics that concentrates on the ways in which words are related to one another. For example, fluent readers and writers know that *house* is to *houses* as *bird* is to *birds*—they have generalized the word knowledge or morphology of the *–s* ending in English. Students also need to know how words can be combined to form phrases and sentences, which we call syntax. These syntactic rules or "patterned relations" govern the way we can combine words to form phrases and sentences. For example, fluent users of English understand that the verb form "to be" changes and is the most complex, irregular verb in the language. Fluent language learners understand the differences between the following uses of the form:

- I *am* tired.

- I will *be* tired after running.

- Boys will *be* boys.

- Cats *are* felines.

Importantly, grammar has always been a part of the classroom. However, as Gribbin (2005) notes, "A persistent question throughout the years is to teach grammar or not to teach, along with how much to teach and when" (p. 17).

At this point, we should acknowledge that we do not advocate traditional or decontextualized grammar instruction (i.e., diagramming, fill-in-the-blank worksheets). In their analysis of the effectiveness of formal grammar instruction, Andrews et al. (2006) noted that there was little evidence to support this approach. In contrast, Feng and Powers (2005) noted that the use of students' writing as the fodder for grammar lessons resulted in increased knowledge and skills. For example, students' writing from their fluency tasks (e.g., power writing) can be used as a source of information to plan grammar lessons. This will be more useful than generic grammar lessons and will more likely to result in student mastery of the language than whole-class, canned grammar lessons. Figure 3.4 provides a comparison between historical approaches to grammar instruction and those we understand to be effective today.

▼ FIGURE 3.4 COMPARING APPROACHES TO GRAMMAR INSTRUCTION

Historical Approaches	Current Approaches
• Sentence diagramming	• Using student writing as fodder for instruction
• Memorizing definitions of grammar terms	• Using mentor texts to apprentice students
• Identifying parts of speech	• Varying instruction based on student need
• Teaching grammar to the whole class	• Using instructional strategies that are flexibly applied to a variety of grammar structures and rules
• Substitution drills	
• Translation	
• Using a grammatical syllabus to determine when to teach a specific structure	

It is important to recognize that teaching grammar is most effective when it takes place within the context of reading and writing. We must combine a focus on sentence structure, usage, and even paragraph organization with an understanding of the characteristics of text. Traditional methods of teaching writing have taken a bottom-up approach—beginning with basic rules of grammar from which students learn to write sentences, from which they learn to write paragraphs, from which they learn to write essays. As we look at student writing—sentences, paragraphs, and essays—we find at least three sources of errors:

1. Knowledge of rules

2. Knowledge of the writing process

3. Understanding of the characteristics of different types of text

Clearly, we must teach the rules that govern the organization of sentences. We can design tasks that provoke errors so that we know which ones to teach. Generative sentences can be used with the whole class to identify gaps in grammar knowledge (as well as vocabulary knowledge).

resources.corwin.com/
thisisbalancedliteracy

Video 10
Students Write With
a Mentor Text

Generative Sentences

One approach to grammar instruction involves students constructing sentences from words that we give to them. Fearn and Farnan call this practice a "given word sentence" (2001, p. 87). We expand on this practice and note the generative nature of this strategy, which carries the writer from the word to the sentence to the paragraph level.

This strategy allows students to expand their sentences and use the language and mechanics that are necessary in order to convey information. Essentially, we identify a letter or word and the place in a sentence where the word will be used. Our students then write sentences with the given components.

For example, in their study of a gradual release of responsibility for writing instruction, Fisher and Frey (2003) asked students to write the letter *v* on their paper. The next instruction was to write a word with the letter *v* in the third position. We then listed these words on the dry erase board. Students were able to see the variation of words that share this characteristic—*love, have, give, dove, advice,* and so on. Following this, we asked students to use their word in a sentence. A sample of the sentences included these:

- I love my family, especialy James.

- The dove is a sign of peace.

- You best get some advice on that hairdo.

On this particular day when we focused on the letter *v* in the third position, we created an independent assignment from this generative sentence activity. We asked students to use the sentence they had written as a topic sentence for a paragraph. The paragraphs were due the following day. Students understood that a paragraph could be 3, 5, or 8 or whatever number of sentences necessary to convey the idea they wanted to share. Consistent with the gradual release model, we had students create the topic sentence in class, so they were well on their way to completing a paragraph on their own. The successful completion rate of this type of homework was much higher than independent writing assignments in which students had to complete the entire paper at home.

Najimo's fifth-grade teacher used generative sentences to expand his understanding of language. For example, during one class the teacher wanted to focus on adjectives. She asked students to complete the following sentences:

- *Spectacular* in the fourth position of a sentence more than ten words long.

- *Grumpy* in the fifth position of a sentence fewer than nine words long.

- *Rude* in the sixth position in a sentence of any length.

- *Struggling* in the second position of a sentence more than seven words long.

One of the sentences Najimo, an English learner, wrote was, "I were in the grumpy mood on Tuesday." His teacher noticed the errors in this sentence as well as the things he did correctly. During her small-group writing instruction, she asked him about his choice of article (*the*). As he reread the sentence, he self-corrected the error (by substituting the word *a* for *the*). She then turned her attention to his choice of *were* and asked him about it. He said, "Tuesday is past, so *were* is right, right?" They talked for a few minutes about singular and plural versions and the impact that changing the pronoun would have (we were, I was, she was, he was, they were, etc.).

resources.corwin.com/
thisisbalancedliteracy

Video 11
Generative Writing
Lesson

In a generative sentences session, we provide students with a word or phrase as well as a placement requirement for the sentence. In addition to the word placement, which requires students to control the grammar surrounding the word, we can place limits on the length of the sentence to help students develop their sentence fluency. Word limiter activities are helpful for students learning English, as they encourage self-editing and a focus on precision in writing (Davis, 1998). Sentence fluency—using sentences of varying lengths—is also important for English language learners, as it is one trait of good writing (Culham, 2003). Generative sentence sessions allow us to assess both vocabulary knowledge and understanding of grammar. After we have collected student information and provided students with practice during whole-class learning, we can offer instruction that is responsive to the needs of individuals or groups. Of course, students need to learn more complex types of sentences, and this tool can be modified to help students practice a wide range of sentence types.

One approach to grammar instruction is to have students create generative sentences.

THE TRAITS OF STRONG WRITING

Many of the examples that we have included thus far in this chapter focus on skills that are relatively straightforward to teach. We used these examples because the instructional moves of the teacher jump out when we provide concrete examples. But writing well is more than forming letters, creating paragraphs, writing in cursive, and creating sentences.

Working with thousands of student writing samples and many teachers, Spandel (2012) identified six traits that could be used to assess student writing. These are not a curriculum, but rather a way of thinking about areas of potential instructional need. As Spandel noted,

> When you become familiar with those criteria, you are not only prepared to assess writing with greater skill, ease, and consistency than ever before, but you are also prepared to teach it with a confidence and insight you never thought possible. . . . The traits will fully support, complement, and enhance the best of your own curriculum. (2005, p. ix)

The six traits (plus a newer one that focuses on presentation) are the following:

1. **Ideas** are the main message. It is the heart of the message, the content of the piece, or the main theme or idea together with the details that enrich and develop that theme.

Writing well is more than forming letters, creating paragraphs, writing in cursive, and creating sentences.

2. **Organization** is the internal structure, the thread of central meaning, the logical and sometimes intriguing pattern of ideas within a piece of writing.

3. **Voice** is the personal tone and personal flavor of the piece of writing. It includes the magic and the wit, along with the feeling and conviction of the individual writer coming out through the words.

4. **Word choice** focuses on the vocabulary that an author uses. It involves the use of rich, colorful, precise language that moves and enlightens the reader.

5. **Sentence fluency** is the rhythm and flow of the language, the sound of word patterns, the way in which the writing plays to the ear—not just to the eye. And sentence fluency involves the author's use of varied sentence lengths and starters.

6. **Conventions** refer to the mechanical correctness of the piece—spelling, paragraphing, grammar and usage, punctuation, and use of capitals.

+1. **Presentation** zeros in on the form and layout of the text and its readability; the piece should be pleasing to the eye.

Courtney Jenkins uses the rubrics developed by Education Northwest (educationnorthwest.org/traits/traits-rubrics) with her students. Students in Ms. Jenkins's sixth-grade class all understand the descriptors on the rubric and make decisions about areas to work on based on the feedback about their writing that they receive from peers and their teacher. Ms. Jenkins also meets with her colleagues who also teach sixth grade, so they can discuss areas of strength and need identified using the rubrics.

Ms. Jenkins also has key questions that her students can ask themselves and others as they consider each trait (see Figure 3.5). When she noticed that her students were struggling with organization, Ms. Jenkins decided to write aloud for her students. In this case, she used a piece of text she had previously written and reread it making note of the organization. At one point she said,

> I wrote about the Trojan War and specifically what caused the war. I was trying to tell the events in order, but now I realize that I mixed up these two. Helen and Paris traveling to Troy should come first. After that, I can include the information about the Trojan horse. That will help the organization, and my reader won't get confused. I am going to move this paragraph [Helen and Paris] up so that the events are in order.

▼ FIGURE 3.5 KEY QUESTIONS BASED ON WRITING TRAITS

Trait	Key Questions
Ideas	• Does the writing go beyond the obvious? • Are the ideas consistent across the piece? • Do the ideas build on one another? • Is the information accurate?
Organization	• Does the writing hook you and keep you reading? • Do the ideas flow in logical way? • Can the reader follow a logical progression of ideas?
Voice	• Does the writing make you want to keep reading it and share it with others? • Can you clearly imagine the writer's or narrator's point of view? • Does the tone of the writing match the purpose or text type?
Word Choice	• Does the writing make the words and images linger in your mind? • Are words and phrases used accurately? • Do the words and phrases used appeal to the senses?
Sentence Fluency	• Is the writing fun to read aloud? • Can you read it with expression? • Are the sentences different lengths, and do they start with different words or phrases?
Conventions	• Are the punctuation and spelling correct? • Is the grammar correct, or does it cause confusion for the reader? • Is there very little work left to be corrected by the copy editor?
Presentation	• Is the overall look appealing? • Are the margins, spacing, and lines used so that the writing flows?

Later in the same session, Ms. Jenkins noted that she did not have a transition sentence and said,

I think it would help the organization of the paper if I added a transition here. It's the right sequence and it happens in order, but I think it's kind of a surprise for the reader and I think it would be better if I added a sentence. I think I will add this sentence: *The war lasted over 10 years before the Achaean troops tried something new.*

Word limiter activities are helpful for students learning English, as they encourage self-editing and a focus on precision in writing (Davis, 1998).

When she had completed her initial review of her writing, Ms. Jenkins said,

> Sometimes I like to use signal words to help with the organization. I think I'll revise this paper to use the words *first, then, next,* and *finally.* Those terms will help my reader understand that the events occurred in order. And I need to include some information that the events may not have all happened. Remember, we're studying Greek mythology, and some of these are popular stories used to teach and explain the world.

Her focus on the 6+1 traits is not limited to write-alouds. Ms. Jenkins can use direct instruction, interactive writing, or power writing, not to mention small-group instruction, to develop her students' skills in composition. As she notes,

> I need to balance reading with writing. I was taught years ago in my credential program that "every writer can read, but not every reader can write," so I spend a fair amount of time developing my students' skills in writing.

WRITING PROCESSES

Before we conclude this chapter, we think it is worth noting that there is no such thing as "the writing process," as in a fixed set of steps that can be taught and practiced. In fact, the person credited for creating the phrase, Don Graves, wishes that he had said "writing processes" instead of "the writing process," because we all vary the systems we use based on the format and audience for the text we are writing. In addition, he noted that revision is not something that happens on Thursdays, but rather often starts as soon as the piece is being drafted. Graves (as cited in National Writing Project & Nagin, 2003) writes,

> The writing process is anything a writer does from the time the idea came until the piece is completed or abandoned. There is no particular order. So it's not effective to teach writing process in a lock-step, rigid manner. What a good writing teacher does is help students see where writing comes from; in a chance remark or an article that really burns you up. I still hold by my original statement: if kids don't write more than three days a week they're dead, and it's very hard to become a writer. If you provide frequent occasions for writing then the students start to think about writing when they're not doing it. I call it a constant state of composition. (p. 23)

So, it's time to take down the posters that suggest that Monday is pre-writing, Tuesday is drafting, Wednesday is revising, Thursday is editing, and Friday is publishing. These are useful habits to develop with students, but they do not occur in a linear fashion. Students need to learn the various processes and then learn to use them strategically based on the writing task and audience. Over time, students will learn to vary their processes, which can still include the following:

- **Idea development:** Formulating (or brainstorming) ideas that may or may not be utilized later in a writing piece

- **Drafting:** Committing brainstormed ideas to paper to produce a first draft

- **Revising:** Revisiting the draft to add, delete, or change what has been drafted

- **Editing:** Approaching the piece's final form and asking teachers or peers for corrections and feedback on content

- **Publishing:** Finalizing the piece and sharing it with others

In addition to teaching his fourth-grade students that they can vary the processes they use to accomplish the writing task, Andrew Goetz engages them in writing tasks of various lengths. As he noted,

> There is no requirement that everything be written in five paragraphs. I used to have this hamburger poster in my classroom. The top bun was the introduction. The lettuce, tomato, and meat were the details. The bottom bun was the conclusion. That's way too formulaic and mechanistic. That's not how writers really write. My students were becoming little robots trying to fit everything into five paragraphs. Sometimes, they only needed three, and other times they need six or seven, or even more.

There is no such thing as "the writing process," as in a fixed set of steps that can be taught and practiced.

CONCLUSION

For students to learn to write well, they need to understand the

- Purpose for their writing

- Traits of strong writing

- Processes useful in getting ideas down on paper

- Mentor texts that allow them practice with grammatical structures

- Various formats that require different lengths of writing

To accomplish this, they need us to spend time teaching writing, not just assigning or causing writing. Sometimes, these lessons are done with the whole class, using tools such as write-alouds, interactive writing, direct instruction, and so on. Other times, the lessons are with small groups of students or individuals during conferences. Balanced literacy requires that we make strategic choices to ensure that all students learn at high levels.

COLLABORATIVE READING AND WRITING

LEARNING IN THE COMPANY OF PEERS

CHAPTER 4

Jim West/PhotoEdit

Walk into Brielle York's fifth-grade classroom, and you will witness what the principal has called a "well-oiled machine." It isn't that everything is perfect. Ten-year-olds are not known for being consistently quiet and studious. In fact, Ms. York says that that has never been the intent. "I call it 'productive noise,'" she said. The teacher reserves time each day to provide small-group instruction in reading and writing, as described in the previous two chapters. But her ability to do so is compromised if her other students are not engaged in meaningful learning away from the teacher. "I made so many mistakes in my first few years," she said, continuing,

> I started with small-group instruction without taking the time to make sure students knew how to work away from me. And I spent way too much time developing center tasks for them to do. I hardly had the energy to devote to the small-group reading and writing instruction I needed to do.

Her awakening came when she realized that she needed to build her students' independence to make decisions, and couple that independence with evergreen tasks that did not require a large investment of time to develop materials. Evergreen tasks are those that students can do throughout the year without additional instruction once they understand the expectations. As Ms. York notes, "Time away from me means that students have the opportunity to do two things. The first is deliberative practice to strengthen the skills and strategies they've been learning. The second is knowledge building through investigation." Ms. York continued, "But they can't engage in deliberative practice and knowledge *building if they don't have processes that support their self-regulation. That requires that I teach those processes and they use them consistently."*

Ms. York has framed the components necessary for generating the productive noise of student-directed learning:

- Capacity-building routines *to build self-regulation*

- Deliberative practice tasks *that reinforce learning*

- Knowledge-building opportunities *to address gaps, fuel curiosity, and leverage prior learning*

As we noted in Chapter 1, balanced literacy learning requires maintaining equilibrium across the domains (reading, writing, speaking, listening, and viewing), and across instructional delivery modes (direct, dialogic, and independent). Balance is also achieved internally. In this case, meaningful learning away from us requires balancing *purpose* (deliberative practice and knowledge building) with a growing capacity for our learners to self-manage. In the sections that follow, we will examine each of the elements needed so that our students continue learning outside our direction.

THE BALANCING ACT IN LITERACY INSTRUCTION

It is important to balance whole-class with small-group learning. It's also important to ensure that students not working with us in a small-group lesson are engaged in meaningful tasks. Nancy (Frey) discovered that her small-group instruction was continually interrupted by other students in the class who were allegedly working on their own. She recalls instituting rules with her first graders such as "ask three, then me." But it was a failure, as her students didn't really know how to ask for help from others, and the students didn't have the capacity to figure out the complicated tasks she assigned them. When these rules didn't work (even though they seemed to work in the classroom of the veteran teacher next door), Nancy tried making the tasks much simpler. But too many mind-numbing worksheets took a toll on her students, who glumly circled long and short vowels for far too long.

It is easy to give up on teacher-led small-group instruction when the rest of the class is not productive. After all, whole-group instruction seems easier, if only because everyone in the room is doing the same thing. But at what cost? One thing every effective teacher knows is that learning doesn't develop at an equivalent pace for every student. While most fall within a range of expected progress, skilled teachers know they must always be on the lookout for those well ahead of the group, as well as for those who are faltering. Whole-group instruction alone doesn't allow for the kind of interactions needed to monitor progress. This is a major reason why small-group teacher-led instruction is of such value.

It took a while (and lots of guidance, professional learning, and experimentation) for Nancy to figure out how to manage the rest of the class during small-group instruction without sacrificing their learning. Like Ms. York, she learned that the first step is to build the capacity of students to work outside the direct oversight of the teacher.

BUILD CAPACITY FOR SELF-REGULATION SYSTEMATICALLY

Small-group instruction works well when the other students in the class are actively engaged in their own learning. But to do so requires a level of confidence on the part of the student to make decisions, seek help, and self-manage. Consider the first month of school to be a time dedicated to building students' capacity to self-manage. To do so,

1. Identify three highly useful routines you want your students to be able to master when they are working away from you.

2. Calendar your instruction to provide modeling and direct instruction for one routine at a time.

3. Allow students to practice the routine while you assist, coach, and reteach as needed.

Figure 4.1 is a sample calendar of a month of lessons (about 20 instructional days) to apprentice your students into working effectively away from you. It is important to note that during this first month, you aren't spending a lot of time on small-group instruction. The prime-time instruction is dedicated to building your students' ability to work with relatively little direction on your part. Get this right, and small-group instruction falls into place more easily.

The First 10 Days

Communication and cooperation are at the heart of learning, and the first two weeks should include short lessons (10–20 minutes) that highlight the principles of helping, accountable talk, and the practical matter of managing the noise volume of a busy classroom. The first order of business is instilling the values and norms of helping in the classroom.

> Small-group instruction works well when the other students in the class are actively engaged in their own learning. But to do so requires a level of confidence on the part of the student to make decisions, seek help, and self-manage.

▼ FIGURE 4.1 FIRST 20 DAYS OF SPOTLIGHT LESSONS FOR TEACHING STUDENTS TO WORK PRODUCTIVELY IN GROUPS

	Monday	Tuesday	Wednesday	Thursday	Friday
Week 1	**Our Rules** How do we work together?	**Helping Curriculum** Offering help, asking for help, accepting help, declining help.	**On-Task Partners** When prompted, check to see if your partner is on the right page and has the right materials.	**Discussion Partners** What makes for good communication between people?	**Productive Noise Meter** How will sound levels be managed in our class?
Week 2	**Accountable Talk to the Community** Explaining your partner's ideas.	**Accountable Talk to the Knowledge Base** How do you ask questions? How do you show others where to find information?	**Sounding Board** Pairs of students meet to share work in progress and provide responses.	**Accountable Talk for Reasoning** How do you disagree with someone without being disagreeable? How do you respond when someone disagrees with you?	**Paired Response Cards** Pairs of students have one set of response cards and must agree on an answer.
Week 3	**Introduce Routine 1** Focus lesson, guided practice.	**Practice, Circulate, and Evaluate: Routine 1** Observe students and evaluate procedures.	**Introduce Routine 2** Focus lesson, guided practice.	**Practice, Circulate, and Evaluate: Routine 2** Observe students and evaluate procedures.	**Implement Two Routines** Divide class in half; switch.
Week 4	**Tune Up** What is working? What is a challenge? Use this time to reteach and refine.	**Introduce Routine 3** Focus lesson, guided practice	**Practice, Circulate, and Evaluate: Routine 3** Observe students and evaluate procedures.	**Implement Three Routines** Introduce schedule; complete three rotations.	**Assessment Day** Implement three routines; assess individuals or small groups.

Most of these are 10–20 minutes in length. All should be modeled by the teacher first! After each instructional routine has been introduced, use it as many times as you can to reinforce and refine skills.

Source: Adapted from Frey, N., & Fisher, D. (2011). The first 20 days: Establishing productive group work in the classroom. *ILA E-ssentials.* Newark, DE: International Literacy Association. Retrieved from https://www.literacyworldwide.org/get-resources/ila-e-ssentials/8006

Sapon-Shevin (1998) called it "the helping curriculum," and while originally designed for elementary children, we have found it to be a good way to capture the soft skills needed by all adults in their personal and professional lives. Each day, students should be able to answer each of these questions:

- Have I offered help today?

- Have I asked for help today?

- Have I politely accepted help today?

- Have I politely declined help today so I could keep trying?

You know best how these should be expressed in your classroom. But too often they are left unstated until a problem arises. Proactively teaching your helping routines can head off tears and misunderstandings. Third-grade teacher Michelle Radford introduces helping statements to assist her students (see Figure 4.2):

> I introduce these at the beginning of the year, and we add to them as a class throughout the year. Our school has a terrific focus on an integrated approach to social and emotional learning through academics, and this is just one example of that.

▼ FIGURE 4.2 HELPING STATEMENTS

Ways to Ask for Help	Ways to Offer Help
<ul><li>I'm stuck. Can you help me get unstuck?</li><li>I tried this but it isn't working so far. Do you have an idea?</li><li>I don't understand this. Do you?</li></ul>	<ul><li>Can I help?</li><li>I have an idea. Would you like to hear it?</li><li>I can help with that, if you want.</li></ul>
Ways to Accept Help	**Ways to Decline Help**
<ul><li>Thank you.</li><li>I appreciate your help.</li><li>I am glad you came along!</li></ul>	<ul><li>Thank you. I think I have it.</li><li>Thank you. I want to try just a little bit longer.</li><li>Thank you. I need a few more minutes. If I still don't get it, can we talk again?</li></ul>

A second area of focus during these first 10 days is developing *accountable talk* (Michaels, O'Connor, & Resnick, 2008). The principles of accountable talk are deceptively simple and take a lifetime to master:

- *You are accountable to your learning community* to talk to and with one another politely, to communicate clearly, and to ask for clarification when needed. (*"Does anyone else have an idea to share?"* and *"Could you give an example so I can understand your idea better?"*)

- *You are accountable to use accurate knowledge* as you work together, to ask for sources of information, and to show others where you found the information. (*"I found this information on page ___."*)

- *You are accountable to use rigorous thinking* by explaining your logic and reasoning, and to ask one another for further explanations. (*"I think so because… ."* and *"Can you tell me more?"*)

resources.corwin.com/
thisisbalancedliteracy

Video 12
Accountable Talk
in Kindergarten

Initial lessons on accountable talk should feature language frames that are appropriate for your students. Display these frames where students can readily use them, such as on table tents or posters located in proximity to where students will be working together.

Accountable talk doesn't end here, of course, and we will revisit this valuable discussion tool in more detail in the following chapter on whole-group reading instruction.

The third suggested focus area for building students' self-regulatory capacity is in setting norms about noise level. Fourth-grade teacher Luis Alvarado uses this as an opportunity to build vocabulary. "Together we make a list of sound-level words and phrases, like *buzz, hum, racket, so quiet you could hear a pin drop,* and *rumble,*" he explained. "Then we cluster the terms and put the clusters into rank order from quietest to loudest. I keep the list and set the noise level as a visual reminder of appropriate and disruptive noise levels" (see Figure 4.3).

▼ FIGURE 4.3 NOISE LEVELS

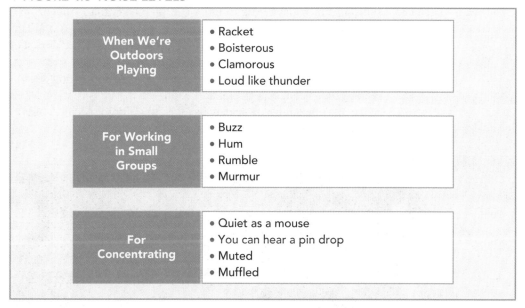

When We're Outdoors Playing	• Racket • Boisterous • Clamorous • Loud like thunder
For Working in Small Groups	• Buzz • Hum • Rumble • Murmur
For Concentrating	• Quiet as a mouse • You can hear a pin drop • Muted • Muffled

Throughout the year, Mr. Alvarado and the class add vocabulary they encounter in their reading. "It ends up becoming a word wall they can use in their writing, too," said the teacher.

The Second 10 Days

This phase provides a means for introducing three low-maintenance (evergreen, or always at-the-ready) routines, while giving students an opportunity to practice the procedures for helping, accountable talk, and productive noise monitoring. For instance, primary teachers might want to utilize low-maintenance centers for students to practice foundational skills. Here are three suggested primary-level routines to get you started:

Primary-Level Routines

1. **A writing station:** In the primary grades, students are often asked to compose based on a topic the class is studying, often in science or social studies. Students write words and draw pictures, expanding their writing as they do so. Student work should be analyzed for areas of strength as well as unfinished learning. In other words, students' writing is fodder for the instruction they receive during whole-class and small-group learning. For this to work, students need to learn to use and replace the writing and drawing materials and to maintain their writer's notebook.

2. **A listening station with headphones:** This task builds listening skills and provides access to more complex texts than students can read on their own. There are a number of computer-based oral language curricula designed for young children, often provided as part of the adopted reading curriculum. Students need to know passwords, how to use the equipment, and what to do when something doesn't work. They listen, as a group, and complete the tasks that are asked of them. For example, they may be asked to point to specific words as they are read, or to complete tasks after the reading.

resources.corwin.com/
thisisbalancedliteracy

Video 13
Accountable Talk
in Grade 5

3. **Word work station:** Here, students practice letter and word sorts using skills that you have already taught them. These sorts can be focused on phonemic awareness using pictures or on phonics knowledge using words. For example, students might be sorting long-*a* sound words and short-*a* sound words. Or they might be sorting words by common spelling patterns (e.g., -*an* or -*at*). Or they might be sorting words based on consonant blends. There are any number of possibilities for providing students with practice. Another option for word work is known as a *word ladder*. Students read clues and follow the instructions, creating new words as they climb the ladder. An example of a word ladder is found in Figure 4.4.

All of these require knowledge of procedures—how to start and stop, how to clean up, where to put completed work, and so on. Notice that these suggested early routines are a mixture of collaborative and independent activities. Don't feel that you need to have everyone working together at

▼ FIGURE 4.4 3-LETTER BLENDS WORD LADDER

Name: _____   Date: _____

Read the clues; then write the words.
Start at the bottom and climb to the top.

The opposite of <u>right</u> or <u>correct</u>
Take away two letters and add "w" to the beginning.

— — — — —

The opposite of <u>weak</u>; if you can lift heavy things you are _____
Add two letters.

— — — — — —

What you sing or hear on the radio
Change one letter.

— — — —

To say the words to a song in a musical way
Take away two letters.

— — — —

The season when it rains a lot and the flowers bloom
Change one letter.

— — — — —

A small piece of thread; a yo-yo has a long one of these
Change one letter and add one letter.

— — — — — —

To take off all your clothes before you take a bath, OR a narrow piece of cloth
Add one letter.

— — — — —

A vacation; you take a car when you go on a long _____
Add one letter.

— — — —

To tear, like a piece of paper or your pants
Take away one letter.

drip

Source: Retrieved from the companion website for Blevins, W. (2017). *A fresh look at phonics, grades K–2: Common causes of failure and 7 ingredients for success.* Thousand Oaks, CA: Corwin. Adapted from the work of Timothy Rasinski: *Daily Word Ladders K–1* (New York: Scholastic, 2012), *Daily Word Ladders 1–2* (New York: Scholastic, 2008), *Daily Word Ladders 2–4* (New York: Scholastic, 2005), and *Daily Word Ladders 4–6* (New York: Scholastic, 2005).

the same time! These preliminary routines typically last 10–15 minutes, which is usually the outside limit of how long young students are able to work away from us. However, throughout the year you can and should add and change routines as they learn how to do them, and as they build stamina. For example, as students progress throughout the school year, they should be able to engage in independent reading, paired reading routines, and expanded word study activities.

Providing students with appropriate language frames is critical to helping them develop accountable talk.

Routines for Older Students

Routines for older students differ, and those in second grade and above are able to take part in those routines that feature more peer-directed learning. Here are three routines for older students to get you started:

1. **Literature circles** (Daniels, 2002) **or book clubs** with peers to discuss a book they have selected for discussion.

2. **Investigatory work related to their science or social studies content** using digital and print texts.

3. **Peer critiques of writing** in which students provide feedback to their peers focused on specific "look-fors" in writing.

Peer critique is a reciprocal writing process designed so that students learn as much from giving feedback as they do from getting feedback. Writing researcher Jay Simmons analyzed peer feedback and responses about writing and found that, in too many classrooms, the majority were composed of global praise ("Great job!") and microedits (e.g., circling misspelled words). More skilled peer responders spent more time offering text feedback about the organization and concepts, as well the writer's craft. ("You might consider using this at the beginning.") Simmons advises that "responders are taught, not born" (2003, p. 684) and that the best way to teach students to do it well is to share one's own writing and allow students to respond to it. This practice enables students to become more skilled in responding rather than evaluating. Figure 4.5 on the next page includes a list of techniques for teaching students to respond to one another's writing.

The notion that the teacher alone is the engine for revising is a false one that reinforces the misplaced belief that the teacher is the only audience. Developing a sense of audience is an essential aspect of writing, yet in most classes we don't provide audiences for students to write to.

resources.corwin.com/
thisisbalancedliteracy

Video 14
Peer Editing and Setting Expectations

Audiences respond. That's what makes them so powerful. We are communicative creatures, and we don't like yelling into a void. It is common practice to provide audiences for very young writers, who read their work from an author's chair to their peers. But that seems to disappear by the intermediate grades. Of course, there are other options besides an author's chair, such as Amazon reviews and movie trailers. But we strongly advocate for putting procedures in place to make the most of peer response so that students come to understand that they have an audience.

▼ FIGURE 4.5 TECHNIQUES FOR PEER RESPONSE

Technique	What the Teacher Does	What Students Do
Sharing your writing	Shares a piece of writing and asks for response Shares rewrites tied to class response	Offers comments on the teacher's writing
Clarifying evaluation vs. response	Shows evaluation is of product Response is to the writer	Understand that response is personable and helpful
Modeling specific praise	Shows how to tell what you like	Understand that cheerleading as a reader is too general to be helpful
Modeling understanding	Shows how to tell what you understood the piece to be about	Understand that reflecting back the piece to the writer is helpful
Modeling questions	Shows how to ask questions about what you didn't understand	Understand that questions related to the writer's purpose are helpful
Modeling suggestions	Shows how to suggest writing techniques	Understand that a responder leaves a writer knowing what to do next
Whole-class response	Moderates response by class to one classmate's piece	Offer response Hear the response of others Hear what the writer finds helpful
Partner response	Pairs up students in class to respond to pieces	Practice response learned in whole-class session
Comment review	Reads the comments of peers to writers Suggests better techniques Devises minilessons	Get teacher feedback on comments
Response conference	Speaks individually with students responding inappropriately	Have techniques reinforced

Source: Simmons, J. (2003). Responders are taught, not born. *Journal of Adolescent and Adult Literacy, 46*, 690. Used with permission.

Ken Ryu stresses the importance of peer response with his sixth-grade students. "I have always emphasized the importance of audience for their writing, whether it be narrative or expository," he says in introducing this practice. "When they start the school year, we begin with discussing the purposes for peer response and how it's different from peer editing." Using the framework described by Simmons (2003), he teaches students about three categories of responses that are useful for their fellow writers:

- *Playback the text* for the writer by briefly summarizing the main points as you understood them.

- *Discuss the reader's needs* by alerting the writer to confusions you had as you read the piece.

- *Identify writer's techniques* you noticed, such as the use of headings, examples, and direct quotes.

"Sometimes they do this face-to-face, but more often lately they do it within a digital environment," Mr. Ryu said. "They insert comments into the margin and code their responses—PT, RN, and WT for the three types of responses I've taught them." Mr. Ryu requires that all writers submit the final version of their paper and the marked-up text of their draft. "I get a good perspective on the writer and the reader," he said. "Sometimes the reader makes a really insightful comment that I hadn't even thought of."

resources.corwin.com/
thisisbalancedliteracy

Video 15
Peer Editing,
Conferencing, and
Small-Group Writing

Peer response allows writers to gain insight into how their words are understood by others. As a writer it is difficult to distance oneself from one's words, and peer response, especially the playback, provides novice writers with a means for hearing their words being interpreted by someone else. It reminds us of a public reading we attended by humorist David Sedaris, who at the time was working on his next book. We watched him edit and revise from the stage in real time. Always entertaining, he still managed to mark on his pages when the audience laughed and when it didn't. At times, he tweaked the turn of a phrase and then read it to us again to see if the change improved it. And while we don't expect our own students to become fabulously successful professional writers, we do want them to understand that writing is a form of communication that is often understood somewhat differently from the way the writer intended. Most important, we hope they discover that revising is an ongoing process based on the questions posed, the connections made, and the insights shared by audiences.

Older students can sustain their time away from us for 30 minutes or more, providing ample time for small-group reading and writing instruction. But just as with younger students, there are procedures associated with each, including materials management, seeking help, and submitting finished work. The details of these and other routines will be discussed in the sections that follow.

USE TIME AWAY FROM THE TEACHER FOR DELIBERATIVE PRACTICE

Deliberative practice, however, is more than just mindless repetition. It is spaced—rather than mass—practice, meaning that the learner has short but regular doses.

Automaticity is an overarching goal for learning to get to transfer. Automaticity is essential so students can use the skill in any new learning situation. We want students to be able to access what they have learned quickly, so they can learn new things. Practice builds automaticity in the application of skills and concepts, or what some have called "unconscious competence." Practice also builds fluency. We aren't speaking strictly of reading fluency, which is a measure of prosody, accuracy, and rate, but rather of a person's ability to utilize learning smoothly. Automaticity is essential for learning how to read, as young children master letters and sounds to decode written language (LaBerge & Samuels, 1974). Other foundational reading and writing skills include print concepts, phonics and word analysis, sight words, spelling, and writing conventions. All of these take time and practice to develop a functional level of fluency such that these skills go underground, and higher order comprehension, expression, and critical thinking can occur.

Time away from the teacher is an excellent opportunity to provide students with the practice they need to fully develop these skills. Practice, when done well, moves learning forward. Deliberative practice, however, is more than just mindless repetition. It is spaced—rather than mass—practice, meaning that the learner has short but regular doses, rather than one Herculean effort (remember trying to cram for a test the night before? That's mass practice, and it doesn't work). Deliberative practice involves five mechanisms (Ericsson, 2002):

1. A willingness to push beyond current levels of performance

2. A clear goal

3. A time to focus intently on the task

4. High-quality feedback

5. An idea of what expertise looks like

In fact, repetition alone only works to a point. Consider any number of things you've done for years (driving, cooking, and teaching, to name a few). In each case, simply doing it for longer doesn't result in improvement beyond an intermediate level of competence. But a deliberative effort to practice for the purpose of improvement results in people who are professional racing drivers, executive chefs, and National Board Certified teachers.

Young children don't typically have such lofty goals when it comes to reading and writing. But helping students set goals, and turning learning into games, can help with deliberative practice. Personal bests are a simple means for doing this. Students love to compete with themselves to beat their previous record. Below are some of our favorite approaches:

- Games such as *My Pile, Your Pile* give pairs of children an opportunity to run through sight words with a partner who plays the teacher, with the card awarded to the child who identifies it correctly. Incorrect responses are given to the "teacher," who then runs through all the cards again until all the cards have been answered correctly.

- Commercial educational board games such as Scattergories and BananaGrams (a simpler form of Scrabble) are other low-maintenance games that are fast moving and engaging for students.

- Digital game apps on tablets appeal to children also.

And remember that while feedback is important, it doesn't need to come from you. The feedback is baked into games as players make adjustments based on their success.

Sixth-grade teacher Dan Fredericks keeps board games on a shelf, and digital game apps on tablets, to foster deliberative practice when students are not meeting with him. "Once a week it's Game Day in my room," said Mr. Fredericks. "While I'm meeting with small groups, the rest of the class is playing a game." He explained that most of the board and card games he has come from garage sales or are donated. "I don't have anything expensive. That way when a piece is lost, I'm not broken-hearted." He smiled.

> Helping students set goals, and turning learning into games, can help with deliberative practice.

The digital game apps are always changing, and he works with his district's instructional technology department to vet games. "Commonsense Media is a great source for reviewing apps and includes teacher reviews, too. I have several students who are fans of Scribblenauts, which is actually a whole series of word puzzles and brainteasers," said Mr. Fredericks. "I like it because the vocabulary is challenging." He winked. "But don't tell them I said that."

SOUNDS AND ORAL LANGUAGE

Emergent readers and writers need lots of opportunities to practice new skills. But, as we have said before, these routines can't be time consuming to create and maintain. There are a number of tasks that students can complete that allow them to practice and apply their developing foundational skills.

- **Syllable clapping center:** A plastic bucket filled with pictures or words on cards and four sets of oversize knit gloves are all the materials you need. Students put on the gloves and clap out the syllables of the words represented by the picture. (We choose adult size gloves because the floppy nature of them adds to the entertainment value while also reducing noise.)

- **Magnetized word parts:** This is another routine that allows students to experiment with onset and rime, this time using magnetized word parts. Children put together different combinations of words; then they write the word and determine whether it is a real word or not.

Kindergarteners Fatima and Benedict used the rimes -*at* and -*an* with single-letter consonant onsets to make a list of words, and then sorted them based on whether they were real words or not (see Figure 4.6). Although a few of the nonwords they identified are in fact words (e.g., *vat*), they are not common to a five-year-old's vocabulary.

▼ FIGURE 4.6 FATIMA AND BENEDICT'S WORD LIST

Real Words		Not Real Words	
sat	dan	dat	zat
cat	can	lat	ban
hat	pan	nat	gan
mat	fan	tat	han
rat	man	vat	kan

Oral language development is essential for emergent and early readers, although a challenge is in getting students to use more academic language. Another simple routine is to place pictures on a table for students to explain to one another. First-grade teacher Sara Takahashi uses photographs and illustrations from discarded curriculum materials from her school to create a "talking folder" of prompts. "In the last few years we have adopted new social studies and science materials," she explained. "I used some of the old student books to cut out photographs that could prompt conversation." She has added picture postcards from places she visits to build out her collection. Students meet at a table with the folder in the center and choose photographs they like; then they explain what is happening in the picture to the other students in the group. "This is a no-fuss, no-muss routine for them," Ms. Takahashi said. "I add photos all the time, so it stays fresh. Magazines are a good source, too."

resources.corwin.com/
thisisbalancedliteracy

Video 16
Whole-Class
Syllable Clapping

Roda Adeyami, who teaches next door, uses a high-tech version of this activity called Tell About It, which she has installed on tablets. The app contains hundreds of photos with prompts, and students answer using the recording feature on the tablet. For example, there is a photograph of a child in the woods holding a magnifying glass, and a prompt that reads, "Where is your favorite place to explore?" Ms. Adeyami says, "The recording feature lets me listen to specific students to gauge their progress in oral language. It's not the only reason I use it. I can put photos of my own in there, too. But it is a way for me to listen in on some authentic language when I need to."

READING FLUENCY

The ability to read smoothly and with accuracy is an essential foundational skill, and it is important to monitor students' progress in this area. Repeated reading is an excellent technique for building oral and silent reading fluency (Jiyeon Lee & So Yoon, 2017). Techniques vary, but the goal is to have students read a passage several times, with improvement each time. One method for meeting this goal is to have short passages available for students to select. Students each read a passage several times, recording their attempts each time, and then listen to the playback to see where they can improve. Fifth-grade teacher Malcolm Smithson uses passages that are related to other current aspects of learning, along with a recording device. "We are going to the natural history museum in a few weeks as a class, so some of the passages I am using right now are about the Mesoamerican display they are featuring," said Mr. Smithson. "I figure I can grow a little learning while I'm at it."

Four students assemble at the table and select a passage they will all use, and their goal is to prepare a podcast their teacher can use at another time for a listening activity. After reading it silently "to get the gist," as one student explained, they each take a turn reading into the recorder. After all four have read, they listen to the playback of each and discuss ways to make it better the next time.

"What I've noticed is that they correct each other's errors. They're especially good at figuring out the prosody and expression needed," Mr. Smithson said. They repeat the reading for a second round, and sometimes a third, depending on the time available. "The thing is, they're reading the same passage at least 10 times," said Mr. Smithson. "They're following along and reading silently as their classmates are recording."

At the end of the routine, they nominate one recording for Mr. Smithson to use as a podcast. He uploads the nominated audio files to the learning management system, where other students can listen to readings for short written responses. "I don't need to rely on professional recordings," he said. "The quality of what they turn out is really good, because they know their classmates will be listening."

Readers theater is a fluency-building routine that couples repeated reading of a passage with the dramatic play of a theater script (Martinez, Roser, & Strecker, 1998). Second-grade teacher Meli Lopez uses short readers theater scripts to encourage repeated reading with her students. She limits the group size to four ("any more than that and they lose the flow," she said) and selects short scripts that they can master in 15–20 minutes. Readers theater is performed as a radio script, so no props or costumes are necessary. Students don't need to memorize their parts, and in fact are discouraged from doing so, as the purpose is repeated *reading*.

> The ability to read smoothly and with accuracy is an essential foundational skill, and it is important to monitor students' progress in this area.

"Eyes on text," Ms. Lopez reminds them.

Over the course of several days, students meet to read together, assign parts, and practice. The payoff is performance, and at the end of the week students perform for the class. "We call it Readers Theater Showcase, and the groups that have been working get a chance to show off their chops," said Ms. Lopez.

Like many of the routines profiled in this chapter, they were originally taught, practiced, and mastered together as a class. "Routines like this take a little more time to establish, but I'm always looking toward the time when I can shift this to a task they can do away from me. They shouldn't be doing the same tasks at the end of the year that they did in the beginning. It keeps it fresh to have new tasks they have grown into."

Next step for Ms. Lopez in readers theater? "We're learning how to write our own scripts using dialogue from books we're reading! I hope to introduce this as another task in the last quarter of the school year," she said.

Third-grade teacher Charlotte Valentine-Diaz uses a routine called *dyad reading* during the second semester of the school year. "During the first semester we are doing it together as a whole class, all at the same time. But after several months, they are so good at it that I shift it to an activity they complete while I'm with a small group."

Dyad reading was developed by Brown, Mohr, Wilcox, and Barrett (2018) as a variation of paired reading. In conventional paired reading, a stronger reader and a weaker reader together read a passage in unison. The passage is gauged in approximation to the weaker reader's current level of performance. But in dyad reading, there is one important difference—the complexity of the text is raised significantly, between two and four grade levels above the weaker reader's current level. Thus, the text is challenging for both. The results have been nothing short of amazing. Brown et al. (2018) reported that after 90 days of dyad reading for 15 minutes a day, both the stronger and weaker readers made significant gains as measured by Lexile reading levels, and in measures of prosody.

> In dyad reading, the complexity of the text is raised significantly, between two and four grade levels above the weaker reader's current level.

Ms. Valentine-Diaz attended a professional learning session on dyad reading and decided to try it with her own students. "Students are paired up, although I don't identify which reader is which. We use the rules outlined for dyad reading (Brown et al., 2018):

- Share one book.
- Sit side by side.
- Track the words with one smooth finger.
- Read aloud together.

- Keep eyes on words.

- Don't read too fast, or too slow.

- Write down unknown words.

- Have fun!

"We did this for 90 days together, and now it is such an ingrained routine that I've shifted it to a task they can complete on their own," said the teacher. "It took me awhile to realize that they can learn from each other. It's just up to me to make sure they get a chance to do so."

KNOWLEDGE-BUILDING TASKS

A third consideration for designing tasks for students to complete when they are away from the teacher is to include those that build knowledge. There are a number of ways to do this, and time invested to introduce the routines will pay significant dividends, as students will understand the expectations of the task. In this chapter, we are providing a wide range of options for students to engage in meaningful tasks away from us. No one we know uses them all. We suggest selecting a few and teaching your students how to use them so that you have more time for small-group, needs-based reading instruction. Then you'll have balance.

Retellings

Practice and repetition occur when students relive and retell stories they have read. Retelling is a practice useful for students to consolidate their understanding of a text. In this context, it is also a form of oral storytelling, and as such provides an additional benefit of fostering oral language development. Retelling requires students to utilize critical thinking skills (Benson & Cummins, 2000):

- Understand the meaning of the text, including plot, character, setting, and themes

- Sequence the story in the correct order

- Infer from and analyze the text

Young children can practice retelling using an interactive whiteboard to tell a story. Children can use the images on the board to demonstrate action as well as involve characters and settings. Interactive whiteboards allow retellings to include imaginative play, too, as children begin to create their own plot variations on familiar stories.

Older students can work together to retell using *text mapping plus* (Lapp, Fisher, & Johnson, 2010). Students work together with an article they have read to develop a graphic organizer to support their retelling of it (see Figure 4.7). Sixth-grade teacher Imelda Rodriguez sometimes assigns text mapping plus as an extension of her small-group instruction: "I often use an informational article during my small-group reading instruction time. This gives my students a way to spend more time with the article outside of my initial instruction."

▼ **FIGURE 4.7 TEXT MAPPING PLUS GRAPHIC ORGANIZER**

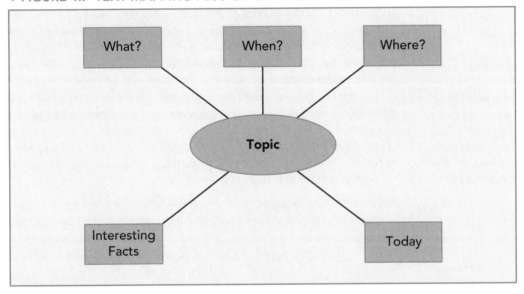

Source: Lapp, D., Fisher, D., & Johnson, K. (2010). Text mapping plus: Improving comprehension through supported retellings. *Journal of Adolescent and Adult Literacy, 53* (5), 423–426. Used with permission.

After meeting with her for teacher-directed instruction, Ms. Rodriguez's students continue their work. Using the text mapping protocol, they coconstruct the graphic organizer to support their retelling with her the following day. For example, in one meeting with Ms. Rodriguez, her students read an informational article on the excavation of the terracotta army of 8,000 life-sized clay soldiers that were discovered in a tomb in China in 1974. When the group met with her again later in the week, they began the lesson by revisiting the article using the graphic organizer they had developed to support their retelling. "It gives me a good way to begin the next lesson. I don't need to retell the information. They do," said Ms. Rodriguez. "The fact that they developed this together means that there's all kinds of academic language being used, even when I'm not witnessing it."

ReQuest

There are a number of ways to get students talking with peers about texts, such as think, pair, share. But when they are away from the teacher, students need more structure than that. One effective way to structure a partner conversation is called *ReQuest* (Manzo, 1969). This approach requires that one student develop questions based on the text, and the other student reads in anticipation of the questions he or she might be asked. It becomes a partner conversation with students taking turns asking and answering questions about the text.

To introduce this procedure to students, we recommend that students first work in partnerships to develop questions. We tend to start this at the beginning of the year, or at another break in the school calendar, by providing the whole class with a piece of text, divided into smaller parts. We like to draw lines on the text to inform students how much they should read each time before pausing to ask questions. (As they become more accustomed to this process, students can identify stopping points.) As part of the introductory phase, we should be the ones who respond to questions from the various groups. In doing so, we can model returning to the text to support the answer, or noting that the answer came from elsewhere, such as personal experiences or other texts.

> The value in this type of questioning is that it develops a habit that allows students to make predictions about where the answer is expected to be, based on the type of question being asked.

Once students understand the ReQuest procedure, they can work in partnerships to ask and answer questions about the text they are reading. When students are new to this procedure, they tend to ask literal questions. We let this happen for several rounds so that students become accustomed to working with a partner to discuss a text. Then, we introduce question types. Some people use Bloom's taxonomy as a way to form questions, and other use question-answer relationship or QAR (Raphael, 1982). The value in this type of questioning is that it develops a habit that allows students to make predictions about where the answer is expected to be, based on the type of question being asked. There is strong evidence that understanding question-answer relationships improves comprehension and even test scores (Raphael & Au, 2005). The QAR method has four types of questions that students can learn to use (see Figure 4.8).

The first two are explicit questions, meaning that the answers can be found directly in the text:

- *Right There* questions contain wording that comes directly from the text, with an answer often found in a single sentence.

- *Think and Search* questions are also derived directly from the text, but the answer must be formulated from information that comes from more than one sentence.

▼ FIGURE 4.8 QUESTION-ANSWER RELATIONSHIPS

In the Text (Book Questions)		
Question Type	**Description**	**Question Stems**
Right There	Words in the question and answer are directly stated in the text. They are explicit, and the words or phrases can be found within one sentence.	• How many … ? • Who is … ? • Where is … ? • What is … ?
Think and Search	Information is in the text, but readers must think and make connections between passages in the text.	• The main idea is … ? • What caused … ?
In My Head (Brain Questions)		
Question Type	**Description**	**Question Stems**
Author and You	Readers need to think about what they already know, what the author tells them in the text, and how these fit together.	• The author implies … ? • The passage suggests … ? • The author's attitude is … ?
On My Own	Readers are required to use prior knowledge. The text may or may not be needed.	• In your own opinion … ? • Based on your experience … ? • What would you do if … ?

The other two types of questions are implicit, meaning that the answer cannot be located directly in the text, and must be formulated by using what the reader knows as well:

- *Author and You* is an implicit question that requires readers to use both information learned from the text and their own background knowledge to answer.

- *On Your Own* questions require readers to use prior knowledge to answer. In this case, the text may or may not be needed.

The students in Sam Escobedo's second-grade class were in the midst of a unit of study on friendships. The students were given choices of books about friendships to read with partners using ReQuest. Each team went to the book bin to select a text. Mr. Escobedo had two copies of each book in a Ziploc bag. Each book had sticky notes indicating places that would be appropriate for a discussion. Shereca and Julius chose *Wings: A Tale of Two Chickens* (Marshall, 1986) and began reading. On the first round, Shereca was the questioner, and she asked

- How were Harriet and Winnie the same? How were the different?

- Who is the stranger?

- Have you ever seen a stranger on TV? What did that stranger try to do?

She and Julius had a great conversation about the first part of the text and what they thought might happen next. Then it was Julius's turn to ask questions, following their independent reading of the next section. Julius asked

- What does it mean, "lick of sense"?

- How could reading help her?

- How does reading help you?

Their conversation continued as they came to understand the message in this book, namely that friends take care of each other. The last question Shereca asked was, "How was Harriet a friend? What did she do?" As they discussed this question, Julius commented, "I think everybody needs a friend like Harriet. She cared a lot and saved Winnie."

Literature Circles

One classroom routine that we can use all year long to engage students in meaningful conversations about texts is literature circles (Daniels, 2002). During these conversations, small groups of students discuss a text that they have all read. These discussions allow students to share their thinking with others and to receive feedback about their thoughts. In doing so, students negotiate the meaning of the text and deepen their connections to the ideas contained therein.

These peer-led discussions provide students an opportunity to engage in argumentation as they make claims, offer evidence, share reasons, entertain counterclaims, agree and disagree, and seek areas of consensus. Literature circles allow students to practice their speaking and listening skills as well as their reading and argumentation skills. And they can do this in meaningful ways, while the teacher is meeting with other students.

For literature circles, or book clubs as some people call them, to be effective, there is some prework that needs to be done. It's not as simple as putting students in a group, handing them each a copy of a book, and expecting that they will talk with one another on a deep level. We typically assign students roles. This requires that we teach the roles, perhaps to the whole class, before starting the book clubs. In some cases, we assign roles to individual students within the literature circle, and in other cases we allow students to rotate roles. Some of the common roles

> For literature circles, or book clubs, to be effective, there is some prework that needs to be done. It's not as simple as putting students in a group, handing them each a copy of a book, and expecting that they will talk with one another on a deep level.

include the following (and note that there are many, many others; see Perenfein & Morris, 2004):

- **Vocabulary enricher:** This role focuses on important words in the reading. Students who perform this role keep track of words and phrases that are confusing or unclear, either marking them in the text or by keeping a log. This student also works in advance to find the meanings of these words to guide the conversation about the meaning of the words but does not just tell others what the words mean.

- **Travel tracer:** This role focuses on characters and how they move across settings. Students who perform this role help the group know *where* things are happening and how the setting may have changed. During the group conversation, the travel tracer describes each setting in detail, either in words or with an action map or diagram.

Rachel Langosch

Literature circles allow students to share their thinking around particular texts.

- **Investigator:** The role of the investigator is to find background information on a topic related to the group's book and to share that information with others in the group. There are several possible investigations, including the geography, weather, culture, or history of the book's setting; information about the author, including her or his life and other works; or information about the time period portrayed in the book.

- **Connector:** This role focuses on making connections between things that are happening in the book and other texts, the world, and personal experiences. The goal is to share some connections that illustrate the ideas in the book and how they relate to things others know and have experienced.

- **Discussion director:** The person who has this role is responsible for keeping the conversations moving. This person welcomes everyone to the discussion and identifies the order in which group members will share. This person also works to resolve conflicts and ensures that every member of the group has an opportunity to share.

In addition to roles, students often need language support to engage in the conversations about texts. We recommend that teachers provide students with generic questions that the group can discuss if they are unsure what else to say about their text. Sample questions can be found in Figure 4.9. In addition, teachers can provide sentence or language frames for students to use if they have something to say but are unsure about how to say it. Sample language frames can be found in Figure 4.10.

▼ FIGURE 4.9 SAMPLE DISCUSSION QUESTIONS

The Story	Setting
What happened in the story?	Where did the story take place?
How can you tell this story is make-believe?	What was the place like?
What happened first, next … last?	Could there be a place like this?
Were you able to predict the ending?	Do you know of a place like this?
Author	**Characters**
What do you know about the author?	Who are the main characters in the story?
Why do you think the author wrote the book?	(Choose one character.) Why is this character important in the story?
What is the author trying to tell you in the book?	Do you know anyone like the characters?
	Do any of the characters change?

In addition to roles and language support, students have to choose the text that they are going to read for the club. Most often, we constrain the choice, offering five or so titles for students to choose from. We share a bit about each choice and the type of reader who might like a particular text. The selections span a range of difficulty and complexity, yet share something in common. It could be that the texts all help students answer an essential question, or it could be that they all build background knowledge on an important science or social studies concept. Or it could be that they all contain specific literary devices that the class needs to learn. It's important that students have some choice and that we balance the groups.

▼ FIGURE 4.10 SAMPLE SENTENCE FRAMES

I can predict that _____ because _____.

The setting of the story is _____ and is important because _____.

I believe that _____ will happen because _____.

Character: In the beginning, _____ (character) was _____ (feelings/traits) because _____ (evidence).

The passage _____ is mostly about _____. One important detail is _____.

If I were _____ I would _____.

The character traits of _____ are _____.

The character is _____ because _____.

Some characteristics of _____ are _____, _____, and _____.

I think that _____ would symbolize the character well, because it represents _____.

I agree with _____ because _____.

This character is like _____ (character/person) as evidenced by _____ (passage).

I think _____ might change the outcome of the story if _____.

We recommend that students identify their top three choices from the five or so we offer, so that we can then use these choices to create the best grouping arrangements. Sometimes students want to read books that are way, way too hard for them at this point in their life, simply because their friends are reading that book. We do not subscribe to the idea that we have to limit students' independent and collaborative reading to a level shown on their most recent assessment, because we know that motivation and interest are important considerations. But there are texts that are currently out of reach for some students, texts that would lead to a high level of frustration.

In Angie Borden's fourth-grade class, the students were studying Native Americans. Ms. Borden shared the following titles with students and asked them each to identity the top three books that they'd like to read:

• *Hidden Roots* by Joseph Bruchac (Scholastic, 2004)

• *The Birchbark House* by Louise Erdrich (Hyperion Books for Children, 1999)

• *In the Footsteps of Crazy Horse* by Joseph Marshall III (Amulet Books, 2015)

- *Indian Shoes* by Cynthia Leitich Smith (HarperCollins, 2002)

- *How I Became a Ghost: A Choctaw Trail of Tears Story* by Tim Tingle (Roadrunner Press, 2015)

As she talked about each title, her students got more and more excited. These are interesting texts that offer a lot of fodder for conversations and connections. Ms. Borden collected her student requests and formed the groups, making sure there was a range of reading proficiencies in each group, but not so extreme that a student would be frustrated.

One group was reading *How I Became a Ghost,* and students were talking about the first chapter. One of the students noted the opening, in italics, saying, "The author tells us that this will be from a ghost, but right now, he's not a ghost. So, I guess he's gonna die sometime in the book, right?"

The students discuss this for a few minutes and then turn to the opening dialogue from the text.

Ryen then added, "I was confused by the work *hoke*, but then I reread that part. Did you all get it?"

Sarah responded, "Kinda. What do you think it means?"

"I think it means *okay* but in another language," Ryen said.

Nick added, "I think that Choctaw is the language. Remember the cover? It says that it is a Choctaw trail of tears, and then he says, 'in Choctaw,' so I think it is the language that these people speak."

The conversation goes on in the group while other groups are discussing their texts. In the meantime, Ms. Borden has invited four students from four different groups to meet with her for small-group instruction. The book clubs can continue without these members for the 15 or so minutes Ms. Borden will be meeting with those students. In this way, Ms. Borden does not create tracked, ability-grouped literature circles but rather intentionally heterogenous groups that can engage in productive collaborations while she works with small groups of students.

Reciprocal Teaching

> Literature circles are good for literature; no surprise there. *Reciprocal teaching* is a better approach for informational texts.

Literature circles are good for literature; no surprise there. *Reciprocal teaching* is a better approach for informational texts. That's not to say that literature circles can't be adapted for informational texts, or that reciprocal teaching is only for informational texts. It's just that these procedures typically work better for different types of texts.

As is the case with literature circles, students have to be taught roles if reciprocal teaching is going to be effective. Unlike literature circles, in which there are a wide range of possible roles, reciprocal teaching has only four roles (Palincsar & Brown, 1984). At each stopping point (first identified by the teacher, but over time identified by students), students use four kinds of comprehension strategies to understand the text:

- *Questioning* the text by asking literal and inferential questions of one another

- *Clarifying* understanding through discussion of how a confusing point might be cleared up (for example, using a dictionary, checking the glossary, asking the teacher)

- *Summarizing* the main ideas of the passage

- *Predicting* what the author will discuss next, based on prior knowledge

Reciprocal teaching enjoys a significant research base that consistently demonstrates a powerful impact on students' learning, in part because they are practicing comprehension and in part because students are discussing texts with others. Over time and with practice, students internalize the comprehension strategies and begin to have a similar internal dialogue when they are reading independently.

For example, the students in Gail Rogovin's fifth-grade class were reading about weather patterns that result from the sun, specifically convection currents. Ms. Rogovin selected a piece of text that was two pages in length. She identified four stopping places in the text and assigned her students to specific groups. Given that her students had extensive experience with reciprocal teaching, she asked that they change roles each section so that each member of the group could get practice with each comprehension practice. Earlier in the school year, she had students stay with one comprehension strategy, so that they could practice it across the text. At this point, Ms. Rogovin is working with her students to integrate strategies. Ms. Rogovin has her students record their thinking on a graphic organizer so that she can review their questions, predictions, summaries, and clarifications later in the day to identify areas of instructional need. The graphic organizer is very simple and includes the four components of reciprocal teaching as well as space for students to identify which section of the text they read for each aspect of comprehension. At the bottom of the tool, Ms. Rogovin asks students to write an overall summary of the text and to ask three questions that are still on their minds. She uses these questions to identify research and investigation opportunities for her students.

> Unlike literature circles, in which there are a wide range of possible roles, reciprocal teaching has only four roles: questioning, clarifying, summarizing, and predicting.

Collaborative Writing Investigations

Students in grades 3 and above are frequently engaged in group investigation tasks, especially in science and social studies. These teams need time to work together on these complex assignments, and the literacy block is an ideal time to do so. Digital collaborative writing tools have made team tasks simpler, in that students can see changes happen in real time. School learning management systems (LMS) provide digital space for teams to store materials in folders, including information resources, original writing, and presentation slide decks. Collaborative tools such as Google Docs and Google Slides give student teams the ability to make revisions and keep current with one another. This is an important advancement from the days in which teams used a divide-and-conquer approach. Perhaps you recall similar experiences from your own schooling, when you and your teammates prepared for a presentation separately, compiling materials at the last minute. It is unlikely that any learning occurred, apart from the section for which you were responsible.

Digital tools have helped students with the collaborative writing process.

Jim West/PhotoEdit

Students in Leanna Gomez's fourth-grade class were studying the biomes of their state as part of their social studies unit on the state's geography. Five students assigned to learn about the desert biome met during the literacy block to compose together in real time. Each had a device, and they logged onto the school's LMS to access their folder on deserts. Ramon asked David to add information he had shared about desert super blooms, which are the name for a phenomenon that occurs in years when there has been a significant rainfall. "You should add pictures of the wildflowers, too," said Abril. In the meantime, she was rereading a section they had written the day before on Native American settlements in the desert. "I'll proofread this part and fix mistakes," she said. Jake and Sabrina were developing a new paragraph on desert animals, based in part on a reading they had done two days ago. "It's in the folder so we can check our spelling," said Sabrina. After 15 minutes, the students stopped writing. David said, "We need to reread this and see if we missed anything. If we're all good with it, we can start making slides tomorrow."

CONCLUSION

A major aspect of balanced literacy is the use of small-group, needs-based instruction. We would go as far as to say that if students are not grouped and regrouped to receive reading and writing instruction in small groups, the class is not balanced. We also recognize that students who are not working with the teacher in a small group can disrupt the learning environment and thus need to be engaged in meaningful learning. During some of that time, students can work independently. But they can only do so for a limited amount of time. We don't expect students to read or write by themselves for an hour or so just so their teacher can get to all of the groups. We also don't want to lower the cognitive demands so that students can work for long periods of time alone on below-grade-level tasks. Those worksheets, which we call "shut-up sheets," don't grow dendrites. That doesn't mean all worksheets are bad, but rather that some are simply designed to keep students quiet and busy. In a balanced literacy classroom, students are also expected to engage in speaking and listening tasks that build on their reading and writing tasks. The key to these tasks is to ensure that they become routine so that the teacher does not spend all of his or her time designing and monitoring the small-group, collaborative learning.

CHAPTER 5

SMALL-GROUP READING INSTRUCTION

TARGETED SUPPORT THROUGH GUIDED LEARNING

iStock.com/monkeybusinessimages

The students in Stephanie Winkler's fourth-grade class have been learning about the concept of the common good in social studies. Ms. Winkler sometimes uses content from science or social studies to inform her small-group reading instruction. In this case, she has identified a group of four students in her class who don't possess the background knowledge needed about how laws in their state are passed. "I'm going to design and deliver two reading lessons based on an article about the state legislative process," she said.

In addition, she has formed another group of students based on their most recent reading proficiency measure. "I just finished my winter informal reading inventories, and I still have a group of students who are reading below grade level. I need to pull them up close for a few weeks to figure out what each student's barriers are. I want to figure out what kinds of scaffolds I am using. Paying attention to how I scaffold tells me some things about what each kid is doing well, and where he or she needs more skill building," she said.

"When they're below grade level," Ms. Winkler continued, "their profiles vary. It's not enough to just rely on a reading proficiency level. I'll be meeting with them three times a week for a while." The remainder of her students are reading near grade level: "I'm using a couple of short novels with them. They're reading it collaboratively, but I am meeting with them at least once a week to highlight a current passage they're struggling with. I have them choose the passage in advance. It gives me some great insight into what they believe they need."

Michael Newman/PhotoEdit

Building phonemic awareness is one potential focus during small-group reading instruction.

There are also two students in her class who need much more support to be successful. Ms. Winkler focuses on advanced phonemic awareness skills with these students. They can sound out basic words and have reasonable sight word vocabularies, but she notices that they are not skilled at deleting and substituting sounds, and they do not read quickly enough to make sense of the text. She meets with these two students daily and sometimes twice per day. During this time, students get practice with segmenting, isolating, and then blending sounds. For example, Ms. Winkler asked them to listen to the word snap and to delete the n sound and then tell her what word would be created. To go from snap to sap, the student must separate the sounds, determine where the n sound is located, delete it, and then combine the resulting sounds. At other times, she may ask students to substitute sounds, such as replacing the b in the word book with an h.

There is evidence that this type of learning is highly correlated with overall reading achievement

(e.g., Catts, Fey, Zhang, & Tomblin, 2001). At other times, Ms. Winkler uses the neurological impress method, an instructional approach in which the teacher reads aloud the same piece of text with an individual student at a slightly faster rate than the student reads independently (Heckelman, 1966). This approach builds fluency with students who struggle.

There are any number of goals that can be accomplished with small-group reading instruction. Balancing literacy learning requires that teachers meet with groups of students to address their needs. Having said that, it is important to recognize that each of the instructional aspects of balanced literacy is important, and there is no need to teach something to small groups that many students need to learn. In that case, whole-class instruction would be more appropriate. Small-group instruction is designed to differentiate learning based on students' current needs.

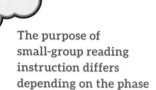

PRINCIPLES AND PURPOSES OF SMALL-GROUP READING INSTRUCTION

The purpose of small-group reading instruction differs depending on the phase of reading development.

Small-group reading and writing instruction forms the keystone of an elementary balanced literacy program. These groups are needs based and responsive, and they are driven by frequent analysis of assessment data. There are some common stages of reading development that can help guide the type of instruction students need (see Figure 5.1). Typically, no more than five students are in the group, such that the teacher is able to deliver scaffolded instruction to move learning forward.

The purpose of small-group reading instruction differs depending on the phase of reading development. Emergent and beginning readers, commonly seen in the primary grades, are coordinating the foundational reading behaviors of decoding, fluency, and nascent comprehension skills to read previously unseen text. This process, which Clay (1991) referred to as the application of strategies "on the run," requires young readers to consolidate early reading skills to build the automaticity they need to read more advanced texts. The leveled texts utilized for emergent and beginning readers are placed on a fine-grained gradient. Children incrementally advance using formative assessment data, particularly running records, phonics assessments, and writing samples, as the text itself is an important source of scaffolding. Frequent assessment is critical, because students who are left too long to linger at a level will not make the gains needed. The importance of frequent assessment and continual advance cannot be understated. Too often, young readers are left to linger for weeks or even months at a single level in static groups that inhibit learning (Fountas & Pinnell, 2012).

While small-group reading instruction is well known in the primary grades, older readers require different experiences, not simply a longer time using the same lesson design and text type. Small-group reading for transitional and fluent readers shifts to the application of an increasingly sophisticated set of comprehension skills. These students, who are typically in grades 3 and above, benefit from the use of texts that are more complex and fittingly stretch the reader. A growing body of research supports the use of more complex texts than have been traditionally used in small-group reading instruction for students in grades 3 and above (e.g., Amendum, Conradi, & Hiebert, 2018; Lupo, Strong, & Smith, 2019). This format is ideal for using more complex texts, as students can receive timely and responsive direct support and scaffolding from the teacher. The shift in small-group reading instruction for the intermediate grades represents an exciting advancement and raises questions about long-held beliefs about independent, instructional, and frustration levels of reading ability.

▼ FIGURE 5.1 PHASES OF READING DEVELOPMENT

Emergent	Early	Transitional	Self-Extending
Emergent readers are experimenting with reading. During this phase they are learning that print carries a message and how books work. They are beginning to recognize letters and words.	Early readers are reading simple texts and have a larger bank of words they can read quickly. They utilize a variety of basic strategies to figure out known and unknown words.	Transactional readers are reading a variety of texts and understand that each has its own unique structure and associated characteristics. When seeking information, they consult more than one source. They are becoming more self-aware of the strategies used.	Self-extending readers read a wide range of texts and apply critical literacy skills to analyze the authenticity and value of information. They continue to acquire increasingly more sophisticated literacy skills through extensive reading and discussion.
• Rhymes, chants, sings and engages in word play • Hears and repeats sounds in words • Names letters of the alphabet and their sounds • Recognizes some words on sight • Possesses book handling skills • Knows the difference between letters and words • Has some 1:1 correspondence • Tells stories using familiar books, relying on a combination of pictures, memory, and text	• Gaining knowledge of phonics (e.g., blends, digraphs, diphthongs) • Uses initial/medial/final letter sounds to figure out unknown words • Sight word knowledge expands • Will self-correct errors when reading aloud • Somewhat disfluent, with hesitations • Vocabulary includes less common words (Tier 2 and Tier 3) • Retells stories in sequence • Chooses books based on interests	• Reads regular and irregular words • Applies structural and contextual knowledge to figure out unknown words • Reads more fluently, and demonstrates basic prosody (e.g., intonation, expression) • Identifies main ideas and key details • Is able to understand simple inferences in texts • Reads longer texts, including chapter books, and series • Identifies favorite authors and genres • Can identify comprehension strategies used in reading	• Text selection reflects a broad reading diet across genres, topics, and purposes • Recognizes age-appropriate titles and authors • Fluent reading includes accurate use of phrase boundaries, timing, and pacing • Locates subtle implications in texts • Reads across texts and identifies points of convergence and divergence • Can reflect on strategic thinking used to make meaning

QUESTIONING THE READING LEVEL FRAMEWORK

Effective teachers know that the premier instructional feature of small-group reading instruction is the scaffolds provided to bridge what readers know and do not know.

Emmett Betts introduced a reading level framework in 1946 that has remained remarkably entrenched for the last seven decades. Betts presented a framework based on two facets of reading: word recognition and comprehension. He stated in order for students to read a text independently, they would need to accurately recognize words at a level of 99–100% accuracy, and correctly answer comprehension questions at a performance rate of 90–100%. A text deemed to be at a frustration level for a student, and therefore to be avoided, could be identified when a student's accuracy dipped below 90%, and her ability to answer comprehension questions was less than 50%. Therefore, he asserted, a student's instructional level was the sweet spot between the two: accuracy of 95–99%, and comprehension at 75–89%. (See Halladay's 2012 analysis of Betts's framework for more detailed information.) However, the source doesn't hold up to the light of day. Betts claimed that these figures were derived from two dissertation studies he supervised; the dissertations themselves did not provide any empirical evidence to support those assertions (Shanahan, 1983).

Halladay (2012) questions several assumptions that the Betts framework appears to be based on. The first is that there is a strong link between decoding and comprehension. While this is true for early readers, it is less so for older readers, as vocabulary knowledge overtakes decoding as a predictor of comprehension (Ouellette & Beers, 2010). A second assumption is that students must possess nearly perfect word recognition in order to read independently, an assertion challenged by findings about older students who read successfully and with good comprehension, even if they have lower accuracy rates of word recognition. In fact, with scaffolded support, students can read challenging text on their own, provided the scaffolds are tailored to address the elements of complexity present in the text (Lupo, Strong, & Smith, 2019; Shanahan, Fisher, & Frey, 2012).

THE CRITICAL ROLE OF SCAFFOLDS

Effective teachers know that the premier instructional feature of small-group reading instruction is the scaffolds provided to bridge what readers know and do not know. The term was coined by Wood, Bruner, and Ross (1976), who studied the ways mothers provided language supports to aid their young children. They explored similar ways in which tutors similarly assisted students through the zone of proximal development (Vygotsky, 1978) such that learners could perform at a higher level than they would otherwise be able to alone. The term *scaffolding* is meant to recall the framework on the outside of a building under construction. It should be no more than needed to provide the worker access and should be dismantled when it is no longer of use.

Scaffolding is not telling, and it is not simply providing hints in hopes that a problem a student is having will simply go away. Scaffolded instruction is investigative; teachers rapidly form a hypothesis about what it is a reader knows and doesn't know in the moment. Based on the hypothesis, the teacher makes a decision about the kind of scaffold that might assist the reader in linking what he knows to what he doesn't know.

Scaffolding is critical during small-group reading instruction.

James Shaffer/PhotoEdit

Scaffolds fall into four categories, from least to most overt: robust questions, prompts, cues, and explanations with modeling (Frey & Fisher, 2010). When a reader stalls, the teacher forms a conclusion about what might be causing the stumble, and poses a question that might assist the reader. For instance, fourth-grade student Tucker and his reading group are reading and discussing a passage about Hermione from *Harry Potter and the Sorcerer's Stone* (Rowling, 1997). However, Tucker is having difficulty associating Hermione's character traits with her actions in the current reading selection. His teacher's hypothesis is that Tucker is not organizing what he already knows about Hermione to confirm this latest incident. The teacher first asks, "What do you already know about the character?" When the question doesn't activate the knowledge needed to move forward, a prompt is provided. A prompt is a bit more overt and provides the student with additional information. The teacher says, "You used that same phrase a few minutes ago when you were describing her character traits to me." A cue is more directive and shifts the reader's attention to a source of information. When Tucker is still having difficulty, the teacher says, "Take a look at the character map we made. You and your classmates identified a key trait of this character. Do you see where it is written here [pointing] on the character map?"

If questions, prompts, and cues have not aided the reader, then a direct explanation is offered and is followed by some teacher modeling. "The descriptive phrase your group listed is that the character has 'a mind of her own.' That means she makes her own decisions, even when the other people around her tell her it's a bad idea. I'll show you another instance of that. Let's take a look back to Chapter 4. Then we'll return to our original question. What character traits is Hermione exhibiting?"

The same process can be used to address gaps in foundational skills. When young children are learning to read, instruction focuses on words that students can recognize by sight (e.g., *and, the, went*) and words that they need to decode (e.g., *hat, stop*). As their reading development progresses, the words they encounter become increasingly complex, and they have to apply more rules and understand that some words are borrowed from other languages (e.g., *café, genre, patio*). Whole-class instruction introduces students to sound-symbol correspondence, and students practice and apply what they have learned independently and with their teacher ready to scaffold during small-group instruction.

We don't just tell students the words when they are reading. Instead we scaffold. For example, a first-grade student was reading the following sentence: The truck went up the hill. The student got stuck on the word *truck*, saying, "Tr-, tr-, tr-, I'm not sure."

The instinct for many of us is to either tell the student the word because it is the longest, and theoretically the hardest, or to ask the student to check the pictures. Neither of these actions will help the student read the word the next time if there is no picture or adult present. Instead, the teacher might say, "You have the first part of the word exactly right. Now, let's focus on the rest of the letters. Let's chunk it. Remember? We put our thumbs over parts and try read smaller parts and blend them together."

The student does so, saying "tr-" and then "uck" and then faster until he says, "Oh, I get it, it's truck. It's a truck. The truck went up the hill." The teacher congratulates him and then asks, "How did you know this word?" pointing to the word *went*. The student responds, "Easy, it's on the wall and I practice my sight words with my dad."

Scaffolding is the key to helping students practice and apply so that they learn. Wood, Bruner, and Ross's (1976) original research on

If questions, prompts, and cues have not aided the reader, then a direct explanation is offered and is followed by some teacher modeling.

scaffolding had two parts: instructional contingency and domain contingency. Instructional contingency involves the amount of help given, as described in Figure 5.2. Domain contingency, on the other hand, focuses the learner on a neglected source of information. The source

▼ FIGURE 5.2 INTERACTION WITH DOMAIN-CONTINGENT MOVE

Instructional Contingency Rubric: Increasing Levels of Help*		
Level	**Definition**	**Sample Teacher Moves**
1. Prompting	Provides no information about anything helpful to use or do; calls on the student to solve the problem.	"What can you try?" "Try that again." "What's that word?" "Were you right?"
2. Prompting with information	Provides some general information; the student must still decide what to use or do.	"You read that word on the other page." "You know this word." "You wrote that word yesterday."
3. Directing	Provides specific information about what the student can use or do to solve the problem; the student must solve the problem.	"Reread and think about what would make sense and look right." "Does that make sense?" "Does that sound right?" "Does that look right?"
4. Demonstrating	Provides all of the information needed to solve the problem by taking the student role and modeling, but the student must still solve.	Teacher uses a card to show the syllables and articulates each part.
5. Telling	Provides all the information needed; no more problem solving is needed.	"That word is *picnic*." "You're right, *picnic*."

*Rubric starts with the least amount of help (prompting) and increases to the most (telling).
Note: Adapted from Rodgers, E., D'Agostino, J. V., Harmey, S. J., Kelly, R. H., & Brownfield, K. (2016). Examining the nature of scaffolding in an early literacy intervention. *Reading Research Quarterly, 57*(3), 351. Copyright 2016 by the International Literacy Association. Adapted with permission.

Source: Rodgers, E. (2014). Scaffolding word solving while reading: New research insights. *The Reading Teacher, 70*(5), 525–532. Figure on page 528. Used with permission.

of information used in domain contingency in the Rodgers study were based on the work of Marie Clay (2013), a pioneer in early reading instruction. This information included meaning, structure, and visual information. Rodgers (2017) defines these as

- *Meaning,* an attempt to make sense in the story: The substitution fits the meaning of the story.

- *Structure,* an attempt that incorporates rules of oral language: The sentence could be read that way up to the substitution and sound right.

- *Visual information,* an attempt that shares some of the same letters. (p. 526)

For example, a student who says the word *man* when the text says *person* is likely using meaning and structure but not visual information. A student who says, "Bill swing a black cat" when the text says, "Bill saw a black cat," suggests that the student has some visual information, but the structure does not work and the meaning is somewhat off. When teachers understand the sources of information that the student is neglecting, they can better target their scaffolds using questions, prompts, and cues, as described above. Notice that the visual information did not include looking at the pictures for clues. We all like the pictures, and readers use the illustrations to help make meaning of the text. But the focus of small-group instruction should be on reading the words in the text. Having said that, when students are absolutely stuck, referencing the pictures might help. But be careful not to rely on the pictures to always do the work. Students need to learn to read.

> When students are absolutely stuck, referencing the pictures might help. But be careful not to rely on the pictures to always do the work. Students need to learn to read.

Rodgers studied one thousand such instructional moves of Reading Recovery teachers, which had been captured on video. She separated the examples into two groups: those from teachers who had above-average outcomes as measured by the national Reading Recovery data, and those whose outcomes were below the average. While there was no difference in the instructional contingency (the amount was similar), those teachers who achieved above-average results exhibited many more instances of domain contingency decision making. Thus, while a teacher relying only on instructional contingency might encourage a student to "try that word again," a teacher using domain contingency orientation considers what the child is using and not using.

Teachers providing small-group reading instruction to students cannot rely on the simple dichotomous decision of whether a student's response is correct or incorrect. There are several complex cognitive moves the teacher must engage in. The first is forming a theory for why the student is giving an incorrect response. What does the child know and not know at this moment? The second decision point is just how much assistance to render (instructional contingency). The rule of thumb is to deliver only enough support to get the student to do the thinking. Be comfortable with underscaffolding. You can always offer more as a follow-up. But it is the third consideration that is perhaps the most important: On what element should the focus of the scaffold lie? For emergent readers, word-level work is a good consideration. For older readers, it is more likely that the focus will lie in one of two broad areas: comprehension and vocabulary.

> Deliver only enough support to get the student to do the thinking. Be comfortable with underscaffolding. You can always offer more as a follow-up.

CONSTRAINED AND UNCONSTRAINED SKILLS OF READING

The National Reading Panel's examination of elementary reading instruction identified skills and concepts essential for elementary students to master. The research summarized in the report clustered into the following domains:

- *Alphabetics*, including phonemic awareness and phonics

- *Fluency*, the ability to read accurately, smoothly, and with expression

- *Comprehension*, including vocabulary and text comprehension

These domains form the core of virtually any contemporary comprehensive reading program. But the distribution of mastery in each domain is not equal across readers at each stage of development. You will recall our discussion in Chapter 1 about constrained and unconstrained reading skills (Paris, 2005): Constrained elements of reading are those that are bounded. In other words, there are finite limits of knowledge needed for mastery. Phonemic awareness is constrained, because there are 44 sounds in the English language. When you know them all, you're finished. There are no new ones to learn, at least within a single language. Alphabetic knowledge is also constrained; there are 26 letters in the English alphabet. Phonics is more complex, as it is the bolting on of the sounds of the language to associated letters and letter combinations. For students making expected progress, mastery of phonics occurs around the end of third grade. A final element of reading that Paris describes as constrained is fluency. This takes a bit longer to master, but oral and silent reading fluency norms typically top out at sixth through eighth grade (e.g., Hasbrouck & Tindal, 2017). These constrained skills are foundational to reading, and in fact are explicitly identified that way in many state standard documents. However, these constrained

resources.corwin.com/
thisisbalancedliteracy

Video 17
Small-Group Guided
Reading in Kindergarten

skills should not be confused with reading. They are essential; they are not sufficient.

Paris goes on to describe the unconstrained skills of reading that, in combination with constrained skills, allow true reading with understanding to occur. Unconstrained skills have no boundaries and develop across an entire lifetime. Your vocabulary is wider and deeper today than it was a year ago. Your comprehension will be more extensive a year from now, because you continue to learn and gain knowledge. Not only are unconstrained skills vital for reading development, but also, "Instruction in high-order reading comprehension should be a specific educational target and treated independently from basic skills instruction" (Tarchi, 2015, p. 80). In other words, comprehension and vocabulary development will not arise from instruction of constrained skills. These unconstrained skills develop through intentional instruction of same. However, the text types used in primary grades have limited usefulness when it comes to comprehension and vocabulary (please note that we did not say *none*). Because the contours of comprehension and vocabulary are constrained in leveled texts—as well as in texts designed to be decodable, have controlled vocabulary, or be predictable in design—young children must have experiences with more complex texts. These experiences occur in the early years through interactive read-alouds, close readings, and shared readings with complex texts that align with their thinking, not their ability to decode.

TEXT TYPES IN THE PRIMARY GRADES: WHICH TO CHOOSE?

Young children must learn to crack the code of written language in order to make inroads toward reading. The foundational skills of reading related to concepts of print, decoding, word recognition, and fluency are taught using several distinctive types of text. However, as Shanahan (2019) notes, each has its unique strengths and limitations. Further, he reminds us that these simplified texts are not the kind that students will be required to read, and that while simplified texts "speed acquisition … they also reduce the learners' abilities to generalize or transfer these skills to the greater complexity of the actual forms that one needs to learn" (Shanahan, 2019, ¶ 18).

Decodable Texts

These texts are highly phonetically regular and oriented toward the alphabetic principle of sound/letter correspondence. The intention is to reduce the number of nondecodable words. Sentences that are highly decodable use repeated patterns that are systematically introduced. "Tim gets a net. Tim gets the pets in a net." is an example of highly decodable text. However, there are shortcomings, especially in the use of very short sentences that possess limited opportunities for meaning making.

Predictable Pattern Texts

These texts introduce and repeat a pattern so that young readers are better able to predict words and phrases. They also rely on sight words to support readers. The song *I Know an Old Lady Who Swallowed a Fly* is a perfect example of a predictable pattern text. With its refrain of "I don't know why she swallowed a fly; I guess she'll die" readers can often anticipate the words without actually attending to them. Children can also rely on the illustrations and sight words, rather than knowledge of phonics, to read.

Controlled Vocabulary Texts

These texts are written to reduce the number of rare words, as measured to a corpus of words that correlate relative to the appearance of words at each grade level. Controlled vocabulary texts introduce new words systematically and use them repeatedly so that students can benefit from practice. Unlike decodable texts, controlled vocabulary texts make broad use of sight words as well as decodable words. Because they draw from a broader range of words compared to decodable texts, some related comprehension instruction is also possible.

Authentic Literature

The use of authentic literature, which comprises texts written for young audiences but not for specifically for reading instruction, has been considerably reduced for small-group instruction since its heyday in the 1970s and 1980s. Most texts used in guided reading programs are not authentic. A major problem in teaching foundational skills using authentic literature is that the opportunity to repeatedly apply skills and practice is not there. A second important limitation is that there are too many rare words present that confound young readers. For these reasons, authentic literature is not used specifically to teach foundational skills. However, it does have an important role in interactive read-alouds and shared reading in the primary grades.

resources.corwin.com/
thisisbalancedliteracy

Video 18
Small-Group Guided
Reading in Grade 5

Leveled texts, generally speaking, are composed of elements of decodable, predictable, and controlled vocabulary texts. But, there is wide variance in the application of each in any commercial program. In fact, some programs suggest that students in the early grades don't need to sound out words, which we find shocking. It is useful to examine the prospectus of any program to see the way these elements are deployed within and across texts. It's also important to know the learning expectations well so that you can determine whether or not the texts will allow your students to develop mastery.

LESSON DESIGN IN PRIMARY GRADES

Young children have limited stamina and attention for small-group reading instruction, and it is important to acknowledge that the cognitive demand is high. These lessons are likely to be about 10–15 minutes in length in early kindergarten, and gradually extend to 20 minutes or so by first grade. Many primary teachers begin with a warm-up using a familiar book, so students can reengage with the act of reading, which is far from automatic for them. This is also a time to assess a student using a running record. We will discuss assessment using running records later in the chapter. The sequence that follows is suggested for use after the warm-up.

Teach the Focus Skill or Strategy

Every small-group reading lesson has a purpose, whether it is to apply a decoding skill, a fix-up strategy, a fluency technique, or a reading comprehension strategy. Each leveled text is engineered to highlight a particular skill or strategy. For example, a leveled text with lots of gerunds demands that the word work focuses on *–ing* endings in terms of decoding, grammar, and syntax. While this step is also short, it is pivotal, as the subsequent reading of the new text is to witness how children apply knowledge of skills and strategies on the run. A leveled text with labeled diagrams requires attention to how this text feature works with the concepts discussed in the main part of the reading. Some of the skills that can be the focus of instruction are included in Figure 5.3.

Many small-group lessons focus on learning how words work in continuous text. Therefore, this part of the lesson is used to reinforce how readers use their foundational skills of print concepts, phonics and word recognition, and fluency to take apart words using their knowledge of sounds, letters, and morphemes. In addition, young children are applying comprehension and vocabulary strategies, such as locating the main idea, using text features, and integrating knowledge of how illustrations and print work together. This portion of the small-group lesson is not a time to introduce a new skill or strategy, but rather to extend their ability to apply what they have been learning in whole-group instruction (see Chapter 2).

Introducing a book to novice readers provides a scaffold for making meaning. Just as we do not enter a library, bookstore, or website and pick the first book we see, we do not expect students to arbitrarily read anything we put in front of them without generating questions.

Introduce the Book

Introducing a book to novice readers provides a scaffold for making meaning. Just as we do not enter a library, bookstore, or website and pick the first book we see, we do not expect students to arbitrarily read anything we put in front of them without generating questions. As students

▼ FIGURE 5.3 SKILLS TO TEACH DURING SMALL-GROUP LEARNING

- Identify features of a sentence, including the first word, capital letters, and ending punctuation.
- Identify long and short vowel sounds in single-syllable words.
- Blend sounds together (including consonant blends) to make a word.
- Segment (break apart) a word into its individual consonant and vowel phonemes (in order).
- Delete phonemes from words to make new words.
- Substitute sounds in words to make different words.
- Decode regularly spelled one-syllable words.
- Identify common spellings for long vowel sounds when seeing a word with a vowel team.
- Learn words that "don't play fair" (irregularly spelled words).
- Read smoothly, not too fast or too slow, and with expression and meaning.
- Read accurately (with few or no decoding mistakes).
- Self-correct or confirm a word in a text by asking "Does this make sense?"
- Reread something when it doesn't make sense or sound right.

progress in their ability to read independently, the teacher should move from introducing the book to having students preview the text to introduce themselves to the book. They might learn to ask these questions:

- What could the author's purpose be for this book?
- How is it organized?
- Why am I reading this book?

Young children benefit from an orientation to a new book, as it introduces language they are likely to need as they read. For instance, if the story involves a ball, use the word and show it to them in the text. Introduce the book in a straightforward and succinct manner. It isn't necessary to provide a long explanation of the book or lots of background knowledge.

As Clay (2005) notes, the teacher should provide the reader a conceptual organization for the reading and should ensure that students are familiar with

- the story,
- the plot,
- the phrases of language that they might never have heard,
- unusual names and new words, and
- old [known] words used in an unusual way. (p. 91)

However, we encourage you to limit the extent of the picture walk, and don't tell the entire story in advance. Students need to learn to read, not only to make meaning from images. Instead, pose a question that is likely to cause students to seek an answer. For instance, you might ask, "I wonder whether the boy is going to be able to get the beach ball out of the waves?" Remind them to apply the targeted reading skill or strategy. For example, you might say, "We've been remembering to blend all of the sounds for all of the letters in the word rather than guessing based on the first letter of the word."

Jim West/PhotoEdit

Young children benefit from an orientation to a new book.

Students Read the Book

Emergent readers usually read aloud, as silent reading behavior is a function of fluency and doesn't happen until they have some reading skills under their belt. If they are reading aloud, remind them to use soft voices so they don't disturb others. As they read, listen in to check each child's ability to process the words, taking anecdotal notes on what each is doing in terms of fluency, accuracy, and use of the targeted skill or strategy. If they are reading silently (this usually happens by the age of 6), ask individual students to read aloud quietly so you can hear them. Scaffold as needed, giving consideration to both the instructional contingency and domain contingency needed. As students are likely to be finished at different times, instruct them to read the book a second time so that you can provide essential scaffolds for individuals.

Check for Comprehension

Reading is ultimately about the ability to formulate meaning, and even in leveled texts for emergent and early readers, meaning does still exist. During the discussion, all students should be participating and adding to the conversation. Refer back to some of the points mentioned during the book orientation, especially the question to be answered at the end of the book (e.g., "So was the boy able to get the beach ball back? How did he do it?"). More general open-ended questions can also prompt further discussion (and students should be encouraged to provide evidence from the text to support their answers):

- What is the story about?

- What did you think about the book?

- Why do you think a character did a specific thing [state what that is]?

- How did the character act or react? Why?

- What did you learn? (for informational texts)

There can be a tendency for students to direct their answers to the teacher, so facilitation is necessary to get them to talk with one another.

Facilitate discussion of the text by asking follow-up probes and encouraging conversation between students. There can be a tendency for students to direct their answers to the teacher, so facilitation is necessary to get them to talk with one another. Deepen the discussion by prompting students to add to their thinking, and ask them to refer back to the text to support their replies.

- What part of the book made you think that?

- What else can you think of?

- Do you agree/disagree?

- Show us the page in the book that makes you think that.

- Tell us more.

- What was important in this book? Why?

It can be helpful to have a list of general comprehension questions and follow-up probes available to draw from. We recommend keeping the list in a transparent sleeve so that you can readily keep it at your elbow to refer to during the discussion.

Brief Writing Task

We ask children to write a sentence or more to amplify the connection between reading and writing. One useful technique is to have a small notebook of primary-lined paper for each child. At the end of the lesson, students can write a sentence that is linked to the book they just read and date their entry. We suggest a notebook, rather than loose paper, as the evolution of their writing over time becomes another source of data for monitoring progress and conferring with students. Depending on the time allotment, students may complete these at their tables, rather than during the small-group reading lesson. But writing should always be part of the small-group learning experience. For example, when reading a decodable text, the writing task requires students to use words with the target phonics skills, and those who need support can use the book to help them.

Remember to review students' writing for evidence of transfer. The phonics lessons should be evidenced in their writing. An analysis of student work allows you to identify which lessons have stuck and where students need reteaching. For example, first-grade texts that introduce the long-*a* vowel should help students when they write words such as *stay, play, gave, name, page*, and so on. If students make repeated errors writing words with long-*a* sounds after instruction, they need additional instruction for the concept to stick. Failure to attend to this gap in learning places students at higher risk for failure in the future.

> While there may be children who have not fully mastered grade-level foundational reading skills, it is dangerous to limit their instruction.

SCAFFOLDING LEARNING IN THE INTERMEDIATE GRADES

As students move into the transitional phase of reading, their instructional needs transform as well. The source of the scaffolding shifts more fully from the text to the teacher. In the primary grades, there is a gradation of the texts themselves, which are engineered specifically for this task. However, students in grades 3 and above are being asked to apply reading skills and strategies to a broader range of texts, especially those that have not been specifically designed for a single purpose. Knowledge building moves to a more prominent place in the language arts curriculum. Students in the transitional phase of reading are increasingly able to consolidate an array of foundational skills and strategies and are becoming more fluent. However, some students fail to progress because they have not become adept at building knowledge from texts. Chall and Jacobs's 1983 seminal study on "the fourth-grade slump" is unfortunately too well known by intermediate teachers, who witness the failure of some students who do not move forward from learning-to-read to reading-to-learn. While there are children who have not yet fully mastered grade-level foundational reading skills of phonemic awareness, phonics, and word recognition, it is dangerous to limit their instruction to these constrained skills. They must have regular exposure to grade-level texts, with scaffolds, in order to keep pace with their classmates who are shifting to reading for knowledge.

As with primary-grade lessons, each session requires a specific focus, often in the comprehension and vocabulary domains. Having said that, some students need remediation, and the focus of their small-group instruction would be on the evidence-based gaps in their learning. For example, a struggling fifth grader who has yet to master decoding of multisyllabic words needs instruction in that area, and likely has gaps in phonemic awareness and fluency. But many students in the upper grades have developed appropriate foundational skills. In these cases, the instructional emphasis shifts in its entirety to further development of the unconstrained skills of vocabulary and comprehension.

Comprehension strategy examples include self-monitoring one's understanding, making predictions, identifying themes and supporting evidence, using text features, noticing the author's purpose and craft, and analyzing the structure of the text. Examples of vocabulary strategies include identifying unknown words and phrases using structural and contextual clues; understanding word relationships, figurative language, and their nuances; and understanding how denotative and connotative meanings of words and phrases are utilized in continuous texts.

LESSON DESIGN FOR INTERMEDIATE GRADES

Older students have likely developed increased stamina, and thus the time for small-group reading instruction is longer—typically 20 to 30 minutes. In addition, these lessons are usually associated with longer texts, including full-length books and articles. Portions of the lesson should also include elements of close reading (see Chapter 2 for a more detailed discussion of close reading) and feature the use of more complex texts that are intended to stretch the reader.

Introduce the Reading and Purpose

If the reading is a new one, provide students with a brief description of the book or article. You don't need to provide an extensive discussion of the text plot, and you certainly don't want to spoil the reading by giving away the major plot points or information. A few sentences are sufficient. What is more important is setting the stage for the purpose for their learning today. Will they be making predictions based on the headings? Perhaps the purpose is to consider what one already knows about the topic, and then examine the table of contents. Or the purpose might be to determine word meanings using contextual clues. If the text is longer, a few minutes spent on reviewing what has transpired thus far in the book or article is helpful for activating prior knowledge.

Structural and contextual clues help students with unfamiliar words and phrases.

Spotlight Vocabulary in Today's Reading

Tread carefully as you consider vocabulary, and resist the urge to preteach all the unusual or unfamiliar terms. If there is a word or phrase that is central to their understanding, and there is no other way to determine the meaning, then of course you need to do a bit of direct instruction. But more often than not, unfamiliar words and phrases can be determined using structural or contextual clues. You might pose a question and invite students to figure out what it means as they read. "Our author uses the term *churn* in the third paragraph. As you read, think about what *churn* means in the context of this story."

Teach the Focus Strategy

As students grow, they must deepen their knowledge of how to apply strategies within increasingly complex text. Remind students of the comprehension strategy (or constellation of strategies) they will want to use as they read. While the small-group lesson isn't the place to introduce a new strategy, it is definitely the time for students to apply what they have learned to a new text. For example, you might remind students that they have learned how to turn headings and subheadings into questions to monitor their understanding. "You'll find that this article has lots of headings, so remember to transform them into questions so you can see if you are able to answer those questions." Alternatively, you might say "This author uses a lot of figurative language and idioms. We've studied some of those in the past, but today we get to really dig in. We're going to identify those words and phrases that are figurative and then analyze them in the context of this reading to identify their meanings."

Students Read the Passage

A challenge of small-group reading is to balance the amount of time reading with opportunities to scaffold and assess. On the one hand, you don't want the students reading silently for 20 minutes in your presence. On the other hand, you also don't want the entire lesson to be filled with discussion and little time with eyes on text. Therefore, it is advisable to zoom in on a passage that students will be able to read within 8–10 minutes. As students read, ask individual students to read aloud to you in a quiet voice, so you can monitor fluency and accuracy.

Pose Text-Dependent Questions for Discussion

Literal-level questions can be used for a quick check of surface-level comprehension, but don't spend too much time there. This is prime time instructionally, so have questions prepared in advance that focus on the structural and inferential levels of meaning. The scaffolding you do, especially as you provide further prompts and cues, should be expended primarily on stretching students to apply critical thinking skills to their reading. If you find that students are stalled at the literal level of meaning, then reconsider whether the text is a good match for your learners and your purpose.

The quality of the discussion is also in play, as you want to facilitate discussion among students, not just with you. Encourage students to address one another, ask questions, and build upon each other's comments. The furniture can either encourage or discourage the quality of the interactions. A kidney-shaped table, which seems to be the traditional choice for small-group reading instruction, seems to squelch student-to-student communication. Consider using a round or square table that conveys an expectation that there is an equal exchange of knowledge and ideas among members of the group.

Debrief the Use of the Target Vocabulary and Comprehension Strategies

Metacognitive awareness of one's learning is an essential skill for intermediate learners to develop. Thinking about one's thinking is a critical process for readers, especially as they monitor their understanding and resolve problems when meaning is lost. Ask students about how and where they utilized the focus strategies in the reading. Be sure to also

Metacognitive awareness of one's learning is an essential skill for intermediate learners to develop.

inquire about the vocabulary spotlighted, if you have not already done so. Press for evidence as you do so. For instance, asking for evidence of how *churn* is understood in the reading reminds students that vocabulary is not about simply knowing a definition in isolation, but is understood as having a function within continuous text.

Students Write at the Interpretive Level

Because the passage highlighted in the small-group lesson has received a level of attention and focus, the writing should extend their understanding. Develop a writing prompt that is aligned with the lesson's purpose and that requires the student to return to the reading. This text-dependent writing task should encourage students to interpret what they have been reading. Avoid prompts that are based on personal experiences that reside outside of the text (e.g., "Write about a time when you were lost") or that are needlessly speculative (e.g., "Would you like to go to the moon, like the astronauts we just read about?"). Instead, craft writing tasks that require students to use the text in their responses (e.g., "The character we read about is lost and terrified. What techniques does the author use to convey those emotions? Use evidence from the text to support your answer."). Because the writing is extended, it can be completed after the small-group lesson is over. Ask students to use a notebook or electronic portfolio so you have another source of data for gauging progress over time.

Lesson design for small-group instruction is essential for student success. Too often we have seen four readers at a table with a teacher who is observing more than teaching, scaffolding, and assessing. Small-group reading instruction is valuable real estate in the balanced literacy block. Utilize those minutes to make the most of the up-close time you have with individual readers.

The methods you use for grouping students, and the responsiveness you exhibit as you move them to better meet their needs, are key to the success of your reading groups.

GROUPING FOR READING INSTRUCTION

The methods you use for grouping students, and the responsiveness you exhibit as you move them to better meet their needs, are key to the success of your reading groups. The two major methods for small-group reading instruction are needs-based and interest groups.

Need-Based Grouping

Needs-based groups are clustered because they are likely to benefit from a particular teaching point. In the primary grades, when the text itself is an important source of scaffolding, students are measured periodically according to their proficiency at a text level. Running records, developed by Clay (1991), can be used to guide instruction. Running records can be used as a measure of reading progress and as a diagnostic tool to gauge how a child is utilizing meaning, syntax, and visual cues to figure out words. The child reads a new text, while the teacher listens and codes miscues (errors). A coding sheet for use with a running record can be found in Figure 5.4. The teacher then analyzes for error patterns, and may create new groups in order to pull together other students who share a similar profile. A second purpose of the running record is to determine when the child is ready to move to a higher level of text. Although training on how to use and interpret a running record is beyond the scope of this

▼ FIGURE 5.4 CODING SHEET FOR MISCUE ANALYSIS

Responses and Miscues	Explanation	Coding	Example
Correct	Calls word correctly	✓	✓ ✓ ✓ ✓ ✓ ✓ The house is blue and white.
Substitution	Calls one word for another	horse / house	horse ✓ house ✓ ✓ ✓ ✓ The house is blue and white.
Omission	Skips a word	— / house	— ✓ house ✓ ✓ ✓ ✓ The house is blue and white.
Insertion	Adds a word	big	✓ **big** ✓ ✓ ✓ ✓ The house is blue and white.
Appeal	Asks for help	A / house	A ✓ house ✓ ✓ ✓ ✓ The house is blue and white.
Teacher told	Teacher tells word	TT / house	TT ✓ house ✓ ✓ ✓ ✓ The house is blue and white.
Rerun	Student repeats words, phrases, or entire sentence	← RR ___ The house	RR ✓ ←✓ ✓ ✓ ✓ ✓ The house is blue and white.
Self-correction	Reader corrects error on own	horse SC / house	horse SC ✓ house ✓ ✓ ✓ ✓ The house is blue and white.

Source: Fisher, D., Frey, N., & Hattie, J. (2017). *Teaching literacy in the visible learning classroom, grades K–5.* Thousand Oaks, CA: Corwin.

book, there are any number of excellent print and video resources designed for that purpose. Importantly, teachers use other data to form groups and plan instruction. In the final chapter of this book, we provide a wide range of assessment tools. It's important to consider literacy learning more comprehensively and to monitor students' progress on each aspect of learning so that needs are identified and addressed early.

A limitation of running records is that as readers become more fluent, it can be more challenging to collect the data. In addition, the cueing systems described in the previous paragraph give way to more mature systems. Informal reading inventories (IRI) are useful assessments to capture the reading performance of students. IRIs are composed of narrative and informational reading passages that have been scaled using a grade level or letter system. These passages are usually 100–150 words in length. The student reads the passage silently and then aloud, as the teacher records miscues. Because the text appears on the teacher's recording form, only the errors need to be written. Each passage is accompanied by postreading questions designed to check comprehension. IRIs are more time-consuming to administer and are not done during small-group reading instruction. Most commercial IRIs have a graded word assessment to initially determine which passage will be a good starting point, as it may take two or even three passages before reaching a level that is deemed as being too difficult. Figure 5.5 is a table of some common IRIs and their features.

Students in grades 3 and above benefit from grouping strategies that are not restricted to a measure of reading ability. The first reason is because the fine gradation of text levels in the early grades gives way to larger text intervals in the intermediate grades. The second reason is because the text itself is less of a scaffold. Comprehension and vocabulary development are more nuanced, and these skills are drawn not only from what occurs within the four corners of the page, but also what is drawn from outside the page.

The chief outside factor that influences comprehension and vocabulary development is knowledge. Students who do not possess requisite background knowledge are disadvantaged compared to more knowledgeable peers. Thus, needs-based groups in the intermediate grades can and should be organized according to gaps that exist. For example, some students who are studying space in science may need more background knowledge about planets, energy sources, or the conditions needed to support life. Small reading groups can be formed temporarily to rapidly build student background knowledge such that they can benefit from content instruction. Initial assessments of student knowledge are

▼ FIGURE 5.5 INFORMAL READING INVENTORIES

IRI	Grades	Special Features
Basic Reading Inventory (Johns)	K–8	• Graded word lists • CD-ROM for administration guidance
Burns/Roe Informal Reading Inventory (Burns & Roe)	PreK–12	• Graded word lists • Silent and oral reading measures • Expository and narrative passages
Critical Reading Inventory (Applegate, Quinn, & Applegate)	K–12	• Evaluates critical literacy skills • Expository and narrative passages • Includes case study examples
Flynt-Cooter Comprehensive Reading Inventory–2 (Flynt, Cooter, & Flynt)	K–12	• Uses sentences for passage selection • Expository and narrative passages
Qualitative Reading Inventory (Leslie & Caldwell)	K–8	• Questions for prior knowledge • Graded word lists • Expository and narrative passages

Source: Fisher, D., Frey, N., & Hattie, J. (2017). *Teaching literacy in the visible learning classroom, grades K–5.* Thousand Oaks, CA: Corwin.

useful for identifying who might benefit from this focused instruction. Conversely, a teacher who relied only on a measure of reading ability would miss this need completely.

Interest-Based Grouping

A second method for grouping students is based on interests. These interests may be student-based, as when a group of students wants to learn more about a specific topic or author. Because student-generated interest groups are usually tied to a unit of study, it can be useful to present options of books or articles for students to read and then survey to cluster students. This is less commonly done for the kind of teacher-directed small-group reading instruction discussed in this chapter. Having said that, these kinds of groups can be especially appealing to older readers. Keep in mind that the teacher is leading the group, and that while there may be variance among readers, the teacher is there to provide instructional and domain-contingent scaffolds. It bears repeating that there is mounting evidence that the presence of teacher scaffolding in mixed-ability reading groups yields satisfactory results for students (e.g., Lupo, Strong, & Smith, 2019).

CONCLUSION

If our students are not meeting with us for small-group needs-based instruction, then we are not implementing balanced literacy. Small-group needs-based instruction is an important aspect of the balanced literacy classroom. Small-group instruction gives time for us to work directly with students on strategies that will help them grow as readers. In these groups, we are facilitating instruction that stretches students to read books that they would not be able to read on their own, to discuss books and ideas within books and develop their understanding about literature and the world, and to read books and other texts that they find interesting and intriguing. Small-group needs-based instruction breathes independence into the balanced literacy classroom. Without expert scaffolding from us during targeted instruction, our readers will not grow in accuracy, fluency, or comprehension of increasingly difficult texts.

As we have noted, text selection is important. And so is grouping. We do not group students based on their reading levels, but rather based on what they need to learn next. Teachers scaffold as students read. As we have noted before, there is no reason to teach something in a small group that should have been taught to the whole class. Small-group instruction is reserved for addressing students' instructional and learning needs. Of course, all students have unfinished learning and benefit from time devoted to their needs. Having said that, this time is critical for students who struggle with reading, as whole-class instruction is not likely to address the gaps in their learning and ensure that they reach high levels of success.

CHAPTER 6

SMALL-GROUP WRITING INSTRUCTION

TARGETED SUPPORT THROUGH GUIDED LEARNING

Billy E. Barnes/PhotoEdit

Darlene Kidder meets with all of her second graders for small-group writing instruction at least once a week. The groups are flexible, shifting and evolving depending on the nature of the writing lessons and students' learning needs. Ms. Kidder monitors her students' writing development using a range of assessment tools and applies the data to form needs-based groups.

While the rest of the class is engaged in independent or collaborative writing tasks, Ms. Kidder is working with four students using a mentor text for guidance. The text is Somewhere Today: A Book of Peace

(Thomas, 1998), and the students are writing statements that are comparable to those in the book to create a class book. Each page presents readers with a photograph and brief poetic statement starting with the words "Somewhere today. . . ." The pages describe specific acts of peace and kindness in different parts of the world. Ms. Kidder asks each member in the group to write a few sentences that start with the words "somewhere today" and are focused on peace. This allows her to assess her students' understanding of the book and their comprehension of the purpose of the selection, as well as their developing writing skills. She has gathered these four students together to strengthen their ability to add details to sentences, something she has seen as a struggle in their previous writing.

"Writers build sentences with the kinds of details in them that make their ideas come alive," says Ms. Kidder. "I can add adjectives to describe an idea. I can also use words that are specific, so my reader understands. And the last part of the sentence should describe the helping action. So, choose one of the sentences you wrote as a possible contribution

to the class book, and let's see how we can make it stronger." Brandi chooses her sentence from her writing journal: "Somewhere today I saw a dog." Ms. Kidder responds, "You wrote an interesting sentence. And I know that you love dogs. Can you tell me more about how you see the dog connected with our theme of peace?"

Brandi thinks for a moment before responding, "I mean that the dog was rescued. It was hurting and the person saved it."

"Oh, I see," Ms. Kidder says. "How can we add those details to your sentence so that the ideas and pictures you have in your mind can come out on paper?" Ms. Kidder turns to the other three students and asks, "Jerome, can you list Brandi's ideas? I'm going to need all of you to figure out how she can build a stronger sentence. Then we'll do the same for each of you." Their conversation continues with Ms. Kidder providing prompts and supports to Brandi and the other students

in the group as they compose sentences. By the end of the lesson, the group has written four sentences:

- Somewhere today, a hurt dog got rescued. (Brandi)

- Somewhere today, a brave firefighter saved a house from burning down. (Jerome)

- Somewhere today, a father packed lunches for his kids. (Payton)

- Somewhere today, a dancer made people smile. (Robyn)

"When you go back to your tables, I want you to choose another sentence you wrote in your journal for this project and make it a stronger sentence. You're going to look to see if it needs more description, and that it contains a helping action," said Ms. Kidder. "I'd like the four of you to meet together again in 15 minutes to show each other the new sentence you wrote and check each other's work to see if all the parts are there."

When it comes to writing, it is fair to say that the majority of elementary students are not performing at expected levels. Results from the 2012 National Assessment of Educational Progress (NAEP) on computer-based writing of fourth graders found that only 14% of students scored at the competent or effective levels. Participants averaged 110 words on a 30-minute timed task, suggesting that writing volume was somewhat low. The tasks varied, but focused on one of three purposes: (1) to convey a real or imagined experience, (2) to explain using information, or (3) to persuade readers about a topic. Students performed best at conveying an experience (17% competent or effective), followed by explanation (15%) and persuasion (10%). Perhaps the results of the 2017 administration will be better. (They were not yet available at the time of publication.)

Anecdotally, we hear substantial discussion about writing in general, and about writing opinion with reasons and evidence specifically. However, a 2016 survey of third- and fourth-grade teachers revealed that they averaged only 15 minutes per day of writing instruction, and their students spent only 25 minutes a day writing, far less than the one hour recommended by the What Works Clearinghouse (Brindle, Graham, Harris, & Hebert, 2016). The surveyed teachers, perhaps projecting their anxiety, reported feeling only slightly positive about their ability to teach writing to their students.

PRINCIPLES AND PURPOSES OF SMALL-GROUP WRITING INSTRUCTION

Students need lots of practice in order to become better writers. But even though writing is typically a solitary activity, it is important that students engage in teacher-directed instruction in needs-based groups, as Ms. Kidder's small-group instruction demonstrated. Indeed, working with students in small groups is key in supporting their growth as independent writers. In these groups, students plan and write in real time, and they discuss their writing with peers and their teacher. This allows for immediate feedback and input. A guided writing lesson begins with a short lesson focused on one writing skill or strategy that will benefit all the students in the group. Students practice using the targeted skill or strategy as the teacher provides scaffolds to mediate their thinking. These lessons typically last 15–20 minutes and include directions to guide their next tasks in collaborative or independent writing. The principles of small-group writing instruction include the following:

- Groups are based on need as determined by assessment of student writing to capture progress toward transfer of learning.

- Teacher-directed small-group lessons include writing skills (conventions, grammar, syntax, and structure) and composition strategies (writing processes).

- Purpose drives writing. Attention to text types and genres, and their associated purposes and audiences, undergird small-group writing lessons.

- Each lesson should build students' capacity to self-assess their writing, and link to a continued collaborative or independent writing task.

- Small-group writing instruction should be infused with dispositions about writing, including self-regulation, persistence, and goal setting.

We will address each of these principles of small-group writing instruction. Our discussion about writing builds on the content of previous chapters, especially as it applies to modeling, direct instruction, scaffolding, and self-regulation. As well, the content of the writing curriculum serves as an extension of the whole-group and collaborative writing chapters (Chapters 3 and 4). There are many applications of small-group writing instruction, depending on the grade and skill level of the students. While the topics and objectives for small-group writing lessons are not necessarily different from those introduced though whole-group writing lessons, the intention with small-group instruction is to provide targeted support to deepen knowledge and skills. In some cases, the purpose is to intervene with learners who need more scaffolding. At other times, it is to extend the learning of students who are ready for more sophisticated writing instruction.

resources.corwin.com/
thisisbalancedliteracy

Video 19
Guided Writing Group

USE STUDENT DATA TO FORM NEEDS-BASED GROUPS

The beauty of student writing is that it can provide us with a clear glimpse into students' transfer of learning. A child's application of spelling conventions serves as a window on his consolidation of phonics, orthographic knowledge, and encoding. A student's informational report suggests how much she knows about the content, as well as her ability to organize it in a coherent fashion. Organizing writing in a coherent fashion means that the core structure meets the author's purpose for writing, such as one of these:

- To describe something

- To sequence steps, or events

- To compare or contrast something

- To identify a problem and possible solution

- To indicate a cause and its effect

Analysis of students' writing informs what should occur next instructionally, in the face of evidence of their strengths and opportunities for growth. This is further balanced with what you witness as students engage in writing. Who is hesitant or distracted, or has difficulty getting started? Those students might need further instruction in planning. Which students have a negative emotional response to revising? Small-group lessons on how to revise without starting all over may be in order. When monitoring student progress in writing and organizing small-group writing instruction, focus on having students meet in groups based on their need, not based on fixed groups determined by what you think of as on, below, or above grade level. This means engaging in ongoing monitoring of student needs, as they shift and change in response to the specific topics we teach. Much of this monitoring can take place during instruction, as you observe and engage with students and their writing, doing daily or weekly checks for understanding. Coupled with evidence found in your analysis of their writing, your responsive teaching benefits your students as you coordinate timely and flexible small-group instruction. There are three purposes: instruction, intervention, and extension.

Instruction

Students benefit from targeted instruction to deepen their writing knowledge. These small-group lessons serve as a continuation of skills and concepts taught during whole-group writing lessons and are designed to drill down to address the group's specific requirements. These lessons bridge the work that is continued in collaborative and independent writing tasks. At the beginning of the school year, and especially with young writers, small-group lessons focus on building habits and routines.

Small-group writing instruction in kindergarten and first grade looks different from instruction in the other grades because of the children's new experiences with literacy and classroom expectations. Importantly, writing develops across phases, as noted in Figure 6.1. Recognizing the phases of writing helps teachers determine the type of instruction students need.

Kindergarteners and first graders may not be used to sitting and working for longer periods of time. Primary teachers often begin with a writing block that is 20 minutes long and then lengthen the writing time as their students develop the ability to write for longer periods. The writing block might begin with a whole-class lesson and then

▼ FIGURE 6.1 PHASES OF WRITING DEVELOPMENT

Emergent	Early	Transitional	Self-Extending
Emergent writers are learning how print works, especially in seeing the permanence of writing.	Early writers possess a larger bank of known letters and words and are able to use them more quickly in their writing. An early writer's work is characterized by storytelling conventions, such as "Once upon a time. . . ."	Transactional writers apply more sophisticated text structures to their work and can utilize structures used by other authors to create original texts. They use their growing knowledge of writer's craft and text types to organize a message.	Self-extending writers write for a variety of purposes and audiences. They select text types and genres to align with their purpose. These writers can use more than one text type within a single composition.
• Writes left to right and top to bottom • Uses known letters and words • Prints name • Uses a mixture of drawing and letters to tell a story • Can "read" own writing	• Writes in sentences • Sequences simple stories • Uses basic conventions and punctuation • Mostly accurate letter/sound correspondence • Uses writing to communicate (e.g., notes, lists, invitations)	• Writes in paragraphs • Uses more complex punctuation • Sentences are largely syntactically and semantically correct • Developing a sense of audience • Revisions are mostly at the local level, to correct errors	• Writes extended texts using multiple paragraphs • Maintains coherence across paragraphs • Revisions are global, and include efforts to reorganize, add, expand, or delete to strengthen the writing • Experiments with writing forms and genres

move to independent writing, where children draw, write, copy, list, imagine, and create using a variety of different types of paper, pencils, crayons, and markers. However, early small-group writing lessons are in order to coach students on how their time is utilized during independent writing. Thoughtful introduction to procedures, checklists, and other protocols and routines, accompanied by scaffolded instruction, is a wise upfront investment to ensure a smooth-running classroom throughout the year.

Kindergarten teacher Ursula Henriksen meets with four children to work on writing fluency and spelling sight words. She begins with a warm-up of sight words flashcards, and an enthusiastic game of My Pile/Your Pile is underway. Ms. Henriksen gives the flashcard to each child who correctly identifies it, and keeps those that the child can't. She repeats her

Early small-group writing lessons are in order to coach students on how their time is utilized during independent writing.

pile of missed sight words until all are gone. "That was fantastic!" says the teacher. "I'm amazed at how many words each of you knows. But can you write those words?" she asks, with a twinkle in her eye. The teacher collects the flashcards and places paper and thick pencils for little hands in front of them. "I wonder how many words you can write in three minutes?" she asks. "They can be any words you know. They could be words on the flashcards, or your name, or any of your favorite words. What questions do you have for me before we begin?"

Jarmille asks if she is allowed to write the name of her cat (she is), and Austin wants to know if it is OK to cross out a mistake and write the word again (it is). With that, Ms. Henriksen sets the ladybug timer to three minutes, and observes their writing. She is especially interested in how they form their letters, their body posture, and their general writing behaviors. She makes a note that Tatiana started in the middle of the paper and then added words above it, and that Austin looks at the alphabet strip sometimes as he writes. Ray has a mature pencil grip, and Jarmille starts most of her letters at the bottom and draws them upward. She also finishes with the most words written—11 in all. Ms. Henriksen asks each child to read the list written, and all of them count the number of words and choose a sticker for their paper. Ms. Henriksen asks each child to find the flashcards that match the words they wrote on their list, which provides her with some insight about their transfer of learning: "I'm doing this with all the students this week to get a sense of their writing behaviors, and to gauge how much they are generalizing from the word work we've been doing. I'll reform next week's groups to do some further targeted instruction."

At other times, small-group writing instruction is used to deepen group-specific knowledge and skills. Fifth-grade teacher Matt Landry meets with small groups to discuss their science investigations. Student teams have been charged with researching and preparing reports on ecosystems. Mr. Landry meets with the group researching the tundra ecosystem to assist them in making revisions. "Planning and revision are two writing processes that are especially challenging for groups," Mr. Landry explains. "It can feel weird to make suggestions for or changes to someone else's work." With that, Mr. Landry revisits the rubric developed for the project, and then asks the five students to pull up the digital document they are developing. "Let's go through each part of your project so far and compare it to the rubric," he says. "I want to hear what you're noticing. Our purpose is to create a plan for what needs to be accomplished next based on what you've already written. I want you to leave here with some agreements about what's next."

Intervention

The work Ms. Kidder does with her small group of second graders in the chapter opening is an example of a targeted intervention. Her ongoing and strategic assessment of her students' writing skills enabled her to isolate a specific skill—using details at the sentence level—and thus shape an appropriate lesson to address student needs. Small-group interventions can address almost any student need, from letter knowledge, spelling, and mechanics to more complex writing tasks such as organization, idea generation and development, coherence, and unity.

Carolyn Bern's fourth graders are working on organizing an opinion text. However, several students have struggled with doing so. Their writing is unorganized and wanders off topic, even though they had been given a template to list and categorize their ideas. Ms. Bern models how she plans to write her opinion piece using the template she had furnished, using a think-aloud process:

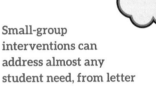

> In my opinion, everyone should drive a hybrid car. Ok, I stated my opinion about hybrid cars, but I need reasons. If I don't have some good reasons, I'm not answering the reader's question, which is "Why?" So I need to list some reasons on my planning sheet to answer the *why*. One reason I think people should drive hybrid cars is that they use less gasoline, so that's one I'm going to list [writes this down]. When I write my opinion piece, my next sentence is going to be one reason for my thinking. This is one way that you can structure your opinion texts today. Make sure you state your opinion and then follow up with a reason.

Small-group interventions can address almost any student need, from letter knowledge, spelling, and mechanics to more complex writing tasks such as organization, idea generation and development, coherence, and unity.

Ms. Bern then asks Marla, one of the three students she has gathered for this purpose, to share her planning sheet with the group. Marla reads her opinion aloud. "My opinion is that students should learn to code. But now I am thinking about why people should code." Ms. Bern says, "I'm going to ask you some questions to help you name your reasons." Within a few minutes, Marla has identified the following reasons and written them on her planning sheet:

- Computers are important and everyone works with computers and we need to know how they work.

- I read *Hello Ruby, Adventures in Coding* by Linda Liukas and in this book the author shows how easy coding can be.

After Marla lists her reasons, Jorge and Damon explain the status of their writing and discuss their reasoning. Once all the students have clarified their opinions and have listed two reasons, Ms. Bern gives them further direction:

> Build out your planning sheet so that you have at least three reasons to support your opinion. Then write one paragraph that includes your opinion and your reasons. Use the success criteria for opinion writing we discussed to see if you have met all the goals. I'll confer with you tomorrow to check in with each of you.

Extension

There are many students who love to write and are developmentally ready and eager for new challenges, or who take to a specific genre. Small-group instruction is an excellent way to engage, motivate, and challenge such students. Such small-group work is suited to all genres of writing and writing strategies. Several fifth graders in Garrett Hollander's class had been meeting online after school to play a popular multiplayer video game. These students had been trading tips with each other, but needed a more organized way to warehouse their ideas. After talking with Mr. Hollander, they decided to build a blog to share tips with others. Over several weeks, Mr. Hollander met with them occasionally in small groups to preview their writing and pose questions to the group to improve clarity. "It helps that I know almost nothing about the game," said the teacher. "It lets me ask authentic questions as a reader. It's helping to build their sense of audience."

Several advanced writers in Monique Harper's first-grade class became intrigued with geocaching after experiencing several outings with an afterschool youth organization they belong to. Given that Ms. Harper's class was studying map location and cardinal directions in social studies, Ms. Harper met with the four students to plan a presentation to the class on geocaching. The children composed short captions to accompany the photographs taken on one of their geocaching outings and shared their knowledge with the class during social studies.

Importantly, small-group writing instruction is not limited to students who struggle with writing. Instead, teachers meet with groups of students strategically to guide the learning of students as they increase their ability to convey their thinking using the written word. The time spent on this is a good investment, as writing is the flip side of the reading coin, and investment in writing can pay off dividends in reading.

Small-group writing instruction is not limited to students who struggle with writing. Instead, teachers meet with groups of students strategically to guide the learning of students as they increase their ability.

USE SMALL-GROUP INSTRUCTION TO TEACH A RANGE OF WRITING SKILLS AND STRATEGIES

Whether for instruction, intervention, or extension, small-group writing should reflect the breadth of the writing standards. It is essential that teachers recognize that writing is the braiding of "affective, cognitive, linguistic, and physical operations" and that therefore our instruction reflect all of these dimensions (Troia, 2013, p. 298). A narrow focus on conventions incorrectly telegraphs that writing is about being "right." However, exclusive attention to writing processes signals that accuracy doesn't matter, only ideas. A balanced apportionment of skills, strategies, and processes communicates the complexity of writing and the need for continuous attention to its development.

Writing Skills

Students benefit from instruction in the use of conventions, and authentic student writing is an excellent source to draw from. This is far superior to commercial products that create manufactured errors for students to edit. Use recent student writing to provide additional instruction for needs-based groups. Second-grade teacher Sarah Killbuck gathers common writing errors she sees in her students' writing. "I rewrite them so no one is specifically identified," she explained. "Instead, we can focus on the errors themselves. I'm seeing a lot of run-on sentences right now, so I've been collecting those." Ms. Killbuck met with small groups to tackle several examples, asking students to correct the writing. One spotted in a student's journal read, "I like to see my little baby sister after school because she is cute and I like when she laughs and she plays with her food at dinner she makes a mess." The teacher had them read the sentence aloud several times so they could hear the rambling nature of the sentence.

The sentence was written on sentence strips, making it possible for students to literally slice it up using scissors. Using prompts to scaffold their understanding, the students reconstructed it to read, "I like to see my little baby sister after school because she is cute. I like when she laughs and plays with her food at dinner because she makes a mess." One of the students in the group wrote the word *because* to build the last sentence. "We do sentence-level work using sentence surgery to carve down sentences that are too long, as well as to combine sentences that are too short and choppy. They like to see how they can easily fix errors. But the real secret, I think, is that the errors are genuine. These errors reflect their writing development, and attention to them helps them move forward as writers," remarked Ms. Killbuck.

> A narrow focus on conventions incorrectly telegraphs that writing is about being "right." However, exclusive attention to writing processes signals that accuracy doesn't matter, only ideas.

After performing sentence surgery, they are tasked with doing similar work in their journals. "I want you to find at least one run-on sentence in your writing journal that can be rewritten," Ms. Killbuck told the group. She put her hand up to forestall any protests. "I've read your journals this week, and all of you have at least one. That's why you're here. If you have trouble finding one, come see me and I'll help you."

Students perform sentence surgery to fix errors and refine their writing.

Composition Strategies

Writing doesn't begin when pencil touches paper or fingers make a keystroke. It begins with discussion. Oral language is an essential ingredient in composition. Perhaps that is why Education Trust's analysis of written assignments includes opportunities for discussion as a quality indicator (Dabrowski, 2016). Small-group writing instruction should include discussion of ideas as a strategy for planning. In fact, planning and revision are the two composition strategies that writers struggle with the most and should be a focus of many lessons (Graham, 2006).

These high-level composition strategies serve as gatekeepers to effective writing. Ineffective planning negatively impacts content, coherency, and organization. Ineffective revising strategies mean that the writer fails to develop the metacognitive skills needed to improve writing.

The ability to revise is rooted in developmental factors, and young writers are more likely to revise at the local level (e.g., conventions, spelling) than at global levels (e.g., text structures, meaning, and organization) (MacArthur, Graham, & Harris, 2004). While there is growth from grade 4 to grade 6, in particular, even students in this age group appear to be better at correcting substantive errors than in detecting them

(Limpo, Alves, & Fidalgo, 2014). Thus, elementary writers remain necessarily dependent on their teachers to show them where revisions should be made. Small-group writing instruction is ideal for this. However, if the revisions we routinely show students are confined to local-level corrections such as mechanics, children will not grow in their capacity to make meaningful revisions. Is it any wonder that novice writers often fail to distinguish between editing and revision?

Revisions of one's own writing can be especially challenging during small-group instruction, and are best left to writing conferences during independent writing (see Chapter 8). But small-group writing instruction is an ideal format for discussion of revisions using writing samples. Anchor papers developed for use with state writing standard frameworks are an excellent resource for these lessons. They are authentic student work, not contrived, and are linked to distinct levels of writing rubrics. Third-grade teacher Tiana Reynolds uses anchor papers from her state's frameworks to provide guided instruction about revision. "Our state uses five-point holistic writing rubrics, and there are great anchor papers for teachers to use for consensus scoring purposes. My grade-level colleagues and I have reproduced these to use in guided instruction," she explained.

> Writing doesn't begin when pencil touches paper or fingers make a keystroke. It begins with discussion. Oral language is an essential ingredient in composition.

Ms. Reynolds invites four or five students at a time to meet with her, and she reviews the writing rubric they will be using. Today it is narrative, and the students are given a copy of an anchor paper that scored a 2 out of a possible 5, as well as the picture prompt the child viewed. "This child saw this picture and was asked to write a story about what might have happened," Ms. Reynolds tells them. She tells students the score and shows students where some of the errors occurred. "The writer has a description of the picture but doesn't tell a story," she explains. "If you were helping this writer, what could you tell him to revise to improve his score? Use the rubric to help you." Yasmin peers at the rubric and then says, "He doesn't have an opening, and he doesn't have a closing. That's where he should start." The discussion progresses, and soon the children are consulting the rubric again. "What did this writer do well?" asks Ms. Reynolds. Emma replies, "His sentences sound right." The teacher replies, "Tell us more about that," and Emma says, "Listen when I read it out loud. Like the words are all in the right order."

Next, Ms. Reynolds gives them an anchor paper that was scored as a 4 on the 5-point scale. "This one will be trickier," she says. "The scorers said that the writer didn't use 'vivid word choices.' What does that mean, and what advice could we give this writer?" After discussion about word choice and "lively sentences," the lesson draws to a close. "You got a picture prompt this morning to inspire a story. As you plan your story and write the first draft, use the rubric to score yourself. Later this week we'll meet again to discuss how you revised your writing."

Small-group writing instruction should include discussion of ideas.

LINK PURPOSE AND AUDIENCE TO TEXT TYPES AND GENRES

Small-group instruction lends itself to deeper exploration of the text types and genres elementary students compose. Young writers, however, may be tempted to focus solely on the form while overlooking the purpose. Each of the major text types serves a purpose:

- Narrative text types are used to convey real and imagined experiences.

- Informational text types are used to explain ideas and processes.

- Argumentative text types are used to persuade.

Without a full understanding of the purpose and the audience, the quality of the writing suffers. It is analogous to building a physical structure—a house, an apartment building, a retail store—without an understanding of what purpose it will serve, or who might live and work there. For too many students, the purpose of writing is to please an audience of one: the teacher. Of course, children need to learn how these text types are structured, just as an architect needs to understand how a multistory building is safely constructed. But as another notable architect said, "Form follows function." Purpose and audience should not be uncoupled from the writing structures we teach.

All students, when they are introduced to new forms of writing, need practice and support. Sixth-grade students in Rita Patel's class have been learning about dramatic structure in narrative writing, and they have had many experiences with identifying how authors have used these elements (exposition, conflict, rising action, climax, falling action, and resolution) in the short stories, plays, and books they have read. Ms. Patel has introduced story mapping as a writing tool for planning a personal narrative they will compose, and she has identified several students who are stalled. Ms. Patel meets with four writers, and asks them to bring their story maps with them, even if the maps are not complete (see Figure 6.2).

▼ FIGURE 6.2 DRAMATIC STRUCTURE PLANNING TOOL

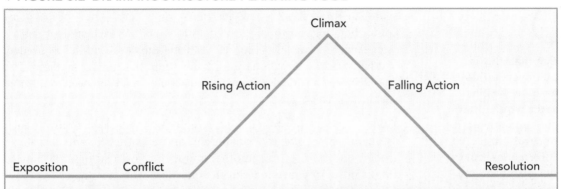

Exposition	Conflict	Rising Action	Climax	Falling Action	Resolution
Who are the characters? What should we know about them?	What problem will the protagonist confront?	What are at least three actions that lead up to the climax?	What is the turning point? What event will change the protagonist's fate?	Will the protagonist be successful, or fail?	What is the outcome to the conflict?

online resources ⬀ Available for download at **resources.corwin.com/thisisbalancedliteracy**

"I belonged to a writer's workshop when I was in college," she began. "We would meet together about once a week to help each other. The feedback was really important to me. Talking to another writer helped me get unstuck more than once." She collects their partially completed story maps and redistributes them so that each student has someone else's story map. "Remember that your purpose for this personal narrative is to describe a time when you succeeded at something you thought you might fail. Telling a great story is going to be really important, and dramatic structure is the backbone of a great story," Ms. Patel continued. "But a story isn't worth a thing if there's no reader. Your audience is one another. Finding out what your audience understands about your story is really helpful."

"Take a few minutes to read what the person has so far. Each map has gaps, so think about a few questions you'll have. I have some sticky notes here for you to write the questions on." As each student reads a story map and writes questions, Ms. Patel provides scaffolds as needed. "What question do you have for Jamir about the conflict he faced? Has he explained it enough for you to understand, or do you need some more details?" she asks Elise.

Summarizing is an important skill, as many writing tasks require that students summarize or synthesize information from a variety of sources.

When each of the students has completed the task, she returns each student's story map to that student, and asks the students to pair up to ask questions of one another about their own stories. "Be sure to make notes to yourself about the questions you're being asked," says Ms. Patel. Again, she listens to their conversations, prompting and cueing as needed to facilitate the discussions. Once they complete these conversations, the students reverse roles and again engage in questions for one another. With the guided writing lesson drawing to a close, Ms. Patel says, "You've had a chance to meet with a fellow writer to resolve some gaps you have in your dramatic structure. Your next step is to rework your story map. Tomorrow, you'll check in with the person who asked you questions to give an update. You are each other's audience, so hearing from your reader is one way to tighten up your story."

Yvette Ramirez's third-grade students are learning to summarize information. This is an important skill, as many writing tasks require that students summarize or synthesize information from a variety of sources. Ms. Ramirez has assembled several writers who need additional instruction on summary writing. She is using a video clip about avalanches as a subject to summarize. (They are studying weather-related hazards in science.) Ms. Ramirez said, "We use written summaries all the time in our writing to explain things. You're all writing informational reports with your groups in science, and being able to summarize facts accurately is part of the success criteria for those reports." She continued, "I'd like to show you a way to chunk the information into bite-sized pieces."

She plays the four-minute video and discusses the main points, and then plays it a second time, stopping at three different points so that students can write one sentence (and one sentence only) stating the main point. "This is a starting point," explains Ms. Ramirez. "Reread those three sentences you wrote to see if anything really important got left out." Francisco says, "I don't have anything in my sentences about how the park rangers use explosions so there won't be a big avalanche." Ms. Ramirez asks, "Why do you believe that's important for your audience to know, Francisco?" The boy replies, "Because we're supposed to include stuff about what to do about weather disasters, so I need that in there." Ms. Ramirez smiles. "Sounds like a good reason to me! Add a sentence about that, and reread it to see if you're satisfied." The students revise and finalize a brief summary of the segment and add it to their writing research notebooks.

Ms. Ramirez used a variation of the GIST technique proposed by Cunningham (1982). Teachers segment a reading into manageable chunks, usually a paragraph or two each. The essential information in each text chunk is converted into one sentence. Therefore, a reading divided into five chunks must be represented in no more than five sentences. This technique, whether using video or print text, provides the teacher with opportunities to discuss sentence construction and conventions as well as content. Key points for using a GIST summary writing approach can be found in Figure 6.3.

▼ FIGURE 6.3 THE GIST OF GIST

- Identify a text you want students to summarize (not too long).
- Read the entire text first to understand the article globally.
- Decide on natural break points, especially major points, where summarization should occur.
- Chunk the text into smaller segments of one or two paragraphs each.
- Model for students, thinking aloud about how you compose a single sentence that addresses the main idea of the segment.
- After repeating for each segment, reread your GIST sentences aloud for students, and make any revisions necessary to smooth out the text you've written.
- Guide students as they apply the GIST writing strategy to another piece of text.

Video 20
GIST Strategy

BUILD STUDENTS' CAPACITY TO SELF-ASSESS

Perhaps nowhere is self-assessment more crucial than in the act of writing. Because writing is ultimately an individual activity, writers should be actively assessing their writing during composition. (A colleague of ours would say that revision begins with the fourth word written.) In addition, they should be developing the habit of rereading what they have written to monitor their progress and compare it to established success criteria. No child should have to be solely dependent on the teacher's determination of whether the writing meets the requirements or not.

Rubrics provide students with opportunities to gauge their own progress and make decisions about their writing. While we will discuss rubrics in more detail in the assessment chapter (Chapter 9), suffice to say that students need lots of opportunities to use rubrics in order to refine their ability to accurately determine where they are in their writing, and where they are headed. Very young writers are not likely to be able to read and understand a traditional rubric; a developmental writing continuum can serve a similar function. In either case, the purpose is to build the child's capacity to self-assess.

Fourth-grade teacher Steve Newell is meeting with five students he identified after having individual writing conferences over the previous two weeks. He formed this group to do a bit of intervention work with them, as he discovered that they did not have a good grasp of the informational writing rubric he had introduced the previous month. Mr. Newell has asked the students to bring a current piece they are working on for either social studies or science, and he has made copies of the informational writing rubric for each of them.

He begins by asking the students to focus on the first criterion, which is conventions. "Let's read what's considered proficient, and then check your draft just on that indicator," he says. "It's about using capitals and punctuation, and spelling and stuff like that," says Connor. "That's right. So circle any errors you are picking up in the first two paragraphs," says Mr. Newell. He observes as his students mark their papers, occasionally asking questions when they miss something.

Rubrics help students make decisions about their writing.

Next he says, "Let's move on to a more challenging one, 'Elaboration of Evidence.' It says, 'Develops the topic with facts, definitions, concrete details, quotations, or other information and examples related to the topic.' Go back through the first two paragraphs of your paper. This time, use a yellow highlighter any time you find an example of elaboration of evidence." The students go back to their papers, but among them they generate few highlighted examples. Mr. Newell asks each student to share what he or she highlighted, and the group discusses the rationale for each. "We didn't have a lot of examples to share, though. Based on what you discovered about your paper, what will you do next?" asks Mr. Newell. Lizette begins to name what she'll do, when Mr. Newell interrupts. "Make a checklist for yourself, Lizette. I'm already hearing a solid plan." Each of the students explains what he or she will do next as it applies to conventions and elaboration of evidence, and has prepared a sticky note as a checklist. "I'm going to circle back around to you tomorrow on the status of your checklist," says Mr. Newell. "Then we'll take on the organization criterion on the rubric. You got this!"

Younger writers can self-assess, too, and first-grade teacher Selena Rodriguez wants to steadily build their ability to do so. She is sitting with samples of her students' writing spread before her on a low table, moving the writing samples around to group students with similar writing abilities together. It is mid-September, and the children have been involved in whole-group writing for about three weeks. She began her instruction first in a whole group and waited before implementing small-group instruction. Her initial focus was on establishing the habit of writing. Now that the school year is underway, and her students are beginning to write narratives, she is ready to meet with small, needs-based groups for instruction and for intervention.

Ms. Rodriguez is going to introduce a developmental writing continuum (see Figure 6.4), to the students in small groups, and let them gauge their own writing with her guidance. "They need to see where they're at, and where they're headed," says Ms. Rodriguez. "It's early in the year, and I've got a wide range of writers," she explains. "Several of them didn't attend kindergarten, which is not compulsory, so school is really new to them."

Three students who are emergent writers join her at the table, where she has folders of their writing samples. "I am so proud of the writing work you've been doing," she begins. "I want to show you how other children learn to write, so you can see where you are right now and where you are going as a writer in your first-grade year." Ms. Rodriguez unveils a large poster showing writing samples in the right column (the left column is for the teacher's use) and thinks aloud about each one. Then she says, "Can you choose one of your writing samples, and put it next to the example you think best matches yours?" The children move around the low table, each with a writing sample in hand, and Ms. Rodriguez guides them to the correct category. "It will take some practice for them to get good at doing this," Ms. Rodriguez remarks later, "but it will aid them in setting writing goals for themselves when we start doing so in a few weeks."

INFUSE DISPOSITIONS ABOUT WRITING IN EACH LESSON

Small-group writing instruction provides an excellent opportunity to build the dispositions of students about their writing. The highly personal nature of writing can cause some students to be anxious about their skills and their ability to complete tasks. A lack of confidence in one's writing can be a barrier to beginning, or persisting, in cognitively demanding tasks. While writing skills and strategies are taught to show children *how* to write, dispositions speak to a willingness to apply them. There is a social and emotional component to writing, and it should not be overlooked. Confidence, persistence, and passion to write form

▼ FIGURE 6.4 DEVELOPMENTAL STAGES OF WRITING

Stage Description	Sample
Pre-literate	
Scribble Stage—Starting point any place on page, resembles drawing large circular strokes and random marks that do not resemble print or communicate a message	
Symbolic Stage—Starting point any place on page, pictures or random strokes/marks with an intended message	"I am happy."
Directional Scribble—Scribble left to right direction, linear, intended as writing that communicates a meaningful message/idea	"I am playing."
Symbolic/Mock Letters—Letter-like formations, may resemble letters but it isn't intentional, interspersed with numbers, spacing rarely present	
Emergent	
Strings of Letters—Long strings of various letters in random order, may go left to right, uses letter sequence perhaps from name, usually uses capital letters, may write same letters in many ways	
Groups of Letters—Groupings of letters with spaces in between to resemble words	
Labeling Pictures—Matching beginning sounds with the letter to label a picture	
Environmental Print—Copies letters/words from environmental/classroom print, reversals common, uses a variety of resources to facilitate writing	
Transitional	
Letter/Word Representation—Uses first letter sound of word to represent entire word, uses letter sound relationships	(I went home.)
First/Last Letter Representation—Word represented by first and last letter sound	(cat)
Medial Letter Sounds—Words spelled phonetically using beginning-middle-end sounds, attempts medial vowels, uses some known words, more conventionally spelled words, one letter may represent one syllable, attempts to use word spacing, writing is readable	(My cat is brown.)
Fluent	
Beginning Phrase Writing—Using all of the above skills to construct phrases that convey a message connected to their illustration	I PLA wif my dog
Sentence Writing—Construction of words into sentence formation, maybe multiple sentences, writing is readable, may use punctuation, known words spelled correctly, topic focused, beginning-middle-end with detail	I play with my frind. We like to jump rop!

Source: Courtesy of West Hartford Public Schools.

three essential dispositions about writing (Piazza & Siebert, 2008). These researchers developed a writing dispositions scale for students in grades 4–6 (see Figure 6.5).

▼ FIGURE 6.5 WRITING DISPOSITIONS SCALE

Confidence	Persistence	Passion
• My written work is among the best in class. • I am not a good writer. • Writing is easy for me.	• I take time to try different possibilities in my writing. • I would like to write more in school. • I take time to solve problems in my writing. • I am willing to spend time on long papers.	• Writing is fun for me. • Writing is my favorite subject in school. • If I have choices during free time, I usually select writing. • I always look forward to writing class.

Source: Adapted from Piazza, C., & Siebert, C. F. (2008). Development and validation of a writing dispositions scale for elementary and middle school students. *Journal of Educational Research, 101*(5), 275–286.

Fourth-grade teacher Ernesto Sanchez asked students to respond to the statements in this scale in the first weeks of school as part of his efforts to get to know his students. Based on their responses, he meets intermittently in small groups to provide intervention or extension. "The students who scaled high on the passion index are ones that I meet with to do extension lessons with," he said. "I've introduced some more unusual genres to them to feed their creativity." In the last month the group has had some extension lessons in reverso poems (poems that can be read forward and backward, each with a different message). "I introduced them to the work of Marilyn Singer and her reversible verse picture books," he explained. "Next month we're going to dive in to writing graphic novels."

Mr. Sanchez also meets regularly with another group of students who scaled low in writing confidence. "They're reluctant to share, so the focus of our lessons is on identifying things they know lots about and letting them become the expert," he said. "So they each name something of their choosing, and then they research it and write up a short explanation as a handout. Then they teach the rest of us." He chuckled. "I already know a lot more about how to do a bicycle kick in soccer, raising chickens in the backyard, and some of the finer points of Minecraft. But what I really like seeing is their confidence. They know the content, so we can focus on how best to teach Mr. Sanchez something he knows nothing about."

Sixth-grade teacher Lara Kennedy has similarly capitalized on her students' topical interests to boost their writing dispositions. "All of my students are required to complete at least one resident expert project each quarter," she explained. Students in Ms. Kennedy's class propose a topic, and once it is approved, they are responsible for developing an entry on the topic on the class's learning management system. The entry should include a short advertisement to persuade classmates to view their project, a written informational piece about the topic, and a short video explaining their own personal experiences. "It actually gets to all three text types—argumentative, informational, and narrative—as well as having a multimedia component," she said. Ms. Kennedy meets with small groups who are at similar points in their production. "We don't talk about content, because their topics are different. We talk about workflow and task completion." Ms. Kennedy acknowledges that complex projects like this can be daunting for sixth graders. "That's exactly why I meet in small groups with them. They're individually accountable, but I also want to build their sense of persistence," she said. "They need to see how large writing tasks like this get broken down into digestible steps."

CONCLUSION

Small-group writing instruction is a crucial linchpin in a balanced literacy classroom. *Instruction* of writing is key, as discussed in Chapter 3, as merely causing writing to happen will not deliver breakthrough results. Children need time to write, and the following chapter is devoted to independent writing. But without instruction at the whole-class and small-group levels, the risk of leaving too many students on the sidelines increases. Small-group writing instruction provides a means for teachers to gather up writers with similar instructional, intervention, or extension needs. To be clear, there is little benefit to putting a small group of students at a writing table and simply watching them write. As with small-group reading, there is active teaching occurring. Domain-contingent scaffolds (Rodgers, 2017) in the form of questions, prompts, and cues are used to promote the use of writing skills and strategies.

What we choose to teach communicates volumes to students about what matters. Our attention to their writing, and our commitment to teaching them in small, flexible groups that are attuned to their evolving needs, tells them that writing is important. And it also tells them that *they* are important.

CHAPTER 7

INDEPENDENT READING

PRACTICING, APPLYING, AND EXTENDING LEARNING

iStock.com/noipornpan

Nichole Juarez's fourth-grade students are spread around the classroom reading. Some are sitting in their desks, one is in a big comfy chair, and several are lying on the floor in the reading area. One thing is evident: They are immersed in reading. They are all reading different things. Some of the students have chosen to read novels, and other students are reading information on websites using their devices. A few students are reading expository texts in magazines, and one student is reading a graphic novel.

The minutes tick by, and students continue to read. Ms. Juarez meets with students individually during this time, typically four students per day, to monitor

their progress. Each day, students read for a sustained amount of time. Ms. Juarez has a lot of reading material for the students to choose from during independent reading. Some of this material is in the classroom library. For example, there are picture books, novels, comic books, magazines, manuals, and even a kid's cookbook in the library. In the corner of the classroom dedicated to the class's topic of inquiry, there is a basket of books on the topic that they are exploring. Additionally, Ms. Juarez uses Google Classroom and has a folder of reading material in it about the topic of the inquiry as well as other websites with interesting reading materials.

Students in upper grades are not the only students who can participate in independent reading. Kevin Smith's first-grade students routinely read every day for 20 minutes. When Mr. Smith first started independent reading in his first-grade classroom, he never dreamed that students could read for a long period of time. But what he found is that by gradually increasing the time students spent reading independently, his students were soon reading for 10 minutes, then 15, and then 20 minutes.

Source: Photo by John Graham.

In Mr. Smith's classroom students often read while he is teaching small groups. When you visit his classroom, you see a group of students working with him in a small group. The other students in his class are either independently reading or working collaboratively at centers. One must-do task in Mr. Smith's class every day is for students to read on their own from their book boxes. The book boxes contain several books, mostly selected from their small-group instruction. In addition, there is at least one book from the classroom or school library that students have selected (Figure 7.1). Mr. Smith has organized a beautiful library with a variety of narrative and expository texts. The students read texts from these book boxes for about 20 minutes at some point during the day, although not all students are reading at the same time. Students also work collaboratively in small groups and meet with their teacher for needs-based instruction.

As noted in these two examples, there are many options for ensuring that students engage in the practice of reading. And there are some things that are consistent. For example, during independent reading, students read on their own for a sustained period of time. Additionally, students often have choice in what they are reading and choose texts that interest them. In the primary grades, students also read familiar books from their small-group instruction time, whereas in the upper grades, students read for their book club meetings. Students are provided with a steady diet of reading materials. Independent reading is not focused only on narrative texts. Students may be reading poetry books, graphic novels, songs and rhymes, nonfiction books, or reference books. They may be reading magazines based on topics of interest. The reading material doesn't all have to be in print form. Students can read from devices or from computers. They can read electronic books as well as materials downloaded from the internet.

Students need to read, and read a lot. There is evidence that students who are struggling readers spend more time doing activities about reading, like worksheets or skill lessons, and less time actually reading (Allington, 1977).

WHY INDEPENDENT READING?

Students need to read, and read a lot. There is evidence that students who are struggling readers spend more time doing activities *about* reading, like worksheets or skill lessons, and less time actually reading (Allington, 1977). This is important to note, because the goal of reading instruction is to ensure students become independent readers who choose to read. And we're pretty sure that doing a lot of worksheets rather than actually reading is counter to building interest in reading and may actually interfere with their willingness to read. What they need is to experience success with reading itself. Success builds motivation.

Although Allington was one of the first researchers to point out the problem that some students do not read a sufficient volume of words per day to develop skills and habits, his findings have been documented repeatedly in the ensuing decades. For example, there is evidence that independent reading is a powerful tool for developing students' fluency (Kuhn, Schwanenflugel, & Meisinger, 2006). Kuhn and her colleagues found that sustained reading is associated with student achievement in comprehension as well as fluency. We are not suggesting that independent reading caused students' comprehension and fluency to improve. Instruction matters. But reading widely is the practice that allows all of the instruction to stick. Without practice, students don't get sufficient opportunities to apply all of the things that they have learned in whole-class and small-group instruction.

Further evidence for our claim that practice is important comes from a study done by Anderson, Wilson, and Fielding (1988). They correlated the volume of reading that students were doing with students' scores on annual standardized reading tests. They found that students scoring in the 90th percentile on standardized tests read texts, on average, 21 minutes per day, while those scoring at the 50th percentile read texts approximately 5 minutes per day. Furthermore, students scoring at the 10th percentile read actual texts less than 1 minute per day. Obviously, the students who spent little time reading did not perform well on assessments. The students scoring at the higher percentile ranks were reading books, texts, and other materials that required concentration and comprehension, whereas the students reading less per day were more likely to read only skill-based materials like flashcards or worksheets.

Vocabulary Increases

In addition to improving fluency and comprehension, independent reading increases students' vocabularies. In fact, reading is one of the more effective activities students can do to improve their vocabularies

(Nagy, Anderson, & Herman, 1987). Again, it's the practice effect. Teachers teach vocabulary and word solving, but students need to practice. Reading exposes students to words. The more a student reads, the more words she will be exposed to (Duff, Tomlin, & Catts, 2015). When students know more vocabulary words, their background knowledge is built, and they have increased comprehension of text.

During independent reading, students enjoy a variety of reading materials.

Bill Aron/PhotoEdit

HOW INDEPENDENT READING MIGHT LOOK

Independent reading does not have to be implemented in any one specific way. It can be implemented in ways that work for you and your students. What is important is that students have daily time with books to simply read. We explore the issue of choice and then consider the differences in independent reading for younger versus older students in elementary school.

Student Choice

We read to learn, to enjoy, to inquire, and to inform ourselves. Don't you? As adults we don't read to answer questions at the end of a passage or to take a test on a text selection. As an adult, you have a great deal of choice in what you are reading. Students need some choice in the materials and topics they are reading during independent reading. Of course, we don't always have choice in what we read. Nor do our students. Sometimes we

We are not suggesting
that independent
reading caused students'
comprehension and
fluency to improve.
Instruction matters.
But reading widely
is the practice that
allows all of the
instruction to stick.

read because we need to, or we are asked to. Sometimes students read because they need to practice. Whether they are reading by choice or not, there is no evidence that readers can independently learn from texts they cannot read. Thus, independent reading should be a time when the text selections are comfortable for students.

Christine Albeitre provides her second-grade students the opportunity each month to identify a topic that they would like to learn more about. She helps the students brainstorm their interests and writes a list on chart paper. Then the students vote on which topic they want to explore next. Once students identify a broad topic, like dogs or superheroes, Ms. Albeitre goes to the library and collects several books on the topic. She displays these books in the tray at the bottom of her whiteboard, and students are welcome to read the books during independent reading time. This provides students with choice, but it is constrained by the theme that they have agreed to learn more about. Students talk with each other about what they are learning and trade books with peers as the month progresses.

Sue Ann Johnston's fifth graders are also involved in voicing their ideas about what to read. The students choose topics based on a current event in the news. For example, when there was news about unusual flooding in nearby states, students chose to read about natural disasters. Ms. Johnston finds books in the school library that match what students have requested as reading material, but often this is not enough. She also retrieves and downloads reading materials from websites that have child-friendly articles. Students also provide URLs of websites they have discovered on their own that align with the topic. She does a check for appropriateness and then posts the URLs in a digital folder for all students to access.

What students are reading is as important as how much they are reading and how engaged they are in the reading. For years, students were encouraged to read only what was at their independent reading level, but this limited access to grade-level material as well as topics that were of interest to them. As we have noted, you can't independently learn from texts you cannot read. But motivation plays an important role in reading. A student who really wants to know more about horses, for example, especially if that student has a lot of background knowledge on the topic, will be able to read a more complex text than might be assumed by a measure of reading level. In addition, there are times when students read a book that is well below their reading level because it is of interest and they want to be able to talk with others about it. Did you read (and even enjoy) *Harry Potter*? It's well below your reading level, but it is a cool story.

Independent Reading in Kindergarten

Caitlyn Ross's kindergarteners participate in independent reading every day. There are a couple of ways that Ms. Ross incorporates independent reading into the day for her busy and active students. First, each child has a book bag, which is a plastic bag filled with three to five books. Ms. Ross places several texts in each student's book bag that the students have previously read with her during small-group instruction. The children practice their reading with these early leveled texts, which are often decodable or have controlled vocabulary. These books typically contain a significant number of sight words, which allows for additional practice in recognizing words. These texts provide a chance for students to practice their phonics skills while reading on their own.

When the children first arrive at school each day, they sign in and place their personal items in their cubbies. Then, they go to their book bag boxes, which are in plastic tubs kept on the floor along the carpet area of the classroom. Each child finds the book bag labeled with his or her name. The children find a place in the room that they feel comfortable sitting, but also where they will not be too distracted by other students, and they begin reading. The children have practiced the routine of finding a place to sit many times, so finding a place to sit and read is a smooth process. The children then have about 10 minutes to read at the beginning of the school day.

What students are reading is as important as how much they are reading and how engaged they are in the reading.

Ms. Ross meets individually with students during this time. She confers with them and takes notes about what reading behaviors she is noticing. She may also check for fluency and comprehension. To check for fluency, Ms. Ross listens to the child read one of the texts and takes notes. She often takes a running record on the book the child reads to her, so she can note the accuracy of the child's reading, what mistakes the child is making, and what strategies the child is using while reading. She will also ask a couple of comprehension questions. She might simply say, "Tell me what happened in the story."

Ms. Ross's kindergarteners have many other opportunities to read throughout the day. When Ms. Ross is teaching small groups, students engage in collaborative and independent tasks. One of the tasks is independent reading. Children can read texts from their book bag or select texts from the classroom library. These library books have been carefully organized to provide students practice with skills and concepts they have learned. There are picture books that allow students to talk with a partner about what they see happening. Sometimes students read in pairs during this time, with one student reading the text aloud and the other following along.

Independent Reading in Third Grade

Jennifer O'Neil's third graders read independently during her literacy block. Ms. O'Neil devotes at least 120 minutes each day to literacy. She starts her reading block with a whole-class lesson focused on a teaching point for the day. Then students work on their reading and reading responses, while she meets with small groups. Ms. O'Neil or the school librarian has met with each student to discuss interests and genres. They work to ensure that each student has a balanced diet of texts, including narrative and informational options. As a result, all students have a book they are currently reading and at least one up-next text that they plan to read. Some students read faster than others and need to be able to change books out as they finish. In addition, students have access to magazines and news articles. Some students have WebQuest lists and use their devices to read material on specific topics from websites. Others have textbooks from science or social studies that they enjoy browsing. The materials are not assigned to students based on topics; students choose these materials based on their interests.

In Ms. O'Neil's class, the students read independently for about 20 minutes per day. But that is not the only reading they are doing. They are also involved in close reading lessons, collaborative reading tasks, small-group reading instruction, and reading during science and social studies. Some students begin independent reading when Ms. O'Neil finishes the whole-class lesson and begins meeting with small groups. Other students are working collaboratively, discussing the texts they are reading. And still others are writing about their reading. Each day, every student is provided time to read independently, but Ms. O'Neil does not have the whole class read at the same time.

Independent Reading in Sixth Grade

Like Ms. O'Neil's third-grade students, Trini Andelian's sixth-grade class also spends time independently reading. Ms. Andelian's literacy block is 90 minutes long. She also starts her literacy block with a whole-class lesson, after which students work collaboratively or independently. She ends the literacy block with a class meeting, where students share what they read and learned. Students in her room meet in book clubs and also meet with her for small-group instruction.

Because all the students are in an assigned book club, they often meet during the literacy block to discuss their book, after they have all read to an agreed-upon stopping point. During the book club meeting, students might be rereading passages, discussing what they read, or working together to comprehend the book and to write about their reading. On some days they are reading their books so that they will be ready for book club discussion. But the majority of students read their book for book club at home, because they want to spend the class time talking about the book.

resources.corwin.com/
thisisbalancedliteracy

Video 21
Independent
Reading Block

In addition to their book clubs, students in Ms. Andelian's class are typically working on an inquiry project. These inquiry projects provide students an opportunity for a dive deep into a topic about which they have posed an inquiry question. Some last a month; others several months. For example, Osmar wants to understand the history of car engines and figure out what type of engine will be next. He thinks solar power is too complicated for cars but wants to know more about new ways to power vehicles. While researching, students read and take notes on the information they are gathering. They will use this information during their independent writing time. Students may be researching online, reading reference material, or reading nonfiction books. Osmar has learned about steam power and internal combustion. He is also exploring battery power and the benefits and drawbacks of that system. Suffice to say that he reads a lot as part of his inquiry project and has written several essays about things he has learned. In fact, he often selects texts about engines that would be considered well above his reading level and works hard to comprehend the texts, in large part because he is motivated. Interestingly, for his book club, he chose to join the group reading *Merci Suárez Changes Gears* (Medina, 2018) because his teacher introduced it, noting that it was about an intergenerational family and was funny.

In Ms. Andelian's class, on a given day and given the range of tasks they complete, some students may be reading for up to 60 minutes. Not every day, but it does happen that some days students read a lot. This may seem like a long time, but it flies by for the students who are focused on what they need to accomplish based on their reading choices and inquiry tasks. Ms. Andelian's students have voice and choice while reading, are meeting on their own in book clubs, and are also reading and researching topics that they are passionate about. During this time Ms. Andelian is providing small-group instruction, but she is also conferring individually with students about their reading. When conferring, Ms. Andelian takes notes about how students are approaching text, what they are working on, how well they are comprehending, and the goals that they are setting for themselves.

HOW TO ORGANIZE FOR INDEPENDENT READING

The first thing we do when preparing for independent reading is to organize the reading materials. You will want a classroom library that has a wide array of genres. Reading materials in the classroom library can include narrative books like picture books, early chapter books, and chapter books. Other types of narrative books that students enjoy reading include comic books, graphic novels, and poetry. Young children enjoy reading along while singing familiar songs and saying nursery rhymes. The library should also contain a variety of expository texts. The wider the variety of expository books, the richer the library will be for students. You can include expository picture books, memoirs, personal experiences, travel experiences, and science and nature writing. Some teachers even put textbooks in the library to supplement reference materials such as dictionaries and a thesaurus.

Listening to Reading for Younger Readers or Those Who Need Support

Some students need additional support while reading, and listening to books read to them is an effective scaffold. Younger students may not yet be able to read favorite picture books you have shared with the class. Also, English learners may need to have texts read aloud as they follow along with the text. You can record yourself reading a book on an electronic device and have it available for student use. Students can use headphones so that when they are listening to books it is not noisy and distracting to others.

Whisper Reading

Many teachers of younger students implement whisper reading in their classrooms, because the students are emergent readers and are reading aloud. Whisper reading is when students practice reading aloud at a whisper sound level. You can also use *whisper phones,* which students hold to their ears while reading aloud. A whisper phone is a phone handset that is not connected to anything. These are available for purchase at teacher supply stories, but you don't really need to buy anything, you can create "phones" by having students hold blocks up, or print phones on heavy cardboard and cut them out.

PRACTICES FOR INDEPENDENT READING

There are practices that students can engage in to be successful during independent reading. Students need to be developing habits so that they will be able to help themselves find reading material that they want to read, and that they can read for longer periods of time.

Knowing How to Select a Book

As previously mentioned, some of the material that students may have available to them to read are books from small-group instruction with you. For other texts, students can choose what to read so long as they can read the text independently. Learning how to choose books is an important skill that needs to be taught and practiced. Students need to choose books that they are able to read with enough accuracy that their comprehension does not break down. As we have noted earlier, if they are highly motivated based on a topic, they can read texts that are more complex. One general rule is that students should not make more than three to five errors every 100 words while reading independently. However, another easier way to help students know if a book is right for them is to encourage them to read the first page or two, then pause and see if they can remember what they read. Encourage students to ask themselves:

- Do I know what I read? Students can ask and answer the "5 W's and 1 How" questions to do a quick check after reading the first couple pages of a book. With this strategy students ask themselves who, why, what, when, where, and how to check their comprehension.

- Can I visualize what I am reading? Readers create images in their minds while reading. If a book is too hard, students probably won't have a clear image about what is happening in the book.

> Students need to choose books that they are able to read with enough accuracy that their comprehension does not break down. If they are highly motivated based on a topic, they can read texts that are more complex.

- Am I able to figure out the meaning of the unknown words in the book? The book should be accessible enough that the student can use context to understand or confirm the meaning of most of the unknown words encountered.

- Did I page through the book to check the table of contents or other text features? Have students read the back of the book, peruse the table of contents, and check the pictures and other features in the book to see if these help them understand the content.

Sometimes students may really want to read a specific book and, as a result, will work harder to read that book.

In addition to identifying a book that is at a level that students can read with enough accuracy that their comprehension doesn't break down, students need to consider whether they like the book and want to read it. Sometimes students may really want to read a specific book and, as a result, will work harder to read that book. This will likely take more concentration and the deployment of a lot of strategies, including monitoring comprehension and word solving. Other times they might choose a book just because everyone else is reading it, even if it is *way too hard,* so encourage students to be self-reflective and honest with themselves when they do their comprehension check. Encourage students to ask themselves:

- Do I understand what the book is about? (see the bullet points above for ways students can check).

- Do I find the book topic interesting?

- Is the length of the book good for me? It should not be so long that students believe they can't read it, or so short that it does not provide enough challenge to be engaging.

- Do I like the book? Have students ask themselves this question after they examine the book, and after looking at the back literature, checking the table of contents, and looking at the pictures or text features, if there are any.

Knowing How to Abandon a Book

Some students may have trouble picking a book because they don't know what they like, or all the books seem boring to them. They may not be choosing any book to read, or they may be frequently abandoning books after reading only a few pages. When this happens, sit with the student and help her go through the routine of picking a book, asking her to be honest about a book's topic or interest level and not to just dismiss the book after looking only at the cover.

Other times you may find that students are struggling through a book, or reading it so slowly, that they are making limited progress. Students need to know that it is perfectly fine to abandon a book after giving it a good try. It helps for students to engage in some self-reflection before giving up on a book so they can choose to leave it, not just abandon it because they didn't focus or were trying to get out of the independent reading time. Have students ask themselves:

- Why don't I like this book?

- What can I learn from how I picked this book? Maybe the student picked the book hastily, or perhaps the book was picked deliberately but wasn't as good after the first few pages as the student had hoped.

- What am I looking for in the next book I pick?

Stamina

Some readers have stamina when reading independently and are able to read for extended periods of time. Others do not. Thankfully, there are ways to develop reading stamina. Stamina includes students' ability to sit for a while and read, maintain attention, and reengage themselves when they get distracted. The first thing you will want to do to build stamina with your students is talk about effective and efficient reading habits and how readers sit and read for a while, but may stop to think about what they are reading, reflect, or check their comprehension. Sometimes readers just need to move about and refocus their attention. These are reading behaviors you can discuss and practice with your students. Students will also need to know how to reengage themselves if they lose attention. These are all natural behaviors that readers use when reading independently, but your students may not be aware of them. They need practice to develop these habits.

After talking about what effective and efficient reading behaviors look like, help students build the stamina to read for longer periods of time. One way to do this is to set a goal in the beginning for a shorter amount of time than the extended time you are working toward; perhaps this might be five minutes. Discuss the goal with your class by saying,

> We need to build our stamina, or our ability to stay focused for longer amounts of time. Today, we're going to read for five minutes. We will be working at implementing the behaviors we have talked about before. Can anyone remind us of some of the behaviors we should practice?

Then, once the five minutes are over, have the students discuss and reflect on how it felt to read for that amount of time. Your students might need practice with five-minute increments several times per day before extending the amount of time in one sitting. Over a week or two, lengthen the reading time slightly until the students work up to the

Students might choose a book just because everyone else is reading it, even if it is way too hard, so encourage students to be self-reflective and honest with themselves.

length of the independent reading you hoped for. By working on independent reading incrementally, you can increase your students' stamina to read for longer periods of time.

Keeping Reading Records

Another good habit for students to practice during independent reading is keeping records about what they read. Students don't typically stop and think about the number of words they read each school year (and they probably don't need to). As mentioned earlier in this chapter, words read per year increase students' vocabularies and their ability to comprehend. Having students keep records of their reading can help them self-reflect on their development as readers. Students can keep a reader's journal in which they record the titles and authors of the books that they read as well as a quick set of notes about the book and to whom they might recommend it. They can also include thoughts and reactions, interesting lines, inspirations for their own writing, and questions in their journals. If it helps the students, they can also record the number of pages in each book so they can watch their growth as readers in reading longer texts.

Note that we focused on a reader's journal and not reading logs. There is some evidence that reading logs can be demotivating for students and actually reduce reading volume (Pak & Weseley, 2012). The journal is not used for accountability or to keep records of students' comprehension. The point of a reader's journal is just to keep track of the number, type, and length of the books that the students are reading so that they can reflect on their own progress, celebrate their successes, and set goals for themselves. For instance, a student who loves informational texts has recorded reading 20 of them in a row. That student might set a goal of reading one narrative book next in order to expand her reading diet. The reader's journal can be useful during conferences between the teacher and the student and can also help involve families in encouraging reading out of school, as students could also be recording books read at home after school and on the weekends.

READING CONFERENCES

Teachers play an important role during independent reading, from ensuring students have books to read to monitoring their reading habits and diet to talking with students about their reading. Reading conferences are brief meetings between teachers and students focused on the texts students are reading. During the conference, students typically read aloud part of the text, identify trouble spots, and perhaps talk about difficult vocabulary terms. Teachers may do a comprehension check with some students to make sure that the students are able to talk about their reading, and also to check that the book is a good fit for them. Conferences are a way for you to assess a student's reading and to provide individualized instruction on the books that are being read during independent reading (Gill, 1996). These conferences also provide students an opportunity to verbalize the strategies that they are using when they get to something difficult or confusing in the text.

resources.corwin.com/
thisisbalancedliteracy

Video 22
Reading Conference

Conferences have many purposes, but there are two main goals:

1. *To increase students' ability to be self-reliant* in comprehending texts

2. *To help students set goals* for themselves in reading so that they can continue to grow as readers

To increase self-reliance in accessing and comprehending, you can listen to students read for accuracy and fluency and give them tips on how to help themselves apply fix-up strategies when they come to words they don't know. You can also encourage them to read with feeling and emotion, known as prosody (Rasinski & Padak, 2013). Your focus is not to correct their reading, but to reinforce their skills in helping themselves as readers (Porath, 2013). You can take notes on the conferences so that you can record student progress and keep track of goals. There are four general steps to reading conferences:

1. A comprehension check

2. An accuracy and fluency check

3. A teaching point

4. Goal setting

Step 1: Comprehension (and Engagement) Check

To get started with a conference, you will want to first ask the students how they are doing with the books and texts they are currently reading. Foster a growth mindset, and reinforce their efforts and the work they are putting into building their reading skills and habits. In a reading conference, you want the student to do most of the talking, while you take notes. You might start out by asking these questions:

- Can you share with me what you have been reading?

- What do you like best about what you are reading?

- What do you like the least (if anything)?

- Tell me about this book. What is going on in the book? Tell me more. (Ask students to focus on one book in particular.)

Step 2: Accuracy and Fluency Check

To check students' reading accuracy and fluency, you can ask them to read a passage to you. After listening to the students read, ask them to reflect on the strategies they were using with text. You can ask these questions:

- How do you think you did while reading?

- What parts were hard? What was easy?

- How do you think you helped yourself?

If you notice students tried a strategy to figure out an unknown word or read a sentence more fluidly, you could ask this:

- I noticed you stopped here (point to the word or phrase) and worked at it. What did you do? How do you think you helped yourself? Would you try that again in the future or try something different?

Step 3: A Teaching Point

After talking about the book and the strategies that the students are using while reading, you can reinforce a teaching point. Depending on the students and their needs, you might provide a quick individual lesson on figuring out a word, applying a comprehension strategy, or taking notes. Teaching points will vary based on the students' needs and the text they are reading. Students will come to words that they don't know when reading the text, and you could show them how to use the context to figure out the unknown word's meaning. You could also show them how to skip the word, read a little more, and then go back and reread to try to figure out what the word means using context clues. You can also quickly teach, or reinforce, a comprehension strategy to help the students self-monitor their own comprehension while reading. Comprehension strategies you could focus on include these:

- Self-monitoring for meaning

- Visualizing

- Retelling

- Summarizing

- Predicting

- Inferring

- Analyzing

- Discussing characters' thoughts and feelings

- Identifying main idea and details

Step 4: Set a Goal

It is important to set concrete reading goals during reading conferences.

At the end of the conference, set a reading goal with the student. It is best if the students set the reading goal themselves, but you will probably need to help them think about what they are doing, and what they are working on, so they can articulate the goal. Perhaps a student is getting stuck on unknown words but has been working to identify the root word. This student could set a goal like this: *When I come to an unknown word, I will take the word apart and look at the root word.*

If you are working with a student who is working to read a book more fluidly, the student might set a goal like this: *I am going to try to read the dialogue as if I am talking.*

Or, if a student really wants to work on a strategy you have just spent a couple of minutes teaching, the goal might be about the teaching point: *I am going to stop at the end of each chapter and predict what I think will happen in the next chapter.*

Encourage students to write their goals down in their reader's journal, so they can remember what they have chosen to work on. Mike Levine, a fourth-grade teacher, has students write their goals on index cards and then tape the index card to the corner of their desk as a reminder to them about their goal. Students don't have to work on their reading goal only during independent reading; they can work on it during the day, any time they are reading.

TAKING INDEPENDENT READING HOME

In addition to the independent reading time teachers provide students during the school day, to meet the standards and ensure that all students achieve at high levels, students have to engage in distributed practice outside of school. The correlational data about reading volume and achievement we presented earlier in this chapter was based on reading that students did outside of school. When students become more motivated to read, as is likely to occur when they are reading on a regular basis, it's more likely that they'll read at home. There are a few things that we can do to encourage students to increase their at-home reading volume, and one of them we have already discussed—provide students opportunities to talk about what they are reading during school. In addition to these very valuable discussions about texts, the following three actions can help:

Access

If there is little to read in your house, you're less likely to read. To raise the volume of reading outside the school day, students must have access to texts. There have been a number of efforts to "flood" students with things to read (e.g., Elley, 2000), to address the need for students to have access to reading materials. The International Literacy Association (ILA) recommends a minimum of seven books per student in the class. That would mean that a classroom library for a group of 28 students would need nearly 200 texts for students to read. In addition to classroom libraries, school libraries can be additional resources that provide students with access to texts. The ILA (2000) recommends a ratio of 20 books per child for school libraries.

However, Neuman's (2017) study of 15 childcare centers serving 501 children in an urban area demonstrated that there was little impact from a book flood alone, noting, "The results of our study suggest that access to such books may be necessary, but it was clearly insufficient to enhance early literacy skills" (p. 18). Yes, students need access to books, and they need to read those books, which is more likely to occur when the remaining two factors are implemented.

David Young-Wolff/PhotoEdit

Peer-led book talks promote student interest in reading.

Choice

When students have choice over their reading materials, they are more likely to read. We noted the value of choice earlier in this chapter. Choice is key to motivation and academic independence (Schunk, Meece, & Pintrich, 2013). We can assign reading for students to do, especially during class time when scaffolding is provided. But to increase reading volume, we have to expand the amount of choice students have in what they read. Students who have opportunities to choose their own books develop elaborate strategies for selecting books and are more likely to become intrinsically motivated readers. In their studies of reading motivation, Guthrie et al. (2007) noted, "Students expressed that they like both making their own book choices, as well as having close, trusted others choose books for them" (p. 306). Choice does not necessarily mean "read whatever you want," but it might. For example, students could be provided a choice of texts based on a theme or essential question under investigation. Or students could be invited to continue reading their independent reading text. Or students might be offered free range to read what they want.

Book Talks and "Blessing Books"

When trusted others make recommendations about a text, potential readers are more likely to read it. To promote wide reading outside the school day, students need recommendations from others. Book talks conducted by trusted adults and peers can spur voluntary reading. Gambrell calls this "blessed books" (Marinak & Gambrell, 2016) and suggests that teachers talk about several books that readers in the class might enjoy. These books are then placed on a special shelf, face-forward if possible, for students to select. Wozniak (2011) conducted an intervention to increase voluntary reading among sixth graders in her school using book talks to anchor the program. Teachers spent 10 minutes three times a week introducing books to their students. Students were also provided with 15–20 minutes of unrestricted reading time, including time for short partner discussions, using any book in the classroom. In this investigation, "There were no guidelines, so their discussions took on different forms" such as discussing what was happening in the book or making recommendations (p. 20). Students were free to talk about their reading, rather than having to provide the kind of school-bound book report that is dutifully delivered but rarely deeply felt. The results of the intervention included positive changes in measures of reading attitude, self-efficacy, and reading outside of school.

Students can "bless" books, too. As Hudson (2016) notes, primary students can conduct peer-led book talks, promoting interest while also learning about one another as readers. Hudson modeled book talks herself, introducing a few titles each day, and included some specifics about the title and name of the author as well as a brief description of characters and plot. Most important, she added recommendations. Within a short time, her first-grade students were leading book talks each week on a rotating basis.

To our thinking, balanced literacy involves students reading widely, at home and at school. You may want to share the correlational data with parents during an open house and impress upon them the value of having their children read independently at home every night. In fact, at-home reading is way more powerful than most other types of homework given to elementary students (e.g., Hattie, 2012). Growing readers takes time, specifically time on task, and independent reading provides the practice time for students to develop their habits for reading.

CONCLUSION

Students need to spend a concentrated amount of time actually reading, at school and at home. They need to read books that they can read, and they need time devoted to increasing their total reading volume. The amount of time students read independently will grow as the students develop as readers and as they get older. Increasing reading volume helps students learn to understand what they are reading, builds reading fluency, and increases their vocabularies. Just like learning to play everything from a piano to basketball, learning to read requires practice. Without sufficient practice, the amazing instruction that you have provided won't stick. Practice does not make perfect; it makes permanent. And that's what we're looking for—readers who develop habits for reading and understanding.

CHAPTER 8

INDEPENDENT WRITING INSTRUCTION

PRACTICING, APPLYING, AND EXTENDING LEARNING

iStock.com/Liderina

Sarah Vang's fifth graders are immersed in their writing. When a visitor walks into the classroom, students don't look up; they just keep writing. Ms. Vang launches the writing block in her classroom with a whole-class lesson. Once students are writing, she calls a few students to a table for small-group writing instruction. Ms. Vang's students are working on opinion writing and have proposed topics to write about. They have read a lot on their topic and are ready to write a draft of their essay. Six students are working in the computer area and have devices out. They are still researching their topics, so they can add evidence to their writing in order to support their opinions. Other students are spread throughout the room, sitting in various places. Some are at their desks. One student is sitting on the floor under the whiteboard with his back against the wall; another one is under her desk, using the floor as a place to organize her growing draft. Most of the students have a writing folder with various drafts in it from previous days. They know how to work with a peer if they get stuck in their writing. After Ms. Vang finishes meeting with a small group for writing instruction, she confers with individual students to assess and advise.

INDEPENDENT WRITING

Independent writing contributes to children's developing sense of agency as they learn the power and influence of their words. They also learn by writing, a phenomenon that underpins writing-to-learn approaches (Klein, Arcon, & Baker, 2017). During independent writing, students compose original texts, write about their reading to deepen comprehension, or address essential questions through inquiry and investigation. Overall, students participate in writing processes for various purposes. But the purposes for engaging in independent writing are up to us as teachers to set forth.

We as authors do not advocate for long, unstructured, and unfocused periods of time for students to "just write." The three of us write professionally, and we can't imagine how frustrating it would be for someone to announce that we were to write for 30 minutes at 10:00 a.m. just because it is writing time. Each time we compose, it is with a purpose in mind. We owe our students the same consideration each time they write independently. In doing so, they practice writing skills and composition strategies taught during whole-class and small-group writing instruction. In sum, writing

- Is part of learning to think reflectively

- Extends student learning about content

- Allows students opportunities to communicate their thoughts and ideas

As noted in previous chapters, writing processes do not follow a strictly linear set of steps (despite classroom posters to the contrary). Unfortunately, some students have been taught that the writing process happens in a proscribed sequence. Often, writers revise and edit even as they are drafting. A piece moving to completion may have multiple iterations of publishing, as writers test their drafts with an audience; it is not just a once-through process. If fact, it is good practice for students to finish up a piece they plan to publish and ask others to read it before going through a final revision and editing process. Not all writing needs to be published, but if the writing is being written with an audience in mind, then students need to have opportunities for feedback from that audience (see Figure 8.1).

▼ FIGURE 8.1 WRITING PROCESSES

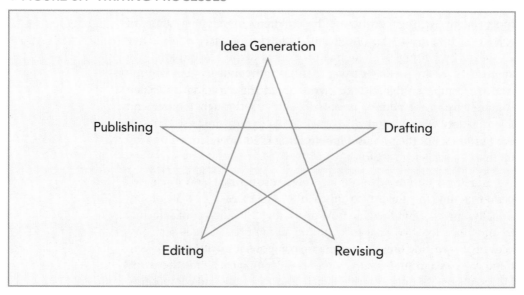

AUDIENCE AND PURPOSE ANCHOR AUTHENTIC WRITING

But when the purpose is not clear, independent writing becomes a compliance activity, with little of the kind of complex thinking we hope our students will experience. Our ability to communicate the purpose for writing influences the usefulness of independent writing. Students must understand the task and the purpose for the task. In part this is accomplished with a high-quality writing prompt.

WHEN THE PURPOSE IS NOT CLEAR, NEITHER IS THE WRITER

A writing assignment or prompt should result, ideally, in the kind of writing one is seeking as a teacher. However, students interpret unclear writing tasks quite differently from one another, and this variance influences the product (Flower, 1990). Moreover, novice writers rely on prior knowledge of writing schemas and may not closely examine the task they are being asked to do. Therefore, while an assignment may ask the writer to analyze and interpret, a novice writer may simply summarize, focusing instead on a familiar format such as the ubiquitous five-paragraph essay. These schemata are not simply "untaught"; they must be confronted intentionally.

Flower (1990) studied the reading-to-write processes of college freshmen in their composition courses; we find that our students in elementary school engage in similar processes. Students in Flower's study were tasked with reading an article that offered conflicting evidence. Flower identified three strategies the students used. Many relied on what she called a *gist and list* approach, where they searched for the main idea and listed key points, staying focused only on what the text itself had to say about the topic, a strategy she described as "fast, efficient, and faithful to the source" (p. 235) but devoid of any construction of new knowledge. In essence, it is a summary of an article but nothing more than that.

Other students focused solely on personal response, or what Flower termed *TIA* (true, important, I agree). While these students engaged in some evaluation, unlike the first group, their responses were confined to existing knowledge. In other words, they judged but did not question: "It is a one-way communication in which the student selects or rejects the claims of others but does not appear to listen to what the voice in the text is saying about them" (p. 236). This type of writing has its place as a personal response, but it does not challenge the writer to examine ideas that conflict with one's worldview.

A third, much smaller group was able to leverage both of these habits—extracting evidence from the text and examining existing understandings—to question both the text and themselves. In other words, they transformed knowledge to reach new and original insights. The researcher called this third approach *dialogue,* as it described not only the interaction between text and reader but also the critical thinking and writing necessary to engage in comparison, explication, reasoning, and contextualization of ideas. Figure 8.2 summarizes Flower's three reading-to-write strategies.

It is noteworthy that each of Flower's approaches has a place in the reading and writing diet of students. But they become problematic when there is a mismatch between the task facing student writers and the approach they have selected to use. A well-designed writing assignment or clear task is a first step in helping students correctly match the task with the approach.

▼ FIGURE 8.2 THREE READING-TO-WRITE STRATEGIES

	Gist and List	True/Important/ I Agree (TIA)	Dialogue
Student's reading and writing behaviors	Locating main ideas, themes, or arguments of the author Identifying key details Explaining the substantive message of the piece	Identifying points of agreement Dismissing or ignoring points of disagreement Locating an organizing idea to use as a springboard for response	*Gist and List and TIA behaviors, plus* Questioning the text and one's assumptions Examining points of agreement and disagreement equally Qualifying textual information with other sources Building new knowledge on a foundation of existing knowledge
Focus	Accurately conveying the information in the text	The student writer's interpretation	Constructing an argument using comparison, cause and effect, explication, reasoning, qualification, contextualization of ideas
Use of evidence	Textual evidence to replicate knowledge	Evidence is extracted from prior knowledge and experiences to comment on a text	Textual evidence, prior knowledge, and the student's inferential understanding of the text to transform knowledge
Best for . . .	Summaries Precis writing	Personal responses Persuasive writing	Analytic writing Argumentation

WRITING TO A WELL-DESIGNED PROMPT

So how to reconcile aligning writing purpose with reading purpose? Well-designed writing prompts can guide reader/writers to engage in the thinking and learning that should result from independent writing. The prompts we give to students launch independent writing, for better or for worse. A vaguely worded writing prompt leaves some students stranded, as they struggle to execute a plan for their writing. Effective prompts provide information about what students are going to write about, identify what the student needs to write, and note the purpose, audience, and form for the writing (Calfee & Miller, 2013). An informative prompt about a narrative text might read, "After reading Chapter 5 in *Because of Winn Dixie* by Kate DiCamillo, write about the actions of the character, Opal, and how her actions changed the story plot. Describe what Opal did and how this affects the story. Be specific, and provide an example from the text."

In this case, the prompt focuses on a single piece of text. Other prompts require that students compare texts. And still other prompts require that students take what they know and respond. For example, a prompt might read, "You live in a city that has watering restrictions to conserve water during a drought, and you notice that the sprinklers at a local park are broken, and water is being wasted. Write a letter to the city letting them know about the problem and asking for the problem to be fixed. Quote sections of the ordinance to support your request. "

Authentic prompts set students up to write for a purpose that is specific and clear. Effective prompts identify an audience and require that students plan their writing and then revise to ensure they meet the expectations. Writing prompts of this nature can help students grow exponentially as writers, because they are set up for success. A well-designed writing task should guide students in responding to that prompt. As such, the basic components of a writing assignment or prompt are the following:

1. Topic

2. Audience

3. Format, structure, or genre to be produced

4. Success criteria for the task

Oliver (1995) studied the effects of these prompt elements by examining the interaction of audience, task, and style to determine what worked best as writers developed. She found that students did best when the prompt specified the audience, real or contrived, and when the topic statement was direct (e.g., "make a recommendation to a fellow student"). It should be noted that all three components—audience, topic, and structure— should be present in a well-designed writing prompt. Students should be able to parse a writing assignment such that they can answer the following questions:

• What is my purpose for writing this piece?

• Who is my audience?

• What is the task?

• What will it look like when I do it well?

The Literacy Design Collaborative (www.LDC.org) proposes that good writing prompts can be formulated using prefabricated task templates that allow teachers to customize. For example, the following argumentation task template invites students to compare two conditions:

[Insert question] After reading _____ (literature or informational texts), write a/an _____ (essay or substitute) that compares _____ (content) and argues _____ (content). Be sure to support your position with evidence from the texts.

This template can be used as a springboard for writing in any number of subject areas. In each case, the writing task specifies the purpose and task in detail. For example, the LDC provides the following examples of the use of their writing frames for students in first grade:

- After reading *Garden Helpers*, about insects that are helpful, write a report that explains why not all insects are bad. Use what you know from *Garden Helpers* to write your response.

- How do animal families care for their young? After reading "Animal Families," write a report that describes what you have learned about how animal families take care of their babies. Use what you know from "Animal Families" to write your response.

For students in third grade, the LDC offers the following examples, again using their templates:

- Is pizza a nutritious food product? After reading the two provided articles, write a report in which you answer the question and explain your reasons from a health and science point of view. Give an example from the articles to support your opinion.

- Would you recommend *Charlotte's Web* to a friend? After reading this book, write a book review in which you answer the question and explain your reasons with reference to the author's use of story-telling strategies. Give several examples from the book to support your opinion.

A Note About Emergent Writers

Matching tasks and approaches for students in kindergarten and first grade looks a bit different than in other grades. That is because much of what the children are working on is unlocking the conventions of print and representing their messages in letters, words, and sentences. Young children benefit from tasks that expose them to print and familiarize them with how print works (Coker, 2013). Writing prompts for emergent writers are designed to use what they know in order to gain early experiences with representing ideas. Consider how this prompt, which is read to children, engages their nascent literacy practices:

How would you solve Duncan's problem? After listening to *The Day the Crayons Quit*, draw a picture about your solution. Add words you know to explain your picture.

Much of the independent writing young children are engaged in is for very short periods of time. As discussed in previous writing chapters, kindergarteners are writing in various ways and settings. They are writing at the writing center, writing in the play area, writing at the listening center, and writing at the art center. They can and should be engaged in short independent writing spurts throughout the day.

The writing of some kindergarteners initially looks like scribbling. Soon it includes pictures and labels, and then pictures and words strung together in short sentences. They apply their growing knowledge of phonics to their writing, with closer and closer approximations to correct spelling. During independent writing time, the teacher confers with students about their prompted writing, listening to children tell their stories as they point to the pictures and the words they have written.

Students who are writing independently rely on routines, as well as the teacher's focus on building the capacity of novice writers to engage in writerly behaviors that build stamina.

CLASSROOM CONDITIONS THAT SUPPORT INDEPENDENT WRITING

Classroom organization is vital for independent writing. This is especially true given that in many cases there are multiple activities taking place in the room, including guided instruction and collaborative learning. Students who are writing independently rely on routines, as well as the teacher's focus on building the capacity of novice writers to engage in writerly behaviors that build stamina. In addition, attention to choice sustains independent writing and builds motivation, a crucial writing disposition.

Routines

Students need to establish routines in order to help themselves write independently when the teacher is busy working with other students in a group or conferencing individually with students. Routines can include helping themselves stay organized. Students will need a writing folder so that drafts can be kept in one place in an organized way so that they are not writing on multiple pieces of loose paper that can get lost in their desks or backpacks. Children of all ages benefit from keeping their writing drafts in a writing folder. They can access their drafts whenever they want, or need to, and they can review work they have already produced in order to expand on a piece or to continue writing in a specific genre. Students working on devices can develop good habits early on for labeling writing folders in word-processing apps and labeling their drafts.

Because movement can be an issue, use a consistent signal for students to transition. After whole-class writing instruction is done, Rick Johnson signals his second graders about their transition. "Here's our schedule for this morning. Before you move, think about where you are going and what you'll need." After a pause, he says, "45 seconds to launch," reminding students they should be ready to write within the allotted time. Students gather up their writing materials and fan out around the room to places where they are comfortable writing. Some are in the library area, sitting on the floor, using clipboards as a writing surface, while others are at their desks. Some of Mr. Johnson's students are settling at the teacher's big table, because he has a small-group writing lesson to share with them.

Students benefit from finding comfortable spaces for writing.

Michael Newman/PhotoEdit

Writerly Behaviors

Accomplished writers have specific writing habits, and students should have writing behaviors as well. Students should develop habits of getting settled into their writing right away. They should know what to do if they have trouble getting started writing—perhaps they sketch out their thinking in a writer's notebook.

Often students cannot get started with their writing. It helps to implement a simple routine that works well. Simply giving thinking time is highly effective in helping students focus on a topic and plan how to go about their writing. However, this should be paired with actionable results, lest the thinking time turns into unproductive time. To make thinking time useful, have graphic organizers, concepts maps, and paper for brainstorming. Encourage students to engage in freewriting by setting a timer for themselves and writing words and sentences for five minutes as a warm-up. Keep in mind that power writing (Chapter 3) is a form of freewriting that can interrupt a temporary writer's block. Students should also be advised to consult previous entries in their writing journals.

Signal students to ready themselves with their writing materials, and then ask them to think about how they will form their writing, what their personal writing goal is for the day, and how they might approach the task (Lassonade & Richard, 2013). A student who has difficulty in getting started may need further support in understanding the prompt, the purpose, the audience, and available resources.

Stamina Building

Students need to develop the ability to write for extended periods of time. Writing for extended periods develops their writing skills and also increases the amount students will learn in content areas when composing informational, argumentative, and narrative texts. Kindergarteners can work up to writing for 20 minutes, while students in grades 1–6 can work on writing up to 30 minutes and more. (Recall that the What Works Clearinghouse recommends a cumulative 60 minutes per day of writing.) What the students are doing during writing time may differ by age. Younger students will be illustrating, drawing, and labeling as well as writing sentences. Older students may dive into their writing and write for 30 minutes, stopping only to check notes, organize, revise, or edit as they go.

Choice in Writing

Students need to exercise choices in what they are writing, the genre they are writing in, and in the development of their topic. This doesn't mean that it is a free-for-all experience. Having said that, choice is an important lever in motivation, which in turn influences their learning about writing and their learning of the content they are writing about (Hiebert, 1994). Involving students in the development of the topic helps them to engage with what they are writing about, and lessens the "cookie cutter" effect in which all the students' writing in a classroom looks the same (Boscolo & Gelati, 2013).

CONDITIONS THAT SUPPORT THE DEVELOPMENT OF WRITING PROCESSES

A goal of independent writing is for students to practice the writing processes that drive composition. These iterative processes gradually become internalized, and accomplished writers are able to enact these processes on their own. But novice writers benefit from classroom environments designed to create the conditions that apprentice students into these habits. Two essential elements of writing—adopting the stance of an audience, and revising to strengthen writing—foster independent writing.

Peer Response as Audience

When students write for their peers, they have an authentic reason to write and an audience with whom to share their writing. It is not necessary to wait until a piece is completely polished to engage students in peer response. In fact, we would argue that it is too late. Peers can serve as excellent thinking partners for each other as they develop and revise their writing. As Graff and Birkenstein (2010) note, academic writing requires that students engage in a series of moves, much like a conversation. In their words, "Writing may require some degree of quiet and solitude," but writers can develop their arguments "not just by looking inward but by doing what they often do in a good conversation with friends and family—by listening carefully to what others are saying and engaging with their views" (p. xxvi).

Peer response propels independent writing forward.

Bob Daemmrich/PhotoEdit

As discussed in Chapter 4, peer response is an excellent means for propelling independent writing forward. Set up expectations to ensure that peer response is purposeful and powerful. This includes the management of how to work together, but more important, expectations for the review should focus on *how* to discuss writing based on identified criteria for success. To do this, students need to know exactly what the expectations are for effective writing. You can develop these expectations during whole-group writing instruction and when working with students during small-group writing instruction. Then, students can work together on their pieces to find areas that are confusing or unclear or that include extraneous details. Students can work together this way (Graham, Harris, & Hebert, 2011):

- One student reads a peer's writing.

- The reader stops when something is unclear.

- The partners discuss together how to revise for clarity.

- The author fixes up the section.

Revision During Independent Writing

As our students' teachers, we are also their audience. The quality of the feedback we offer can aid or inhibit the revision process. The National Writing Project and Nagin (2003) define revision using a gerund:

> In revising, a writer approaches a rough draft with an editorial eye, identifying and deleting extraneous subject matter, focusing the material, determining what needs to be amplified and what needs to be cut. . . . Writers need to learn revision strategies, and teachers can help by modeling the process, showing drafts of their own or someone else's writing and demonstrating how revision can transform and clarify a piece of writing. Students then learn that writing is a continual process of transforming or re-seeing their work. (p. 26)

You will recall that young writers are not especially good at noticing what needs to be revised, although they are more effective at revising what has already been identified for them. Unfortunately, in too many classes revising is really just making the changes the teacher recommended, with little thought beyond minimal compliance. ("I'll just make these changes she wrote on my paper and then I'll be done with this!") But how well do our stated values about writing mirror the feedback about revisions that we provide to students?

Lee (2009) interviewed 26 teachers about what they valued in the development of student writing. They spoke of the importance of focusing on a writer's strength, and emphasized that good writing was more than accuracy of conventions and mechanics. Teachers in the study said that the usefulness of feedback was contingent on their students' ability to understand it. Most important, they said, revision was necessary for the development of skilled writers. The researcher then analyzed the written feedback of these same teachers on their students' papers and found the following:

- The majority of the feedback focused on errors, mostly about conventions and mechanics.

- They used error codes their students did not understand.

- They assigned a single grade for the initial attempt and did not create opportunities for meaningful revising.

The last finding is particularly disturbing, because without revising, students fail to develop the stamina and persistence needed to engage in complex writing. The feedback we offer to young writers must reflect what we value in writing. Procedures that don't allow space for revision communicate to students that a one-and-done approach is how accomplished writers compose. (We assure you it is not!)

These procedures are entirely in our control. One way to ensure that students are afforded opportunities to revise is to create a protocol that asks them how they revised. Jago (2002) offers some advice on this subject. She requires her students to attach a self-assessment to their final revision:

1. What changes did you make from draft to revision?

2. How did these changes improve your essay?

3. What do you like best about the revised work?

4. What would you continue to work on if you had more time?

5. What else do you want me to know before I read your paper? (p. 108)

The shift in ownership for revising empowers novice writers. Revision, loved or not, becomes less about *something the teacher makes me do*, and more about *assuming responsibility for my efforts*. Strong writers know they're never done, just that time ran out.

WRITING CONFERENCES

As described in Chapter 7, individual conferences with children focus students on monitoring their current work, getting feedback, and setting goals. Time spent in conferring with students about their writing yields critical assessment information for the teacher to gauge progress and determine next steps. We utilize steps that parallel reading conferences when we talk with young writers about their compositions and dispositions:

1. A composition check

2. An accuracy and fluency check

The shift in ownership for revising empowers novice writers. Revision, loved or not, becomes less about *something the teacher makes me do*, and more about *assuming responsibility for my efforts*. Strong writers know they're never done, just that time ran out.

3. A teaching point

4. Goal setting

Step 1: Composition (and Engagement) Check

Ask individual students to bring two completed writings, two pieces that are in progress, and their writer's notebook and power writing fluency chart. Begin by asking them to give you a tour of their completed and current pieces, prompting them to tell you more as needed. Find out about their level of writing engagement and dispositions by inquiring about what they like best about writing and what they like least about it or where they are having difficulty. Depending on the students' replies, this may be a teaching point.

Step 2: Accuracy and Fluency Check

Ask students to show you their power writing graph and their writer's notebook of daily power writing. This is time when you can discuss trends in the quantitative student data, leading to discussion about salient points (e.g., "You really surged in the number of words per minute two weeks ago. Why do you believe you grew so much?"). The writer's notebook includes power writing that the students have reread, circling errors they caught. If you see that the student is noticing most of her errors, then you have reason to believe her self-monitoring is consistent. However, if you detect a pattern in errors that she missed when rereading her power writing, make note of it. This should be a focus of future small-group writing intervention.

Step 3: A Teaching Point

Turn your attention back to a piece that is in progress, and ask students if there is a place where they are stuck. This isn't time for you to extensively read and comment, but rather is designed to build students' revision skills. A writing conference, after all, is a two-way street, and students should be encouraged to take the lead in the discussion. Ask them how you can help. Ownership is a key disposition young writers need to develop, and it takes practice. The use of a single-point rubric (discussed in detail in Chapter 9) can assist students in building self-assessment habits. Again, take notes about what it is that students are requesting.

Step 4: Goal-Setting

The goals set in a writing conference don't need to be long-term and complex. The purpose of this phase of the writing conference is to set actionable steps for what is to occur next. The goal should be linked to an aspect of writing discussed in the conference; perhaps a goal about power writing, or next steps to revise a current piece. Third-grade teacher Kristin Baltierra uses a two-part carbonless phone message pad purchased at an office supply store to record agreed goals. Ms. Baltierra writes the goals down for the student, her name and the date, then tears off the original and gives it to the student. The note has sticky edge, which allow the student to place it in her writer's notebook. The carbonless copy remains in the message pad, which allows the teacher to keep a record of the goals set with the student.

WRITING TASKS THAT PROMOTE LEARNING THROUGH WRITING

Writing tasks contribute in different ways to how and what students learn. Some writing tasks prompt students to be metacognitive in their thinking, especially in the case of written reflections. Other tasks prompt students to analyze information, or to interpret and explain (Klein et al., 2017). Students need a range of writing tasks and aligned purposes, so they have the opportunity to apply cognitive, behavioral, metacognitive, and affective skills. Additionally, students can work through information and content by writing, and in this way, writing promotes learning content.

Involving students in inquiry and protocols on how to dive into an inquiry project can help advance their learning of content through writing (Akhavan, 2008). Using a protocol is a way that students can approach their writing to help themselves get started quickly. For instance, students may want to investigate a topic using this protocol: Think of an essential question that can guide their thinking, investigate it, and write. The protocol includes students crafting a compelling question to address, locating information and taking notes, and reporting on findings. If students are working on writing in science, they may keep notes of an experiment and then write an explanatory report about what occurred in the lab. A protocol to guide this experience? Check notes in science journal, focus on the text structure to explain what was observed, sketch out how to explain what happened in a notebook, and then write (Akhavan, 2018). Subject areas such as science, social studies, and mathematics require students to integrate content into their writing. This type of writing lends itself to students representing their learning in a variety of ways, including using graphics and illustrations, presentation software, and other multimedia applications like a webpage or word-processed text that looks like a report, brochure, or booklet.

Argumentative Writing

Argumentative writing requires students to extend their thinking about a topic, using evidence and reasoning to support their claims. It also requires that students read text in order to research a topic so that they can understand the topic deeply. This allows them to take a stance and make a claim about an issue. Argumentative writing goes beyond persuasive writing, as the writer provides reasons for and against various points about the issue (claims and counterclaims). In argumentative writing, the student needs to address counterclaims, not just argue for one side of an issue. Argumentative writing usually begins in sixth grade and is an extension of work in grades K–5 on writing opinions with evidence.

Summary Writing

Summary writing requires students to select important points from a text and connect the points in a cohesive manner—this is a rather sophisticated skill (Klein et al., 2017). The GIST summary writing strategy (Chapter 6) is a tool for shaping summaries, as it assists students in drilling down to the main points without getting lost in the details. Summarizing is a reading comprehension strategy, and working through writing a summary on specific content helps students learn the content.

Reflective Writing

Writing tasks that require students to reflect are primarily metacognitive in nature. Students may evaluate their own learning about a topic and then write about it. Students can discuss their current level of understanding of a subject and what their plans are for furthering their learning.

WRITING ACROSS THE SCHOOL DAY

Independent writing in the classroom does not necessarily mean that all students are sitting at their desks at the same time and writing quietly. Some of the independent writing students do is integrated into other tasks in the balanced literacy classroom. These shorter spurts of writing add up, as students build the habit of composing routinely. The following sections include examples of the ways in which teachers can ensure students are writing independently for a significant number of minutes. None of us use all of these techniques, but we use some of them to ensure that writing volume is sufficient.

> Independent writing in the classroom does not necessarily mean that all students are sitting at their desks at the same time and writing quietly. Some of the independent writing students do is integrated into other tasks in the balanced literacy classroom. These shorter spurts of writing add up, as students build the habit of composing routinely.

Annotations During Reading

Students can take notes about what was read to them as they think about text features, text structures, story elements, and information gleaned from text, especially during close reading instruction. (See Chapter 2 for more details on annotation.)

Word Wall Writing and Generative Sentences

At the word wall writing center, children use individual whiteboards and select words from the large word wall to turn into sentences. They write their sentences on the whiteboard and share with a peer at the same center. Set boundaries and limiters using a generative sentence technique. (See Chapter 6 for more details on generative sentences.)

Listening Center

Primary teachers often use a listening center to augment reading of more complex texts. In the listening center, students listen to a book or text and then write about what they thought about the book. Depending on the focus for the week, students may write about characters, plot, or action. Teachers may record themselves reading a book, so their students hear them reading. They can record a prompt at the end of the reading to get students engaged in writing and illustration.

In listening centers, primary students listen to text and then write and draw in response.

Mary Kate Denny/PhotoEdit

Social Studies or Science Center Writing

There is always something interesting to write about at the social studies or science center. We introduce a RAFT writing process to students as part of perspective taking (Santa & Havens, 1995). Once they have practiced the procedure in whole-group writing instruction, we move it to centers. RAFT stands for *role, audience, format, and topic,* and frames a short writing prompt to respond to the reading. We write a RAFT prompt on the inside cover of picture books for students to write in response to. Students might be studying a social studies theme, such as symbols in second grade. The reading *F Is for Flag* by Wendy Cheyette Lewison (2002) is accompanied by the following RAFT prompt:

Role: You are an American flag

Audience: Our town

Format: A letter

Topic: Why I have 13 stripes and 50 stars

Students write their responses in their writer's notebooks, or turn them in as evidence of their work.

School Library Visits

There are many ways to incorporate writing before or after school library visits. Coordinate with your school's librarian or media specialist for methods to infuse writing into this time.

- Have children use 11" x 4" paper strips to write "reviews" of books. Children write a sentence about the book on one side, and on the flipside of the paper draw a picture. Then they put the paper in the book, so there is a "flag" sticking out of the book letting others know the book has been reviewed by a student. Many of these one or two sentence reviews start with "I like ___ because ___" or, "The best part was _____."

- Develop a school library recommendation board filled with reviews written by students at the school. This review board can be used to spotlight specific titles while increasing interest in books and materials related to schoolwide and grade-specific themes.

ORGANIZING MATERIALS FOR INDEPENDENT WRITING

Students need a place to collect their writing, especially the brief writing they do in centers, during power writing, and during idea generation and freewriting. A writer's notebook is a place where students take note of and collect ideas for writing. For younger students the journal could be pages of paper stapled together with a cover. For older students the journal could be a spiral notebook. The journal writing should include prompt writing as well as reflective writing the students engage in, and on topics that they choose. We want students to see, and be proud of, the accumulated writing they have done over the course of the year. A thick notebook filled with so much writing is motivating and fosters a sense of accomplishment.

Writer's notebooks give students a sense of pride in their work.

Michael Newman/PhotoEdit

To facilitate journal writing, it is effective to teach thinking strategies so that students can dive into the writing. Morning arrival is a good time for journal writing, as the teacher takes attendance, lunch count, and other administrative duties. Students in Karen Eyller's first-grade classroom are greeted with a short writing prompt each morning as part of the morning message:

Good morning! Happy Wednesday! What is your joy today?

The children sit with their writer's notebooks while Ms. Eyller encourages them to plan their words and think about how they might write their words. She encourages them to "see the words in their minds first" and then begin to write. Ms. Eyller incorporates this writing into discussion during her morning meeting routine.

Teachers can also provide examples of journal writing with annotations about the strategies used in the margins. It is also effective to teach meta-cognitive strategies during journal writing. Students can reflect on their writing focus, stamina, and process, and write a statement explaining how well they feel they worked or how much they accomplished. We also want to keep students organized, as lots of loose paper tends to get lost in backpacks and crowded desks. Students can decorate their note-books and fill them with ideas, doodles, writing, pictures, illustrations, and other items that inspire their writing. The notebook is a place where students can brainstorm writing topics and write parts of different texts they are composing. They can keep collections of beautiful language, hooks to start their writing, and vocabulary words that interest them. In addition, they can keep track of writing on sticky notes, quick-writes, observations, and short summaries.

Students need to be in charge of their materials for writing. One reason for this is that being responsible for staying organized develops good writing habits, but also it reduces the preparation teachers need to make. During the time most of our students are doing independent writing, we are engaged with other students either in small-group instruction or in individual conferences, so the students need to be in control of their writing. This means they need access to materials and implements such as the paper, pencils, colored pencils, markers, and devices used for a variety of writing applications.

Older students may be composing on devices as well as by hand, and they also need methods for organizing. Too often, students use incon-sistent methods for naming files, and then spend valuable time trying to locate them. (Nine different files titled "Essay" is not going to help!) Introduce students to a digital organizational system using the learning management system (LMS), and teach them a file naming convention so they can locate their work.

- Name of assignment (be sure to provide them with a name)

- Student's last name and first initial

- Date of file

So for example, the file title ElectricCarsEssay_HendersonJ_102419 gives you and the student a consistent means for locating work efficiently on the LMS.

During independent writing, students are also practicing keyboard-ing skills that they have been working on during small-group and whole-group writing instruction (see Chapters 3 and 4). Students will need to have a copy of the color-coded keyboarding model (explained in Chapter 3) at their desks to help them develop automaticity while drafting and revising their pieces. A quick reference guide to cutting, pasting, and deleting text should also be readily available to students in poster form in the room. They are also using spellcheck software, so be sure that students know how to run a spellcheck themselves. Students are anxious to publish their work, too. Programs that go beyond simple word processing, like Padlet, Story Bird, and Glogster, give students an opportunity to write articles and other texts, add pictures, and then download and print their writing in a final, polished form.

SPOTLIGHT ON THREE CLASSROOMS

Classroom organization varies by grade level and scheduling, and getting started does require a bit of investment in getting independent writing up and running. Here is a spotlight on three teachers as they develop independent writing in their classrooms.

Kindergarten

In Janene Mueller's kindergarten classroom, the children are spread out around the room writing. They have writing folders, and there is a paper station set up in the back of the classroom where children can go help themselves to three different types of writing paper and pencils. Ms. Mueller has also stocked the paper station with crayons and markers. When students need paper or a pencil, they stop working and go to the paper station without having to ask permission. During the first few weeks of school, Ms. Mueller showed the children what she expected during writing time, and the children regularly self-reflect on their work during writing. Not often, but occasionally, a student spends too much time retrieving writing materials. When this does happen, Ms. Mueller has a gentle conversation with the child, providing a reminder of the class work expectations. There is a large word wall that can be seen from multiple locations in the room, and Ms. Mueller has created a variety of word banks with the children and written them on chart paper hung around the room. When visiting Ms. Mueller's classroom, you might see children up near the word wall figuring out how to spell a word, or copying a word from a word bank.

Third Grade

Ricardo Saenz is a third-grade teacher, and he has started using writer's notebooks with his class. It is January, and students have returned from winter break. Before they started using writer's notebooks, the children kept both their planning and their drafts in writing folders. The writing folders were kept in bins near each grouping of four desks. Now that the students are using writing notebooks, they think, plan, and draw in the notebooks and retrieve their writing folders and paper from the writing center once they are ready to begin a new piece. There is a busy hum in the classroom as some students share their thinking and what they have added to their notebook today.

Fifth Grade

Jay Reynolds's fifth-grade students are writing on devices. All students have their own devices, and the students are working with Google Docs to draft their pieces about a topic they are investigating. Some students are working in pairs, listening to each other read the texts aloud and discussing the meaning of sentences and words together. Other students are paired up, but the two students are not talking, as they are making notes on each other's pieces in Google Docs using the edit features of the application. The room is fairly quiet, but you can hear the murmur of conversation from the few pairs of students working together to write. In baskets near the groupings of desks are students' writing notebooks and writing folders. Some of their writing is drafted out by hand on paper and is later typed into a Google Doc and saved in a drive. As Mr. Reynolds conferences with students, he sometimes checks on students' progress by checking their writing from his own device and leaving notes in the margins to prompt students' thinking.

CONCLUSION

Writing is used for a variety of purposes and practices, but overall the focus is on communication. Independent writing is the time when students practice writing so that they can write fluidly and with confidence. Some independent writing tasks allow students to make their own choices about what they are going to write and how they approach the processes of writing. However, students need and deserve to be provided with specific tasks and well-designed prompts to efficiently work through their process of responding. The writing processes utilized during independent writing are not linear; students may revise and edit as they draft. Therefore, we need to create the conditions necessary to support students throughout these processes, including peer response and conferring with the teacher.

9 ASSESSMENT AND INTERVENTION IN THE BALANCED LITERACY CLASSROOM

NOTICING AND RESPONDING TO STUDENTS' NEEDS

David Young-Wolff/PhotoEdit

Fourth-grade teacher Maren Granville pulls up the detailed records she keeps to monitor her students' progress. Some of the information she utilizes comes from her school district's interim benchmark assessments. The reports are helpfully color coded to visually denote student progress, using green, yellow, and red to signal relative status toward end-of-year goals.

"These [benchmark assessments] are good because they give me a report of my kiddos' progress toward the state assessment," she said. However, a limitation is that they only happen twice a year. "It's just not frequent enough," said Ms. Granville. "I need to know how they're doing, and so do they."

Ms. Granville, who is a racing enthusiast, uses the metaphor of lap times to gauge a driver's progress toward winning. "Lap times are useful because of the frequency of the measure and what they are used for in decision making," she said. "But it would be crazy if the timing data weren't shared with the driver."

Ms. Granville uses the racing theme to talk about the importance of using literacy assessments formatively in the learning lives of her students. She administers frequent assessments so that students can track their own progress, using the same flagging procedures used on the racetrack.

"I'm the race director in the classroom, so I have to signal them when they are on track to complete and when they aren't," she explained:

- Green flag *means, "Race: You are on track and making expected progress. Your race plan is successful so far."*

- Yellow flag *means "Caution: You're falling behind. Watch for instructions to adjust your race plan so you can pick up your speed."*

- Red flag *means "Stop: Something is wrong with your current race plan. Consultation with the race director is needed to assess together and make a plan to rejoin the race."*

"I want my students to understand that we assess ourselves frequently and adjust the plan when something is off," she said. "Instruction, assessment, and intervention are all linked. When a driver isn't making expected progress, she and her team adjust the plan and fix what isn't working well. There's no shame at all in that. That's a formula for winning."

PURPOSES OF FORMATIVE EVALUATION

It is difficult to imagine how any of us would make much progress in our endeavors without frequent checks. Many of us wear tracking devices to gauge our daily activity levels and adjust them as needed. For instance, what's your reaction when your device reminds you, "Your activity level is usually higher at this point in the day. Take a few minutes to walk or climb some stairs to get back on track"? Such reminders draw our attention to an aspect of our lives that we know is important but can be easily overlooked due to competing demands.

The effect size of formative evaluation, 0.48, reported in Hattie's 2018 analysis, is above the average teacher effect size of 0.40, indicating that the practice is an important accelerant for student learning. Assessment systems in the classroom can have a similar effect for students, but only if we provide students access to the data and make sure our students are actively engaged in decision making.

We can use assessments summatively or formatively. Summatively, they can be used to measure end-of-unit or end-of-year goals. Formatively, assessments can provide incremental information about student progress. In fact, some use different terminology to highlight the role of each—formative evaluation and summative evaluation:

- Formative evaluation is assessment used *for* learning.

- Summative evaluation is assessment *of* learning (Hattie, 2012).

This is more than just semantics. It rightly underlines that we can use virtually any assessment formatively or summatively. It simply depends on how it is used. Robert Stake, an assessment researcher, said, "When the cook tastes the soup, that's formative; when the guests taste the soup, that's summative" (Scriven, 1991, p. 169).

In this chapter, we will use this terminology:

- *Assessment for learning* describes specific instruments commonly used by literacy teachers.

- *Formative evaluation* is the process of making instructional decisions, gauging student progress, assisting students in developing goals, and most important, providing interventions to accelerate learning when students are not yet making expected progress. The process of *formative evaluation* is foundational.

The latter half of this chapter will be devoted to assessments for learning, or using data formatively. In this section, we discuss the purposes of formative evaluation.

USING FORMATIVE EVALUATION

Making Instructional Decisions

Just because you taught something doesn't mean your students have learned what you intended.

As an effective literacy teacher, you know never to equate teaching with learning. After all, just because you taught something doesn't mean your students have learned what you intended. The first function of formative evaluation is to ensure good teaching. Without regularly spaced measures to gauge learning, it is much like teaching in a dark room—how do you ever know if learning is occurring?

This facet of formative evaluation relies mostly on informal checks for understanding of language and literacy. These may come in the form of exit tickets at the end of a lesson, visual gestures such as a thumbs up or thumbs down, or through a short-answer quiz about last week's content after returning from the weekend.

First-grade teacher Arletta Coleridge posts a question about recently taught content for her students to answer as they check in each morning. "I use a tablet for them to sign in digitally every day," she explained. Students select their name (for attendance), their lunch choice, and a word that reflects their emotional status (*happy, excited, confused, sleepy, discombobulated*). "They like that last one in particular," she chuckled. "But it gives me a sense of who I need to check in with early on."

Ms. Coleridge explained that she adds a multiple-choice question about current learning. For instance, one morning she asked her first graders a comprehension question about a story read the previous day. "It gives me great data to know what I need to teach next, or can skip altogether, depending on the answers I get," she said. "I've learned over the years that it prevents me from wasting their time reteaching something they already know, and from moving forward when I really needed to circle back."

Gauging Student Progress

A second purpose for formative evaluation is to incrementally monitor the extent to which individual students are making gains. The description offered by Ms. Granville, the fourth-grade teacher in the opening scenario, is illustrative of this concept. Progress monitoring typically requires a more deliberative approach than that used by Ms. Coleridge with her quick morning check-in.

We usually collect student progress data at specific points in the school year. For example, grade-level interim benchmark assessments are useful for measuring progress toward long-term goals. We may also use skills checklists quarterly to chronicle incremental progress. Many schools use a set of screening tools for kindergarten students to determine what their current level of knowledge is regarding letter recognition, sounds, sight words, and oral language development. We can use these same tools throughout the year to measure and report on progress and to adjust learning as needed.

Without regularly spaced measures to gauge learning, it is much like teaching in a dark room—how do you ever know if learning is occurring?

For instance, when Andrew entered kindergarten, he had already nearly achieved the goal for the end of first grade at his school, which is 100 sight words and 300 easy-to-decode words. During his screening assessment, Andrew read 88 of the sight words and all the easy-to-decode words. Given his high level of literacy achievement on this and several of the other screening tools, his teacher, Jonathan Palomes, knew that he would need to extend Andrew's learning beyond his kindergarten curriculum. We feel the need to point out that the goals his school set for the end of first grade seem reasonable to us, but we do not have research evidence to support those specific numbers.

"My first-grade colleagues were really important. I used their tools as a way to gauge his progress individually," said Mr. Palomes. In addition to a new sight words checklist, he used oral retelling and reading fluency measures that reflected Andrew's advanced reading skills. "That said, his letter formation and writing skills are more consistent with his age group," said Mr. Palomes. "I have to monitor his progress more closely, because he does have literacy skills that are somewhat scattered. Some are typical of an older student, while others are what I expect to see with kindergarteners."

Setting Goals With Students

You have goals for your students, but do they know what they are? A third purpose of formative evaluation is for us to establish goals in partnership with students. Student motivation in reading is closely associated with being able to witness incremental progress toward long-term goals (Guthrie, Wigfield, & Barbosa, 2004). We should do this selectively, as some elements of reading progress take longer to develop. A child's perception that there is a lack of visible progress can have the opposite effect, which is a feeling of discouragement (Förster & Souvignier, 2014). For example, sharing measures of reading comprehension growth every three weeks with a second grader is not advisable, as growth from one level to the next typically takes longer than three weeks to attain. However, measures of volume and personal best data can be motivating. Keeping track of the cumulative number of words they have written each week in their journals or of how many minutes they have read can be rewarding, as the numbers will likely increase across the week and over the months. Tracking mastery of sight words read and new vocabulary words they use in their writing allows students to see that they are accumulating a growing number of words that they "own." In this way, students are able to witness how their daily efforts translate to learning. Providing parents with reports on student-developed literacy goals can be an excellent component of student-led conferences with families.

Sixth-grade teacher Chase Evans meets with his students regularly to monitor student-developed goals. Of major importance to Mr. Evans is the volume his students are reading. "This is precisely the age when competing demands get in the way of reading," he said. "I work in a community that's fairly affluent," he said. "And what I see is lots of sports, rehearsals, and other enrichment activities that fill [students'] schedules. Add the amount of screen time on their devices, and there's no room left for independent reading."

Mr. Evans began the year by sharing evidence with his students about the correlation between reading volume and academic achievement. (See Chapter 7 for a more thorough discussion.) Mr. Evans then challenged his students to keep a reading diary for one week to track the amount of time they spent outside of school reading.

"The kids are blown away when they recognize that most of them do very little in the way of independent reading," he said. Based on their initial findings, he has students develop a goal to increase their reading volume over the course of a month.

Rowan, a student in his class, reported that her average daily reading was two minutes. She remarked, "I have ballet three afternoons a week,

You have goals for your students, but do they know what they are? One purpose of formative evaluation is for us to establish goals in partnership with students.

and youth group at my church one night a week. I realized that if I was going to fit more reading time in, I needed to schedule it." Rowan's first monthly goal was to average 10 minutes a day. "I set up a time tracker on my phone so I could log my minutes," said Rowan. At the end of the first month, she had fallen short of her goal, averaging 7.2 minutes a day. In reviewing her progress with Mr. Evans, she stated that she still wanted to keep the same goal for the following month.

"What might you do differently, so you'll be successful?" Mr. Evans asked. Rowan considered this question, then stated that she realized that waiting until bedtime to read was a problem.

"I fall asleep," she said. "I'm tired." But she also noted that the long commutes to ballet and other events offered possibilities. "Usually I just ride in the car and watch a movie or look out the window," she said. "But I could definitely take my book with me and catch up on some reading during that time," she said.

Rowan's goal of increasing her daily reading volume, while not initially successful in the first month, represented progress. In addition, it leveraged her self-determination to improve. "Rowan's a determined student, and she strives to get better at what she does," said Mr. Evans. "Setting goals with her and the other students is tapping into their increasing ability to make decisions about their choices."

Providing Interventions

Arguably, the most critical function of formative evaluation is as an early alert system for students who are not making expected progress. You have undoubtedly been confronted with observational data that show that a student is slipping behind. She falters during reading instruction, although her group mates seem to be progressing. The written work she produces is labored and brief. The addition of a formative evaluation system in your classroom can increase your ability to trigger interventions early on.

The evidence on early intervention for literacy development is compelling. A series of studies were made of a kindergarten early intervention program that screened for early evidence of reading difficulties, using indicators such as letter identification. Children that scored in the 30th percentile or lower received supplemental interventions and were closely monitored using a response to intervention (RTI) process. Those children who continued to struggle in first grade received additional intensive interventions. By the end of third grade, only 16% of those initially identified as being at risk in kindergarten were still performing below grade-level expectations (Vellutino, Scanlon, Zhang, & Schatschneider, 2008).

> You have undoubtedly been confronted with observational data that show that a student is slipping behind.

There is not a single meta-analysis of in-grade retention that demonstrates a positive academic outcome for students.

And while intervention at the beginning of schooling is optimal, the RTI process has been demonstrated to be effective with older students as well. A related study of fourth graders whose intervention focused on reading comprehension reported similar successes (Gelzheiser, Scanlon, Vellutino, Hallgren-Flynn, & Schatschneider, 2011).

Our enthusiasm for RTI is grounded in a strong evidence base and the contrastive damage of in-grade retention as a default mechanism for students not making expected progress. Hattie's analyses on RTI report an effect size of 1.09, well above the average impact of .40. Now consider the troubling evidence that 50 years of in-grade retention studies have yielded an effect size of -0.32, equivalent to nearly a year's *loss* in progress (Hattie, 2018). In fact, there is not a single meta-analysis of in-grade retention that demonstrates a positive academic outcome for students. Any initial gains disappear within a couple of years of the retention. Without question, caring educators and concerned families have made these retention decisions in the sincere belief that a "do-over" would give the child a chance to catch up. Sadly, the evidence does not support this. Quite the opposite, in fact. Early grade retention is a strong predictor of dropping out in high school (Cratty, 2012; Hughes, Cao, West, Allee Smith, & Cerda, 2017). Given that lack of literacy progress is a primary factor cited in retention decisions, it is vital that children demonstrating early warning signs of failure in reading and writing receive early and sustained interventions.

Palo Verde Elementary School is determined to interrupt this dropout pattern by using response to intervention to intercede on behalf of students displaying signs of reading failure. Like many schools, Palo Verde uses a three-tiered approach:

- Tier 1: quality core instruction, including screening, for all students

- Tier 2: supplemental interventions delivered to small groups in the classroom

- Tier 3: targeted intensive supports delivered to individual students

Abril Silva, principal of Palo Verde, explains that students are screened at the beginning of each year to establish a baseline of literacy and math skills and knowledge. "We use the DIBELs and IDEL (Spanish) as a quick measure of reading skills for our primary students," explained Dr. Silva. "Any student who is flagged for further follow-up is identified, and the classroom teachers prioritize their teacher-based assessments so those children are assessed first." Based on the results of their measures, students are immediately scheduled for additional Tier 2 supplemental interventions in the classroom.

"These are mainly done by the classroom teacher," said Dr. Silva. "They include additional small-group needs-based instruction. The main thing is that we wanted the most highly trained person in the room working with the hardest-to-teach students. We're fortunate enough to have parent volunteers. We deploy them to work during these times with the children who are on grade level. It frees up the teacher to deliver intervention, without sending students out to someone else. It's part of the classroom structure."

Dr. Silva acknowledged that monitoring progress at Tier 2 is a long-term investment. "We don't expect to see transformation in a few weeks," she said. "Minimally, we're looking at an 18-week investment." She also noted that students who have received Tier 2 supplemental interventions are tracked closely throughout their academic years at the school, even if they are not currently participating in an intervention. "That's part of an early warning system, right? Once you see students who have demonstrated difficulty, you owe it to them to watch over them closely. If they stumble, we want to be there to catch them."

A smaller number of students are less responsive to intervention at Tier 2 and require the more intensive targeted supports that Tier 3 offers. "In first grade, it's Reading Recovery or Descubriendo la Lectura," said the principal. "In other grade levels, classroom teachers, our reading specialist, the librarian, and the biliteracy coach are all working with individual students." She explained that in order to minimize disruption of core education, the grade levels organize their schedules to make time for Tier 3 interventions. "It takes some juggling, but to the best of our abilities we want to make sure these most vulnerable students aren't missing out on core instruction." In doing so, the school has embraced the idea that RTI is part and parcel of a viable curriculum, and the fact that some students will need intervention should not come as a surprise to anyone.

> A smaller number of students are less responsive to intervention at Tier 2 and require the more intensive targeted supports that Tier 3 offers.

Dr. Silva attributed a schoolwide approach to RTI as a key to their collective success. In the four years since the initiative began, retentions dropped from an average of eight per year in kindergarten and first grade to zero.

"Retention isn't an intervention," she said. "It's just kicking the problem down the road and hoping for the best." Long-term tracking of these students has allowed them to deliver what she calls "academic booster shots." She said that one dose of intervention isn't always enough, and that they have found success with setting aside eight-week periods for delivering short follow-up Tier 2 interventions for students who remain below grade level. "We don't necessarily sustain these follow-up interventions across the whole year. Instead, we designate a specific period where it is all hands on deck."

These efforts have paid off. Dr. Silva reports that by the end of third grade, the majority of students initially identified in kindergarten are within range of grade-level performance. "It doesn't mean that they're all necessarily *on* grade level," she said. "But the research evidence is that even modest improvements in reading and writing translate to success in school over the long term. And isn't that what we're supposed to be doing?"

ASSESSMENTS FOR LEARNING: USING DATA FORMATIVELY

The tools one uses to make instruction decisions, gauge progress, set goals with students, and provide interventions are crucial. The assessments we highlight here are especially useful for formative evaluation. Some of these are normed, while others are teacher-developed assessments. It is likely that you have your own favorites that are not mentioned here. Our intent is not to provide an extensive review of assessment tools, as there are many fine publications that provide a comprehensive review of instruments. In addition, your reading and language arts curriculum instructional materials probably include a plethora of similar assessment tools. Here, we organize our list by elements of literacy domains and provide illustrative examples of types of instruments to consider in a formative evaluation system for your classroom.

ASSESSMENTS FOR LEARNING IN READING

Reading development in elementary school is breathtaking in its scope. Most children arrive at the age of 5 with little formal knowledge of reading, but some experiential knowledge from being in the company of books. In a short period of time, they are learning the sounds and alphabetics of the language, and how the two work together. In addition, they are building knowledge, evidenced through their growing vocabulary and comprehension skills. Measures of these reading skills and strategies provide you with details about your students' progress in reading. In fact, we like to call these *informative assessments* because they can equip you with the data you need to make decisions about reading instruction and intervention.

Reading development in elementary school is breathtaking in its scope. Most children arrive at the age of 5 with little formal knowledge of reading. In a short period of time, they are learning the sounds and alphabetics of the language.

Concepts About Print

Most young children entering kindergarten have at least some experience with books. Many have been read to since infancy, and these early interactions with caregivers sets the stage for their reading development (Swick, 2009). Concepts About Print was first identified by Clay (1979) as a measure of familiarity with books and the early book handling skills of emergent readers (see Figure 9.1 on the next page).

Kindergarten teacher Keith Wu tracks his students' growing concepts about print beginning in the first days of school. "I meet with each of them for just two or three minutes to get a sense of what they know," he says. Mr. Wu invites each student to a small table where he has several books displayed and asks them to select one. "I start with just asking them about the front and back covers of the book, and I watch them turn the pages," he explains. Over the next two weeks of the school year, he moves on to other questions about locating the title, using directionality, and locating print. "I used to do these all in one sitting," he said, "but I've found that for me, these quick conversations at the beginning of a small-group lesson are more natural. Plus, I can go back to them [the assessments] periodically to chart when they have mastered these skills and to figure out who needs more assistance."

> Kindergarten teacher Keith Wu tracks his students' growing concepts about print beginning in the first days of school. "I meet with each of them for just two or three minutes to get a sense of what they know."

Phonological Awareness

A key substrate of learning to read is the ability to process the sounds of the language. You will recall from earlier chapters that these smallest units of sound are called phonemes, and there are 44 in the English language. *Phonological awareness* (PA) is a broader term that describes a progression of knowledge of how sounds, and eventually phonemes, are manipulated. These skills track developmentally, from early to late phases of PA development (Chard & Dickson, 1999):

1. *Rhyming words* (e.g., away/day/play in the nursery rhyme "Rain, Rain Go Away")

2. *Sentence segmentation* (e.g., clapping for each word in a sentence)

3. *Syllable segmentation and blending* (e.g., clapping twice for the word *pen-cil*)

4. *Onset-rime, blending, and segmentation* (e.g., separating r/at in the word *rat*, and putting the sounds h/at together to say *hat*)

5. *Blending and segmenting individual phonemes* (e.g., separating p/a/t as three distinct phonemes, and putting the three phonemes of h/a/t together to say *hat*).

▼ FIGURE 9.1 EARLY CONCEPTS OF PRINT CHECKLIST

Name: _____ Teacher: _____

Grade Level: _____

Directions: Choose a picture book with large print and a variety of punctuation marks. Tell the child you will read the story but you will need some help. Note responses to the prompts in the right column.

Concepts About Print Prompts

Front of book	Hand book to child upside down. "Show me the front cover of the book."	
Title and author	"This book is called _____ and it is written by _____. Show me where that's written."	
Turns pages	"Show me how to open the book."	
Locates print	Turn to first page of story. "I'm going to read this to you. Show me where to begin reading." Correct response is pointing to a word on first page.	
Directionality on page	"Show me which way to read the words." Correct response indicates left to right.	
Return sweep	On a page with more than one line of print: "Which way do I go when I get to the end of the first line?"	
1:1 correspondence	"Point to the words while I read."	
Beginning and end of story	"Show me the beginning of the story." "Show me the end of the story."	
Period	Point to a period at the end of a sentence. "What does this mean?"	
Question mark	Point to a question mark at the end of a sentence. "What does this mean?"	
Directionality within words	Point to a word with at least three letters. "Show me the first letter in the word." "Show me the last letter in the word."	

Notes:

Source: Fisher, D., Frey, N., & Hattie, J. (2017). *Teaching literacy in the visible learning classroom, grades K–5.* Thousand Oaks, CA: Corwin.

A useful measure of this last stage of phonological awareness is the *Yopp-Singer Test of Phonemic Segmentation* (Yopp, 1995). This assessment is used in the second half of kindergarten and first half of first grade, as students advance in their ability to process the sounds of the language, which is key to developing phonics skills. The Yopp-Singer is a 22-item assessment and is administered individually to students (see Figure 9.2).

▼ FIGURE 9.2 YOPP-SINGER TEST OF PHONEMIC SEGMENTATION

Name: _____ Date: _____

Score (number correct): _____

Directions: Today we're going to play a word game. I'm going to say a word and I want you to break the word apart. You are going to tell me each sound in the word in order. For example, if I say "old," you should say "/o/-/l/-d/."

(Administrator: Be sure to say the sounds, not the letters, in the word.) Let's try a few together. Practice items: *(Assist the child in segmenting these items as necessary.)* ride, go, man

Test items: *(Circle those items that the student correctly segments; incorrect responses may be recorded on the blank line following the item.)*

1. dog _____	12. lay _____
2. keep _____	13. race _____
3. fine _____	14. zoo _____
4. no _____	15. three _____
5. she _____	16. job _____
6. wave _____	17. in _____
7. grew _____	18. ice _____
8. that _____	19. at _____
9. red _____	20. top _____
10. me _____	21. by _____
11. sat _____	22. do _____

Source: Yopp, H. K. (1995). A test for assessing phonemic awareness in young children. *The Reading Teacher, 49,* 20–29. Used with permission. (The author, Hallie Kay Yopp, California State University, Fullerton, grants permission for this text to be reproduced. The author acknowledges the contribution of the late Harry Singer to the development of this test.)

First-grade teacher Lorena Kirby was concerned that one of her students, Xavier, was not making expected progress in phoneme segmentation. Although it was the end of the first semester, Xavier had still not mastered all the items on the Yopp-Singer. Ms. Kirby met with her first-grade colleagues to discuss results and to identify students like Xavier who were demonstrating difficulty with this skill. Ms. Kirby and her team discussed each of the six first graders that had not made expected progress and examined other assessment data about these children. The team identified each of them as being candidates for Tier 2 supplemental instruction, which included additional practice using Elkonin sound boxes (see Chapter 2) and other activities such as Guess the Covered Word, which exposes a secret word one letter at a time.

"What we don't want to do is teach an isolated skill that is artificially separated from all the other learning that they are doing," said Ms. Kirby after the meeting. "That's why we also identified ways we could infuse more practice into our Tier 1 core instruction for these students. So when I am meeting with Xavier in his reading group, I am also specifically asking him questions that give him more practice with segmenting and blending sounds."

Measures of Letter Recognition and Letter Sounds

Measures of alphabetic knowledge, specifically letter recognition, represent the first critical skills of decoding. Some children enter kindergarten already knowing all the uppercase and lowercase letters, while others may only recognize the first letter of their name. A simple way to assess letter identification is to use flashcards of letters, with no pictures to influence students' answers.

"I'm not surprised at the beginning of the year when I learn that a child doesn't know the name of more infrequently seen letters, such *v*, *q*, *d*, and *l*," said kindergarten teacher Cynthia Washington. "But I am concerned when a child doesn't know O, and B, and X," she said. "That's when I focus on having them identify letters in their name," she explained. "I want to see what they already know about the alphabet, because it gives me a good sense of their exposure to print."

Phonics

The school where Ms. Washington teaches uses the CORE Phonics Survey as a way to gauge progress for their students from kindergarten through grade 2 (http://cbl.jordandistrict.org/files/CORE-PHONICS-SURVEY.pdf). "We digitally pass the assessment data along from one grade level to the next to monitor these milestones and to trigger interventions as needed," she said. The CORE Phonics Survey, which is available in English and in Spanish, contains the following items:

* *Alphabet skills and letter sounds*, including long and short vowel sounds

* *Reading and decoding skills*, including CVC, consonant blends, digraphs, trigraphs, *r*-controlled vowels, and multisyllabic words

The teachers at this school assess both accuracy and automaticity. Accuracy allows teachers to identify areas of need and allows them to place students in the right level of phonics instruction. Automaticity provides teachers with information about mastery and decayed learning, and this information is also used to guide instruction.

A simple way to assess letter identification is to use flashcards of letters, with no pictures to influence students' answers.

Cindy Charles/PhotoEdit

"I use some of these results to show my students their progress," said Ms. Washington. "I can tell them, 'In September you knew 7 letter names, and today you know 16!' It gives them a sense of their learning progress, and it is something they can tell their family about. I send home a note with the child sharing the news of their progress so that parents can share their child's success."

Sight Word Recognition

As emergent and early readers learn to read, they acquire a growing ability to recognize some words, especially high-frequency words, using minimal decoding skills. Texts designed for young readers may be composed of 70% or more sight words (e.g., *the, is, a, that, as, and, to*) and easily decoded words (*hat, pig, car*). The most common lists of sight words are the Dolch lists, which are segmented into several lists from kindergarten through third grade (https://sightwords.com/sight-words/dolch/#lists).

Tracking the progress of students as they master sight words can provide an excellent measure of student progress in mastering commonly used words that appear in their texts. Of course, simply drilling students on isolated words is not adequate reading instruction. But using sight word lists can serve as an insight into which students may be lagging in their reading development.

The second-grade team at Harriet Tubman Elementary School assesses its students' sight word knowledge up to three times a year. Robin Hammond explains that "some of our students already know the second-grade list of Dolch words in August, but others are still working toward them. For those that have not mastered all the words, we check in again in November and, as needed, in February."

The results are shared with students and their families, who have expressed appreciation at knowing to highlight particular words as they encounter them during at-home reading time. "We always want them to learn these words in context," said Ms. Hammond, "and this is a simple measure on the reading dashboard. Just as a speedometer gives drivers their speed, it gives us as teachers a way to make sure each child is moving forward."

Oral Reading Fluency

As discussed in Chapter 5, reading fluency is a gauge of a reader's ability to read accurately and smoothly. The ability to do so is an important component of automaticity, which is the recognition of words such that we only need a low level of attention to read them. Reading fluently allows the reader to focus more attention on meaning, rather than decoding individual words. Prosody in reading fluency emerges in second and third grade, as students move from what Chall (1983) called "grunting and groaning" to "ungluing from print" (p. 11). Rate and accuracy are essential components of measures of fluency, as is prosody, which is expressive reading using intonation, phrase boundaries, and pace. The best way to gauge prosody is to listen to students as they read aloud. The reading prosody scale first developed as a measure of fourth-grade prosody for the National Assessment of Educational Progress (NAEP) is easy

Simply drilling students on isolated words is not adequate reading instruction. But using sight word lists can serve as an insight into which students may be lagging in their reading development.

to use and can provide you and the student with a way to discuss progress (Daane, Campbell, Grigg, Goodman, & Oranje, 2005). The prosody scale can be found in Figure 9.3.

▼ FIGURE 9.3 NATIONAL ASSESSMENT OF EDUCATIONAL PROGRESS FLUENCY SCALE

Fluent	**Level 4**	Reads primarily in larger, meaningful phrase groups. Although some regressions, repetitions, and deviations from text may be present, these do not appear to detract from the overall structure of the story. Preservation of the author's syntax is consistent. Some or most of the story is read with expressive interpretation.
Fluent	**Level 3**	Reads primarily in three- or four-word phrase groups. Some small groupings may be present. However, the majority of phrasing seems appropriate and preserves the syntax of the author. Little or no expressive interpretation is present.
Non-fluent	**Level 2**	Reads primarily in two-word phrases with some three- or four-word groupings. Some word-by-word reading may be present. Word groupings may seem awkward and unrelated to larger context of sentence or passage.
Non-fluent	**Level 1**	Reads primarily word-by-word. Occasional two-word or three-word phrases may occur but these are infrequent and/or they do not preserve meaningful syntax.

Source: Daane, M. C., Campbell, J. R., Grigg, W. S., Goodman, M. J., & Oranje, A. (2005). *Fourth-grade students reading aloud: NAEP 2002 special study of oral reading* (NCES 2006-469). Washington, DC: U.S. Department of Education, Institute of Education Sciences, National Center for Education Statistics.

The number of words a student reads correctly provides further insight into the fluency development of your students. Oral reading fluency (ORF) normed expectations are reported as the number of words read correctly per minute (WCPM). These ORF norms for students in grades 1–8 were updated in 2017 by Hasbrouck and Tindal, and can be found at www.brtprojects.org/publications/technical-reports/. The authors note that because these are norms, the goal should be for students to perform in the 51st to 75th percentile range. In other words, reading faster doesn't make you a better reader. There is no reason to cajole a student who is comprehending grade-level texts in this ORF range to read at an even higher rate.

Fifth-grade teacher Dave Chang uses reading fluency measures formatively with students who he has identified for Tier 2 and Tier 3 interventions. Mr. Chang assesses all of his students at the beginning of the school year, and uses these periodic measures to set goals with students who are not yet at expected levels. For his students scoring below the 50th percentile on a measure of ORF, and for those nonfluent in prosody, he shares results as well as the prosody table (shown in Figure 9.3). "I don't want them to obsess on fluency, but I do want them to be mindful. Fluency is a doorway to understanding what they're reading," said Mr. Chang.

Kincaid, a student who in August scored at the 25th percentile in ORF and at Level 2 (Non-fluent) in prosody, set a goal for himself of getting to the 50th percentile by midyear. The boy said, "I was 85 words a minute at the beginning of the school year, and Mr. Chang showed me I was supposed to be at least 110. I always felt like I read pretty slow. I didn't know it mattered, though." Kincaid set a goal of being at 127 WCPM in January. (Norms increase across the school year.) "I know it's a big goal, but I think I can hit it," said Kincaid. "My mom and I are reading the Percy Jackson series together," he said. "I like the books because he's a demigod and stuff. So sometimes I have her [mom] time me for a few minutes when it's my turn so I can see how I'm doing."

"I appreciate what his mom is doing," Mr. Chang added. "Lots of parents don't know that this is a goal they can help with."

Informal Reading Inventories

Many districts use informal reading inventories (IRIs) as a means for creating a comprehensive reading profile for each student. In addition to their breadth, IRIs provide consistency across the elementary years, not just within a single school year. The results are readily understood by teachers and parents, who become familiar with how findings are interpreted. IRIs are criterion referenced, meaning that they assess students against a fixed set of learning criteria, rather than against their age or grade-level group. They come with a gradient of narrative and informational reading passages, as well as word lists, fluency measures, and a script of questions to ensure reliable administration. Because IRIs are administered individually, they are more time consuming, but they are well worth the effort because of the quality of information they yield (Walpole & McKenna, 2006).

The teachers at Grant Avenue Elementary decided to reevaluate the use of IRIs in their school, with an eye toward selecting a tool they could use across grades K–6.

"Over the years, teachers had drifted toward a patchwork of instruments," explained reading coach LaShawn Martel. "Certain teachers or grade levels might use one, but then the teachers in the higher grades used something else. It was hard to track how our students were doing over the course of their time at Grant," said Dr. Martel.

A working group of grade-level representatives, the reading coach, and the district coordinator for language arts met over a period of two months to screen instruments.

"We started with each grade rep polling colleagues to find out what they were using," said Dr. Martel. "Then we got all the IRIs together and talked about features, strengths, and drawbacks."

> Informal reading inventories provide consistency across the elementary years, not just within a single school year. The results are readily understood by teachers and parents, who become familiar with how findings are interpreted.

The Grant Avenue work group used a process designed by Flippo, Holland, McCarthy, and Swinning (2009) to guide their discussions and their decision making (see Figure 9.4 on the next page). "We compared each IRI against what we needed," Dr. Martel concluded. "They're all good, but we wanted to figure out what's good for Grant. There's a renewed commitment to using IRIs consistently, and that's good for our students."

Maze Assessment

There are times when you want to make some decisions about reading materials in advance of instruction, such as when you are preparing to engage in a nonfiction unit of study using a set of reading materials you're not quite sure how to use with your students. A maze procedure is a quick and useful way of gaining a sense of what students can comprehend. The maze procedure bears some similarities to a cloze procedure, but it is faster to administer and especially well suited for students in grades 2–6. The maze procedure is a 300-word passage with every seventh word omitted. For each omitted word, students circle one of three choices that have been arranged in random order. One is the correct missing word, the second is an incorrect word that is the same part of speech, and the third is an incorrect word that comes from a different part of speech. (In a cloze procedure, the student must write in a word, and no choices are provided.) Consider this sentence:

> Avril and Donovan couldn't wait for (<u>school</u>/tree/going) to begin, because it meant seeing (<u>all</u>, me, tray) their friends after a long summer (<u>vacation</u>/laboratory/amazing).

In this example, the underlined word is the correct one. In practice, the correct word is not underlined, and the order of the correct word and the two foils varies. The maze assessment is timed at three minutes, and students read silently and circle the word they believe restores the meaning. The first sentence of the passage is left intact so that students can initially orient themselves to the topic of the text. A free automated maze passage generator is available at www.interventioncentral.org/teacher-resources/test-of-reading-comprehension and generates foils using a list of common English words.

Second-grade teacher Diamond Redding uses maze procedures in two ways. The first way is with the entire class as a way to make some decisions about using reading materials for collaborative and independent reading. She explains, "Next week I'm going to begin a unit in my reading block on adaptations in nature. I've got lots of books included in the unit, more than I actually need. So I did a maze assessment using a passage from the target book to make some choices about grouping for book clubs."

▼ FIGURE 9.4 QUESTIONS TO ASK WHEN SELECTING AN INFORMAL READING INVENTORY

Step I: Examine your own reading instruction and assessment beliefs or perspective. Indicate with a check mark whether a particular IRI is relevant or suitable for your classroom needs.

Step II: Review the content:
_____ 1. What does this IRI measure?
_____ 2. What specific reading behaviors does it assess?
_____ 3. If the IRI is grade specific, is there a variety of assessments for each?
_____ 4. What grade levels and range(s) are included?
_____ 5. Are the word recognition lists embedded in sentences or text, or are they out of context?
_____ 6. Is this IRI available in other languages for my ELLs?

Step III: Questions about passages:
_____ 7. What are the sources of the passages? Are they written for the IRI or are they from actual published children's texts or literature?
_____ 8. Are both expository and narrative texts, in various genres and subject areas, used for the student readings?
_____ 9. Are the readings interesting and appealing to students of all levels?
_____ 10. What length are the passages?
_____ 11. Is the material culturally, linguistically, and cognitively appropriate for all my students?

Step IV: Measuring comprehension:
_____ 12. Do the reading passages rely heavily on background knowledge for comprehension?
_____ 13. Does the opening of the passage provide sufficient information to assist students with little schemata?
_____ 14. Do the comprehension questions include all areas of comprehension—literal, inferential, and critical?
_____ 15. Are there enough comprehension and vocabulary questions per selection?
_____ 16. Are metacognitive questions included?
_____ 17. Does the IRI include pictures or illustrations appropriate to the text, or other commonly used context aids?

Step V: Administering the IRI:
_____ 18. Overall, is the IRI easy to use and understand?
_____ 19. How are data collected on each student? Are the data sheets provided adequate?
_____ 20. Do you have to purchase parallel forms of the IRI, or are they included?
_____ 21. Does the author provide an explanation of each subtest?
_____ 22. What criteria are used to determine independent, instructional, and frustration levels? Do I agree which miscues (errors) will be counted?
_____ 23. Can a teacher easily administer this IRI with her or his own choice of reading selections?

Step VI: Interpreting results and instructional follow-up:
_____ 24. Does the IRI provide instructions for interpreting the results?
_____ 25. Does it provide suggestions for instruction?
_____ 26. Is this IRI going to help me understand the needs, strengths, skills, and strategies of my students?
_____ 27. Will the information I learn about my students be worth the time it will take me to administer this assessment?

Step VII: Reflections on overall suitability:

Source: Flippo, R. F., Holland, D. D., McCarthy, M. T., & Swinning, E. A. (2009). Asking the right questions: How to select an informal reading inventory. _Reading Teacher, 63_(1), 79–83. Used with permission.

Based on other information she has about her students' academic abilities and behavior, as well as their performance on the maze assessment, she identified 10 of her students as being good candidates to read _How and Why Do Animals Adapt?_ (Kalman, 2000) in book club groups. "They did well on the maze passage I gave them. They all scored 80% or higher. Book clubs are new for us. We just finished our first one. We all read the same book for that one. Now I'm going to try two in the room," said Ms. Redding.

The teacher also uses maze passages for monitoring purposes. "I don't make those," she said. "They are already prepared. The whole school uses these [prepared] maze assessments three times a year as a benchmark for all students to measure basic reading comprehension," said Ms. Redding. "They're quick to administer and score."

Measures of Print Exposure

There are a plethora of other reading assessments available—far too many to be named in one chapter. However, one type of assessment that is rarely used, easy to administer, and quite informative are those that measure a child's exposure to print. These most often consist of a few dozen children's book title names, or names of children's book authors, as well as foils (items that are not book titles or authors, respectively). Students are asked simply to check those that are real. Title and author recognition tests are strongly predictive of a child's vocabulary knowledge, spelling ability, verbal fluency, and general knowledge (Cunningham & Stanovich, 1990).

Because sociocultural forces impact what one reads, these lists of real and pseudo titles or names should be locally constructed to reflect current trends. For instance, the original Title Recognition Test developed by Cunningham and Stanovich (1990) includes a lovely book called _Homer_

Price, written by Robert McCloskey in 1951. However, relatively few children might recognize the title today, as it is not as widely read as in earlier decades.

Alyson Burnette uses a title recognition test she devised to gain a sense of the reading habits of her fourth-grade students. "I deliberately choose authors and stories that have not appeared in the reading and language arts comprehensive program we use in our district," she said. During the first week of school, Ms. Burnette gives her students a 26-item checklist called "Real or Fake?" to gauge their exposure. "I try to give a whole range of titles that might have been read outside of school, like the graphic novel *Bone* (Smith, 2004). I also have to watch out for books that have been made into movies or TV shows," she said ruefully. "I've lost a few good titles in the last few years because of movie adaptations." Not all of the books and authors are current ones, however. "I keep *The Westing Game* (Raskin, 1978) on my list because it tells me something about the child who has read it," she said. "That's a kid who loves mystery and uses logic and reasoning," said Ms. Burnette. The teacher also includes the names of authors they will be reading during their fourth-grade year with her. "I've got Christopher Paul Curtis, Alma Flor Ada, and Patricia McKissack on there because we'll be reading them this year," she said. As for the foils? "I use names from my high school yearbook!"

Automatic letter writing is "the single best predictor of length and quality of written composition in the elementary grades" (Graham, Berninger, Abbot, Abbot, & Whitaker, 1997, p. 170).

ASSESSMENTS FOR LEARNING IN WRITING

Continuous attention to the development of students' writing and composing skills in elementary school is crucial in the balanced literacy classroom. However, too often assessment of writing takes a backseat to reading assessments. Yet while you will encounter students who can read but not write well, you won't find a writer who can't read. The ability to write, encode (spell), and compose are integral to reading gains and appear to be woven together at the neurological level in ways that are not fully understood (e.g., Purcell, Turkeltaub, Eden, & Rapp, 2011; Rapp & Lipka, 2011). Regular monitoring of progress in writing skills, including letter formation, writing fluency, spelling, and composition, pays off not only in the area of writing but in reading development as well.

Letter Formation

Young children often learn to "draw" some letters even before they enter formal schooling. However, writing these letters, as opposed to drawing the shapes of them, is a process that takes more formal instruction. Automaticity is a major goal in letter formation, as children learn to write smoothly and legibly. Automatic letter writing is "the single best pre-dictor of length and quality of written composition in the elementary grades" (Graham, Berninger, Abbot, Abbot, & Whitaker, 1997, p. 170).

Most kindergarten and first-grade screening assessments feature an assessment of letter formation. If you don't have access to one, you can create your own to utilize periodically to gauge growth and identify students who need more specialized support. Consider these elements as you assess the letter formation of your students.

- **Uppercase and lowercase:** There is usually a disparity between the number of uppercase letters a child is able to produce (more) versus lowercase ones (less). Ask students to write each.

- **Model or not?** One decision point is whether you want students to copy each letter form or produce it from memory. There is a rationale for each approach, but we like to stick with the same procedure each time to ensure reliability of the assessment.

- **Watch the student write:** There is a temptation with writing assessments to turn away, but the information you gain from actually watching them is invaluable. Are they correctly using downward strokes when writing *b, d, k, t, g, j, p, q,* and *y*? Or are they incorrectly using ascending strokes that begin at the baseline? Are they gripping the pencil correctly? Do they steady the paper with the helper hand? We make note of these actions, as they are temporal and not in evidence once the assessment is completed.

First-grade teacher Catherine Samuels is grateful for the letter formation assessments her kindergarten colleagues collect and analyze. "When I get a new class, I also get all the assessment data the children's teachers collected last year, provided they attended this school," said Ms. Samuels. "To be sure, it's a lot of data, but it's worth it," she said. "I don't have to start from zero in trying to learn about my new students." Ms. Samuels explained the value of the letter formation assessments. "When I first started teaching, I thought this was just about printing, but I realize that it's a valuable glimpse into what else students can do."

Using the kindergarten data as a baseline, she and her first-grade colleagues add new tasks to augment those already mastered the previous year. Ms. Samuels explained that the new tasks involve copying a full sentence posted nearby ("they need more hand-eye coordination and visual memory to do so") and writing a sentence that has been dictated to them ("I get to see their auditory memory in action"). The dictation task, Ms. Samuels cautions, allows for the sentence to be repeated to the student as many times as they request. "But I also make a note of how many times I need to repeat it." She offered that the big challenge for

Young children often learn to "draw" some letters even before they enter formal schooling. However, writing these letters, as opposed to drawing the shapes of them, is a process that takes more formal instruction.

her is to not slip into coaching when a student gets stuck. "If they do get stuck, I just tell them that what they did was fine, and we'll be learning all these new skills this year. My purpose is to figure out what to teach, and to whom," she said. "But I can't make good decisions if I don't know what they can do and not do yet."

Spelling

If there is one area of literacy that has undergone a radical shift since we were in school, it is spelling. Each of us recalls having a spelling textbook with weekly lessons, a list of words to memorize, a bunch of activities to complete for homework, and a test every Friday. But developmental spelling has revolutionized spelling instruction, which is now embedded within vocabulary and writing. Encoding (another word for spelling) is now understood not as an exercise in memorization, but rather as woven into a child's understanding of oral language, reading, meaning, and the rules that govern how words are spelled. Henderson (1990) described developmental stages of spelling that are widely utilized in reading and language arts programs. The ages provided are approximations, as individual students vary somewhat in their development:

- **Emergent:** Uses few or no sound associations (ages 1–7)

- **Letter name:** Spells by sound (ages 4–9)

- **Within word:** Uses familiar patterns to spell one-syllable words (ages 6–12)

- **Syllable juncture:** Uses syllables and double consonants to arrive at spellings (ages 8–12)

- **Derivational constancy:** Uses word origins to spell new words (ages 10+)

As you can see from the age spans for each stage, several developmental groups are likely to be represented in a single classroom. That was the case for fourth-grade teacher Christie Saban. Her beginning-of-the-year developmental spelling screening (see Figures 9.5 and 9.6) revealed that she had three different groups in her class. "The majority of my students this year are early in the Syllable Juncture stage," said Ms. Saban. "That's what I would expect. But I've got five kids who are a little behind. They're still at the Within Word stage. And I was even more surprised to find out that one girl is already at Derivational Constancy."

Ms. Saban said that the developmental spelling screening she does helps her set up spelling groups. "But I'll be doing this again with the Within Word groups at the end of the first quarter," she said. "Some of them are on the bubble, and I want to move them forward as fast as possible."

▼ FIGURE 9.5 DEVELOPMENTAL SPELLING ANALYSIS SCREENING INVENTORY

Directions: I am going to say some words that I want you to spell for me. Some of the words will be easy to spell, and some will be more difficult. When you don't know how to spell a word, just do the best you can. Each time, I will say the word, then use it in a sentence, and then I will say the word again.

1.	hen	The hen sat on her eggs.
2.	wish	The boy made a wish and blew out the candles.
3.	trap	A spider web is a trap for flies.
4.	jump	A kangaroo can jump high.
5.	brave	A brave dog scared the robbers.
6.	smile	A smile shows that you're happy.
7.	grain	One kind of grain is called wheat.
8.	crawl	The baby can crawl but not walk.
9.	clerk	The clerk sold some shoes to me.
10.	clutch	The clutch in the car needs fixing.
11.	palace	The king and queen live in a palace.
12.	observe	I like to observe birds at the feeder.
13.	shuffle	Please shuffle the cards before you deal.
14.	exciting	The adventure story I'm reading is very exciting.
15.	treason	The man was found guilty of treason.
16.	column	His picture was in the first column of the newspaper.
17.	variety	A grocery store has a wide variety of foods.
18	extension	The workers need an extension ladder to reach the roof.
19.	competition	There was much competition between the two businesses.
20.	illiterate	An illiterate person is one who cannot read.

Stop when a child has spelled no words or 1 word correctly out of any set of five.

Source: Ganske, K. (1999). The developmental spelling analysis: A measure of orthographic knowledge. *Educational Assessment*, 6(10, 41–70). Reprinted by permission of Taylor & Francis, Ltd.

▼ FIGURE 9.6 DEVELOPMENTAL SPELLING ANALYSIS INVENTORY PREDICTION CHART

Letter Name (LN)—Students learn about beginning sounds, blends (bl, sl, etc.), word families, and short-vowel sounds. This is the stage in which students are usually taught to read.

Within Word (WW)—Students spell most short-vowel sounds correctly, and they learn about long-vowel sounds and patterns in one-syllable words. In this stage, students can read and spell many words correctly because of their automatic knowledge of letter sounds and short-vowel patterns.

Syllable Juncture (SJ)—Students learn about the conventions of joining syllables in words with two or more syllables. Students are expected to spell many words of more than one syllable. Students consider spelling patterns where syllables meet and at meaning units such as affixes (prefixes and suffixes).

Derivational Constancy (DC)—Students learn that meaning as well as sound and pattern are important in the spelling of the English language. This last stage in the developmental model continues through adulthood.

Inventory Score	Predicted Stage(s)	Inventory Score	Predicted Stage(s)
20	DC	10	WW/SJ
19	DC	9	WW
18	DC	8	WW
17	DC	7	WW
16	SJ/DC	6	LN/WW
15	SJ/DC	5	LN/WW
14	SJ	4	LN
13	SJ	3	LN
12	SJ	2	LN
11	WW/SJ	1	LN*
		0	LN*
			* Children who achieve a score of 0 or 1 may or may not be letter name spellers.

Source: Ganske, K. (1999). The developmental spelling analysis: A measure of orthographic knowledge. *Educational Assessment*, 6(10), 41–70. Reprinted by permission of Taylor & Francis, Ltd.

Ms. Saban went on to say, "There's nothing worse than being stuck in a group that isn't meeting your needs. It's up to me to get them going. 'As fast as we can, as slow as we must.' That's my philosophy for teaching and learning."

Writing Fluency

Accurate and automatic letter formation and spelling contribute positively to writing fluency, which is the ability to compose meaningful text quickly and smoothly. As with any skill, regular practice in writing is necessary for fluency to develop. After all, it is hard to get better at something you rarely do. Yet a national survey of third- and fourth-grade teachers revealed that their students spent only 25 minutes a day in total actually writing (Brindle, Graham, Harris, & Hebert, 2016). At a time when students should be becoming increasingly more fluent in their writing, these findings suggest they get little opportunity to practice.

Daily timed writing provides both practice and assessment data the student can use to monitor progress and goal attainment. These power writing sessions, which are detailed in Chapter 3, contribute to the overall development of literacy and build young writers' stamina to engage in on-demand writing (Fisher & Frey, 2007). Again, the directions for daily power writing are simple. Each day, students engage in three 60-second rounds of writing, when they are asked to compose "as much as you can, as well as you can." You might furnish a word or phrase for students to use as inspiration, but it isn't necessary for them to actually use it. At the end of each round, students tally the overall number of words written and circle any misspellings or other errors they made. After three rounds, students graph the highest number of words written. Because the volume of writing quickly adds up, we suggest that students have a power writing notebook and a sheet of graph paper to chart their progress. It isn't uncommon for intermediate students to average 40 or more words per minute.

Tina Rider meets with her students quarterly to review goals they have set for their learning and to discuss what they are doing to meet them. "Sixth grade is an important year, as they are transitioning to middle school expectations," said Ms. Rider. "One of the data points we look at together is their writing fluency graph and goals," she said. Covelin, one of Ms. Rider's students, had set a goal to average 45 words per minute in timed writing. The teacher and student looked at his third quarter writing fluency graph, noting that he had reached the goal only once in the last nine weeks. More troubling was the fact that this represented a decline from the second quarter.

"What do you think is getting in the way?" Ms. Rider asked Covelin. What followed was a longer discussion about his attitude toward school in general and his social struggles with peers. Ms. Rider later remarked,

"I do daily power writing because I want to build their stamina. But I've found that sometimes just looking at data together with a student can open up other conversations I didn't expect. Their learning is bound up in who they are and how they relate to the world," she said. "Sometimes writing is more than just putting words on a page."

Holistic, Analytic, and Single-Point Rubrics

The qualities and traits of written composition are commonly represented in rubrics. There are two general types of rubrics:

- **Holistic rubrics** yield one overall score for a paper as a whole. A holistic writing rubric might feature four levels, with descriptions for each level of the quality of style and coherence, cohesiveness of ideas, and use of writing conventions. Holistic writing rubrics are easy to use because they yield a single score, and for that reason we commonly use these for large-scale assessments. But they are not very useful for future instruction, because they provide little guidance for how the learner can improve.

- **Analytic writing rubrics** are far more common and provide a means to articulate the characteristics that compose the qualities of writing. These are the familiar rows and columns that describe each criterion in detail. One of the most well known is the 6+1 Trait Writing rubric, which details a range of performance for ideas, organization, voice, word choice, sentence fluency, conventions, and presentation (Education Northwest, 2018).

The mere use of a rubric is not sufficient. While writing rubrics can convey the learning goals, they are not effective without accompanying feedback about current performance and feedback on how to reach the desired level of performance (Wollenschläger, Hattie, Machts, Möller, & Harms, 2016).

But the mere use of a rubric is not sufficient. While writing rubrics can convey the learning goals, they are not effective without accompanying feedback about current performance *and* feedback on how to reach the desired level of performance (Wollenschläger, Hattie, Machts, Möller, & Harms, 2016). In other words, the assessment for learning function is lost on the learner unless there is specific feedback that accompanies it. However, analytic rubrics can be cumbersome for young children, as there is a lot of print to manage. A solution that contributes to the effective use of a writing rubric, while being sensitive to the developmental needs of elementary students, is the single point rubric.

A **single point rubric** provides the student and teacher with a means to communicate using a single dimension of quality. Take, for example, an analytic writing rubric with four column headings—Not in Evidence, Approaching, Proficient, and Advanced. The third column, Proficient, represents the grade-level expectation, while those to the left are below the expectation, and Advanced is above grade-level expectations. Now isolate the Proficient column and place it in the center, with blank columns on either side for students to analyze their own draft writing before submitting it to you. In the left column, they list areas that they feel need more work, and on the right, evidence that they have met or exceeded the learning goals (see Figure 9.7 for an example).

▼ FIGURE 9.7 SINGLE POINT WRITING RUBRIC

Areas That Need Work	Success Criteria	Evidence of Exceeding Standards
	Topic introduced effectively	
	Related ideas grouped together to give some organization	
	Topic developed with multiple facts, definitions, and details	
	Linking words and phrases connect ideas within a category of information	
	Strong concluding statement or section	
	Sentences have clear and complete structure, with appropriate range and variety	
	Knowledge of writing language and conventions shown	
	Any errors in usage do not interfere with meaning	

online resources ↘ Available for download at **resources.corwin.com/thisisbalancedliteracy**

Fifth-grade student Key'ajah uses the single-point writing rubric before submitting her draft research report on the lives of children during the Revolutionary War. As she rereads her draft, she catalogues evidence that she believes she is mastering expectations, as well as items where she needs more work. "I started this [report] last week, and I didn't have a good conclusion then. I worked on that this week," she said, pointing to the single-point rubric she completed last Friday. "Ms. Roberson wrote that I also needed to use more linking words and phrases, so I paid attention to that this week."

Ms. Roberson joined the conversation. "I trade these back and forth with students so they have some direction on what to work on and know where they are already doing really well," said Ms. Roberson. "These rubrics work as a way to be able to show them where they are improving and how to get to the next level. Revisions were always such a chore, because my students would just think I was being mean. You know, 'do it again.'"

At that, Key'ajah laughed. "You're not being mean when you're telling me how to make it better," said the girl.

"What's even better," said Ms. Roberson, "is when you can see with your own eyes that you're making it stronger."

Curriculum-Based Measures of Writing

Students who are receiving Tier 2 and Tier 3 levels of supplemental and intensive interventions require more specialized monitoring of their writing. Periodic analytic writing assessments are a means to closely monitor progress and gauge whether the intervention is having a desired effect. Because this is more time consuming, we do not recommend doing this for the whole class, but rather for those individuals not making desired progress. The process, as described by Gansle, VanDerHeyden, Noell, Resetar, and Williams (2006), begins with giving the student six to ten minutes to respond to a writing prompt. The writing is then analyzed and recorded using the following data (see Figure 9.8 for a recording form):

- Total words written (TWW)

- Average number of words written per minute (AWPM)

- Total words spelled correctly (TWSC)

- Total number of complete sentences (TCS)

- Average length of complete sentences (ALCS)

- Correct punctuation marks (CPM)

- Correct word sequences (CWS)

- Incorrect word sequences (ICWS)

The last two categories, word sequences, require more explanation. A word sequence is composed of two adjacent words in a sentence that are spelled, are capitalized, and make sense (Videen, Deno, & Marston, 1982). A correct sequence is indicated by an upward-facing caret (^), and an incorrect one is marked with a downward-facing caret below the sentence line (ᵥ). Correct sequences are counted for sentences that begin with a reasonable word, and they are also counted at the end when the last word is considered reasonable. Here's an example:

Third-grade student Nico was given six minutes to respond to the following prompt: *What is your favorite way to spend time with your family?*

▼ FIGURE 9.8 ANALYTIC WRITING ANALYSIS TOOL

Student: _____ Grade: _____ Age: _____

Date of Sample: _____ Start Time: _____ End Time: _____

Administered by: _____ Analyzed by: _____

What direction or prompt was given to the student?	
Did the student need encouragement to continue? Explain.	
What are your overall impressions of the writing sample as it relates to content accuracy and adherence to the prompt or direction?	

Please attach the writing sample to this document.

1. Total words written (TWW)   _____
2. Average number of words written per minute (AWPM)   _____
3. Total words spelled correctly (TWSC)   _____
4. Total number of complete sentences (TCS)   _____
5. Average length of complete sentences (ALCS)   _____
6. Correct punctuation marks (CPM)   _____
7. Correct word sequences (CWS)   _____
8. Incorrect word sequences (ICWS)   _____
9. CWS – ICWS =   _____

 Available for download at **resources.corwin.com/thisisbalancedliteracy**

Nico wrote:

> ˆI lik ⌄ to ⌄ goˆ to ˆ ⌄ water ˆ parkˆ. I ⌄ rit ⌄ the ⌄ rits ⌄. ˆI ⌄ lik ⌄ the ˆ tube ⌄ rit⌄.

> ˆMy ˆ sister ⌄ hats ⌄ itˆ. ˆSheˆ got ˆ wetˆ!

An analysis of his writing shows the following:

1. Total words written (TWW): 23

2. Average number of words written per minute (AWPM): 3.8

3. Total words spelled correctly (TWSC): 17

4. Total number of complete sentences (TCS): 5

5. Average length of complete sentences (ALCS): 4.6

6. Correct punctuation marks (CPM): 5/5

7. Correct word sequences (CWS): 14

8. Incorrect word sequences (ICWS): 13

9. CWS − ICWS = 1

The results indicated that Nico, who was new to the school, was a disfluent writer with low output, used punctuation correctly, made significant spelling errors for his age, and did not use any complex sentence structures. Nico received intensive Tier 3 writing support delivered by the reading specialist as well as supplemental reading and writing instruction in small groups with his classroom teacher during his third-grade year. The analytic writing assessments were a way for the educators involved to monitor his progress and gauge his responsiveness to the interventions. Perhaps most important, the analytic writing assessment, which they did monthly, allowed his family to see his improvement. "Writing assessment can be impressionistic, like how neatly it's done, or whether the conventions are present," said Elise Kennedy, the coach. "These series of curriculum-based writing measures have given us a way to measure his progress in very concrete ways."

ASSESSMENTS FOR LEARNING IN ORAL LANGUAGE

Our prime communication modality, regardless of age, is through oral language. From the time we are born, we are hardwired to communicate using speech, facial expressions, body language, and gestures. Oral language development plays a powerful role in learning receptive and expressive written language. As with other literacy domains, assessment of oral language development is of great use in the balanced literacy classroom. However, a challenge is in collecting the data to do so. Checklists are useful for tracking progress in the moment, as when you witness a student telling a joke, asking questions, and furnishing elaborative details. In addition, the availability of recording devices in our smartphones makes it easier than ever to play back more extended oral language examples for analysis.

Oral Language Profile

The classroom offers a rich space for the observation of formal and informal language development.

Formal language generally encompasses academic demands, especially presentations of information, structured group discussions, and academic discourse. Informal language includes social communication and the use of language to build and extend relationships with other people. Both are vital in school. An oral language profile of students might include nonverbal behaviors, such as maintaining eye contact, using appropriate volume for the situation, and taking turns when speaking with others. These skills can be especially useful for primary students.

Michael Newman/PhotoEdit

The classroom offers a rich space for the observation of formal and informal language development.

In addition, the interactions students have with one another in academic settings is important for their learning and for the learning of the other students in the classroom. The increased understanding that collaborative learning is vital has drawn further attention to the need to attend to the quality of the interactions students use in small- and whole-group discussions. A rating scale for observing the use of oral language in group discussions was developed by Butler and Stevens (1997) and has proven to be a convenient way to capture information on behalf of students (see Figure 9.9).

Fourth-grade teacher Keith Gibson meets periodically with his students to examine their contributions during group discussions. Mr. Gibson will film a few minutes of a group working together, and then play it back for the children using the group discussion scale.

"At the beginning of the year, I introduced the scale to them and played excerpts from some video my colleague captured in his own classroom a

▼ FIGURE 9.9 RATING SCALE FOR GROUP DISCUSSIONS

Rating	Descriptor of Quality and Quantity of Information
4	*Very elaborate* comments, opinions, solutions, or replies. Includes category 3 below with greater elaboration of reason, solution (e.g., weighing the alternatives, pro and cons).
3	*Elaborated* comments, opinions, solutions, or replies; i.e., opinions with reason(s), solutions with detail or explanation, generalization with reason(s), comments with details.
2	*Simple* comments, opinions, solutions, or replies; not necessarily a complete sentence. In general, these are remarks or ideas, with no supporting evidence, examples, details, or illustrations.
1	*Irrelevant* comments having nothing or little to do with the discussion or introduced into the discussion without context or explanation; may be complete or incomplete sentences or one or two words.

Source: Butler, F.A., & Stevens. R. (1997). Oral language assessment in the classroom (p. 218). *Theory Into Practice, 36,* 214–219. Used with permission.

few years ago," he said. "He's in another state, so I can be sure we're not looking at video of students they might know."

Mr. Gibson said that he initially used teacher think-alouds to model his own observations and how he associated them with the levels of oral language skills. "Now they can do it on their own," said the teacher. "We get together as a small group, and they only rate themselves, not anyone else in the group." After the students have watched it and rated themselves, he facilitates their discussion of their noticings. "It's really been amazing," said Mr. Gibson. "They're pretty astute. I don't actually have to say too much because they see it for themselves."

Retelling Narrative and Informational Texts

Retellings of text are an excellent measure of reading and listening comprehension. But they can also be used as a means for assessing how a student puts ideas into words. In addition to assessing comprehension, they can provide you with insights about a child's attention, sequencing ability, memory, and oral composition ability.

Younger children can benefit from having a text read to them, thereby lifting the burden of decoding. It is important to say that retelling shouldn't be a memorization task, and students should be encouraged to return to the text to check themselves and organize their recount. There are any number of narrative and informational retelling rubrics available. We feature two in Figures 9.10 and 9.11.

▼ FIGURE 9.10 NARRATIVE STORY RETELLING RUBRIC

Name: _____ Teacher: _____
Title of book: _____
Who read the story?   ❑ Teacher   ❑ Student

	Proficient—3	Adequate—2	Needs Attention—1
Character	Main and supporting characters and their characteristics identified. Examples given to describe characters.	Most main and supporting characters identified. Characteristics are less descriptive.	Characters essential to the story are overlooked. Few or no examples or descriptions of characteristics offered.
Setting	Setting is identified and described in detail using vivid vocabulary.	Setting is identified and description is accurate. Some detail included.	Setting is either not identified or identified incorrectly.
Problem	Central problem of the story is identified. Character motivations or potential solutions included.	Central problem is identified. Character motivations or potential solutions are not included.	Central problem is not identified or is incorrectly identified.
Solution	Solution is identified. Retelling features connections to characteristics of characters. Student relates this to story's moral or theme.	Solution is identified but retelling does not include connection to moral or theme.	Solution is not identified or is incorrectly identified.
Plot	Sequence of story is told in correct order.	Sequence of story is told in nearly correct order, with one or two events out of sequence.	Sequence of story has three or more errors.

Script retelling in the box below, then score quality of the retelling.

	Character: _____
	Setting: _____
	Problem: _____
	Solution: _____
	Plot: _____
	TOTAL: _____

Source: Fisher, D., Frey, N., & Hattie, J. (2017). *Teaching literacy in the visible learning classroom, grades K–5.* Thousand Oaks, CA: Corwin.

 Available for download at **resources.corwin.com/thisisbalancedliteracy**

▼ FIGURE 9.11 INFORMATIONAL TEXT RETELLING RUBRIC

Name: _____ Teacher: _____

Title of book: _____

Who read the story? ❑ Teacher ❑ Student

	Proficient—3	Adequate—2	Needs Attention—1
Main Ideas	Main ideas are identified. Examples are given to illustrate these ideas.	Most main ideas identified. Examples are less descriptive.	Main ideas essential to the text are overlooked. Few or no examples or descriptions of main ideas offered.
Supporting Details	Supporting details are clearly connected to the main ideas.	Supporting details are identified but are not told in association with main ideas.	Few or no supporting details offered.
Sequence	Sequence of retelling is accurate and reflects the order used by the author.	Sequence is similar to order in book, with some instances of "doubling back" during retelling.	Sequence is difficult to discern.
Accuracy	Facts are relayed accurately.	Retelling is mostly accurate, with few errors.	Retelling is inaccurate.
Inferences	Student makes connections within text (e.g., meaning of title, usefulness of information).	Student makes few associations between pieces of information in text.	Student makes no associations within text.

Script retelling in the box below, then score quality of the retelling.

	Main Ideas: _____
	Details: _____
	Sequence: _____
	Accuracy: _____
	Inferences: _____
	TOTAL: _____

Source: Fisher, D., Frey, N., & Hattie, J. (2017). *Teaching literacy in the visible learning classroom, grades K–5.* Thousand Oaks, CA: Corwin.

 Available for download at **resources.corwin.com/thisisbalancedliteracy**

Retellings of text are an excellent measure of reading and listening comprehension.

BobDaemmrich/PhotoEdit

Second-grade teacher Rana Abboud uses retelling rubrics to gauge how her students are comprehending multimodal texts. "It can be so tempting for students to get caught up in the razzle dazzle of videos that feature lots of color, music, and quick edits," said the teacher. "I use these a lot in class, but I also want to make sure they are getting the information contained within." Using the informational text retelling rubric featured in Figure 9.11, Ms. Abboud collects information from individual students. "Obviously I don't want everyone telling me the same information over and over," she smiled. "I appoint a summarizer before we watch the video clip, and then that person knows she or he will be furnishing a complete oral summary to the class. It's a kind of extemporaneous speaking opportunity, too." The teacher noted that she uses three or four video clips a week. "When I think about it, I realize I can collect assessment information on my entire class every month," she said. "It gives me great information to share with them so they can see their growth."

CONCLUSION

We have described a number of ways to balance literacy instruction in your classroom. We noted the value of informational and narrative texts as well as formats for instruction, including direct and dialogic and whole class and small group. In this final chapter, we focused on the powerful role that assessment plays in the balanced literacy classroom. Without data, it's nearly impossible for us to make instructional decisions that result in better learning for students. Some students respond beautifully to our initial instruction; others do not. The assessments we profile allow you to determine which students need additional interventions to reach their goals and become proficient. As we discussed each assessment—and remember that there are many more that we could have profiled—we noted the ways in which a teacher used the tool to make instructional decisions. Ultimately, that's what balance is all about: knowing students' literacy needs well enough to meet them all in the classroom. Yes, it's a balancing act, but one that you can succeed at, and your students will thrive as a result.

REFERENCES

Adams, M. J. (1990). *Beginning to read: Thinking and learning about print.* Cambridge, MA: MIT Press.

Akhavan, N. (2008). *The content–rich reading and writing workshop: A time-saving approach for making the most of your literacy block.* New York: Scholastic.

Akhavan, N. (2018). *The big book of literacy tasks, grades K–8: 75 balanced literacy activities students do (not you!).* Thousand Oaks, CA: Corwin.

Allington, R. L. (1977). If they don't read much, how they ever gonna get good? *Journal of Reading, 21,* 57–6.

Amendum, S. J., Conradi, K., & Hiebert, E. H. (2018). Does text complexity matter in the elementary grades? A research synthesis of text difficulty and elementary students' reading fluency and comprehension. *Educational Psychology Review, 30,* 121–151.

Anderson, R. C., Wilson, P. T., & Fielding, L. G. (1988). Growth in reading and how children spend their time outside of school. *Reading Research Quarterly, 23*(3), 285–303.

Andrews, R., Torgerson, C., Beverton, S., Freeman, A., Locke, T., Low, G.,.. ., & Zhu, D. (2006).The effect of grammar teaching on writing development. *British Educational Research Journal, 32*(1), 39–55.

Avalos, M. A., Plasencia, A., Chavez, C., & Rascón, J. (2007/2008). Modified guided reading: Gateway to English as a second language and literacy learning. *The Reading Teacher, 61,* 318–329.

Balajthy, E. (1987). Keyboarding and the language arts. *The Reading Teacher, 41*(1), 86.

Barack, L. (2005). Kindergarten keyboarding. *School Library Journal, 51*(11), 26.

Bear, D. R., Invernizzi, M., Templeton, S., & Johnston, F. (2011). *Words their way: Word study for phonics, vocabulary, and spelling instruction* (5th ed.). Upper Saddle River, NJ: Pearson.

Beck, I., & McKeown, M. (2001). Text talk: Capturing the benefits of read-aloud experiences for young children. *The Reading Teacher, 55*(1), 10–20.

Benson, V., & Cummins, C. (2000). *The power of retelling: Developmental steps for building comprehension.* Bothell, WA: McGraw-Hill.

Blevins, W. (2000). Lessons: Language arts, playing with sounds. Successful reading and spelling begins with phonemic awareness. *Instructor, 109*(6), 16–17.

Blevins, W. (2017). *A fresh look at phonics: Common causes of failure and 7 ingredients for success.* Thousand Oaks, CA: Corwin.

Boscolo, P., & Gelati, C. (2013). Best practices in promoting motivation for writing. Best practices in writing assessment. In S. Graham, C. MacArthur, & J. Fitzgerald (Eds.), *Best practices in writing instruction* (2nd ed., pp. 202–221). New York: Guilford Press.

Bosman, A. T., & Van Orden, G. C. (1997). Why spelling is more difficult than reading. In C. A. Perfetti & L. Rieben (Eds.), *Learning to spell: Research, theory, and practice across languages* (pp. 173–194). Mahwah, NJ: Lawrence Erlbaum.

Brindle, M., Graham, S., Harris, K. R., & Hebert, M. (2016). Third and fourth grade teachers' classroom practices in writing: A national survey. *Reading & Writing, 29*(5), 929–954.

Britton, J. (1983). Writing and the story of the world. In B. Kroll & E. Wells (Eds.), *Explorations in the development of writing theory, research, and practice* (pp. 3–30). New York: Wiley.

Brown, L. T., Mohr, K. A. J., Wilcox, B. R., & Barrett, T. S. (2018). The effects of dyad reading and text difficulty on third-graders' reading achievement. *The Journal of Educational Research, 111*(5), 541–553.

Butler, F. A., & Stevens. R. (1997). Oral language assessment in the classroom. *Theory Into Practice, 36,* 214–219.

Calfee, R. C., & Miller, R. G. (2013). Best practices in writing assessment. In S. Graham, C. MacArthur, & J. Fitzgerald (Eds.), *Best practices in writing instruction* (2nd ed., pp. 265–286). New York: Guilford Press.

Catts, H. W., Fey, M. E., Zhang, X., & Tomblin, J. B. (2001). Estimating the risk of future reading difficulties in kindergarten children: A research-based model and its clinical implementation. *Language, Speech, and Hearing Services in Schools, 32,* 38–50.

Chall, J. (1983). *Stages of reading development.* New York: McGraw-Hill.

Chall, J. S., & Jacobs, V. A. (1983). Writing and reading in the elementary grades: Developmental trends among low–SES children. *Language Arts, 60*(5), 617–626.

Chard, D. J., & Dickson, S. V. (1999). Phonological awareness: Instructional and assessment guidelines. *Intervention in School and Clinic, 34*(5), 261–270.

Clay, M. (1979). *The early detection of reading difficulties: A diagnostic survey with recovery procedures.* Upper Saddle River, NJ: Pearson.

Clay, M. M. (1991). *Becoming literate: The construction of inner control.* Portsmouth, NH: Heinemann.

Clay, M. M. (2005). *Literacy lessons designed for individuals, part two: Teaching procedures.* Portsmouth, NH: Heinemann.

Clay, M. M. (2013). *An observation survey of early literacy achievement* (3rd ed.). Portsmouth, NH: Heinemann.

Coker, D. (2013). Writing instruction in preschool and kindergarten. In C. A. MacArthur, S. Graham, & J. Fitzgerald (Eds.), *Best practices in writing instruction* (2nd ed., pp. 26–47). New York: Guilford Press.

Cox, C., & Many, J. E. (1992). Stance toward a literary work: Applying the transactional theory to children's responses. *Reading Psychology, 13,* 37–72.

Cratty, D. (2012). Potential for significant reductions in dropout rates: Analysis of an entire 3rd grade state cohort. *Economics of Education Review, 31*(5), 644–662.

Culham, R. (2003). *6+1 traits of writing: The complete guide.* New York: Scholastic.

Cunningham, A. E., & Stanovich, K. E. (1990). Early spelling acquisition: Writing beats the computer. *Journal of Educational Psychology, 82*(1), 159–162.

Cunningham, J. (1982). Generating interactions between schemata and text. In J. A. Niles & L. A. Harris (Eds.), *New inquiries in reading research and instruction* (pp. 42–47). Washington, DC: National Reading Conference.

Curtis, C. P. (1995). *The Watsons go to Birmingham, 1963.* New York: Yearling.

Daane, M. C., Campbell, J. R., Grigg, W. S., Goodman, M. J., & Oranje, A. (2005). *Fourth-grade students reading aloud: NAEP 2002 special study of oral reading* (NCES 2006–469). Washington, DC: U.S. Department of Education, Institute of Education Sciences, National Center for Education Statistics.

Dabrowski, J. (2016). *Checking in update: More assignments from real classrooms.* The Education Trust. Retrieved from https://edtrust.org/wp-content/uploads/2014/09/CheckingInUpdate_Assignments FromRealClassrooms_EdTrust_April2016.pdf

Dahl, R. (1964). *Charlie and the chocolate factory.* New York: Knopf.

Daniels, H. (2002). *Literature circles: Voice and choice in book clubs and reading groups.* York, ME: Stenhouse.

Davis, L. (1998). One hundred words. *TESOL Journal, 7*(6), 39.

De la Peña, M. (2015). *Last stop on Market Street.* New York: G. P. Putnam's Sons.

Duff, D., Tomlin, J. B., & Catts, H. (2015). The influence of reading on vocabulary growth: A case for a Matthew effect. *Journal of Speech/Language, Hearing Research, 58*(3), 853–864.

Duffy, G. G. (2014). *Explaining reading: A resource for teaching concepts, skills, and strategies* (3rd ed.). New York: Guilford Press.

Duke, N. K. (2000). 3.6 minutes per day: The scarcity of informational texts in first grade. *Reading Research Quarterly, 35*(2), 202–224.

Duke, N. K., & Block, M. (2012). Improving reading in the primary grades. *The Future of Children, 22*(2), 55–72.

Duke, N. K., & Pearson, P. D. (2002). Effective practices for developing reading comprehension. In A. E. Farstrup & S. J. Samuels (Eds.), *What research has to say about reading instruction* (pp. 205–242). Newark, DE: International Reading Association.

Easley, D. (2004). Sharing the gift of literacy: How to get your students hooked on books. *Techniques, 79*(8), 36–39.

Eaton, H. A. (1913). Reading poetry aloud. *English Journal, 2*, 151–157.

Education Northwest. (2018). *6+1 Trait Writing rubrics*. Retrieved from https://educationnorthwest.org/traits-rubrics

Education World. (2017). *Teaching keyboarding: More than just typing*. Retrieved May 17, 2019, from https://www.educationworld.com/a_tech/tech/tech072.shtml

Elkonin, D. B. (1963). The psychology of mastery of elements of reading. In B. Simon & J. Simon (Eds.), *Educational psychology in the USSR* (pp. 165–179). London: Routledge & Kegan Paul.

Elley, W. B. (2000). The potential of book floods for raising literary levels. *International Review of Education, 46*(3–4), 233–255.

Ericsson, K. A. (2002). Attaining excellence through deliberate practice: Insights from the study of expert performance. In M. Ferrari (Ed.), *The pursuit of excellence in education* (pp. 21–55). Hillsdale, NJ: Erlbaum.

Fearn, L., & Farnan, N. (2001). *Interactions: Teaching writing and the language arts*. Boston: Allyn & Bacon.

Feng, S., & Powers, K. (2005). The short- and long-term effect of explicit grammar instruction on fifth graders' writing. *Reading Improvement, 42*(2), 67–72.

Fisher, D., Flood, J., Lapp, D., & Frey, N. (2004). Interactive read–alouds: Is there a common set of implementation practices? *The Reading Teacher, 58*(1), 8–17.

Fisher, D., & Frey, N. (2003). Writing instruction for struggling adolescent readers: A gradual release model. *Journal of Adolescent and Adult Literacy, 46*, 396–407.

Fisher, D., & Frey, N. (2007). Implementing a schoolwide literacy framework: Improving achievement in an urban elementary school. *The Reading Teacher, 61*, 32–43.

Fisher, D., & Frey, N. (2008a). *Better learning through structured teaching: A framework for the gradual release of responsibility*. Alexandria, VA: ASCD.

Fisher, D., & Frey, N. (2008b). What does it take to create skilled readers? Facilitating the transfer and application of literacy strategies. *Voices from the Middle, 15*(4), 16–22.

Fisher, D., & Frey, N. (2014a). *Better learning through structured teaching: A framework for the gradual release of responsibility* (2nd ed.). Alexandria, VA: ASCD.

Fisher, D., & Frey, N. (2014b). Closely reading informational texts in the primary grades. *The Reading Teacher, 68*, 222–227.

Fisher, D., Frey, N., Amador, O., & Assof, J. (2018). *Teacher clarity playbook*. Thousand Oaks, CA: Corwin.

Fisher, D., Frey, N., & Hattie, J. (2017). *Teaching literacy in the visible learning classroom, grades K–5*. Thousand Oaks, CA: Corwin.

Fisher, D., Frey, N., & Lapp, D. (2011). Coaching middle-level teachers to think aloud improves comprehension instruction and student reading achievement. *The Teacher Educator, 46*, 231–243.

Fisher, D., Frey, N., & Rothenberg, C. (2011). *Implementing RTI with English learners*. Bloomington, IN: Solution Tree.

Flippo, R. F., Holland, D. D., McCarthy, M. T., & Swinning, E. A. (2009). Asking the right questions: How to select an informal reading inventory. *Reading Teacher, 63*(1), 79–83.

Flower, L. (1990). Studying cognition in context. In L. Flower, V. Stein, J. Ackerman, M. J. Kantz, K. McCormick, & W. C. Peck (Eds.), *Reading-to-write: Exploring a cognitive and social process* (pp. 3–32). New York: Oxford University Press.

Förster, N., & Souvignier, E. (2014). Learning progress assessment and goal setting: Effects on reading achievement, reading motivation and reading self-concept. *Learning & Instruction, 32*, 91–100.

Fountas, I., & Pinnell, G. (2012). Guided reading: The romance and the reality. *The Reading Teacher, 66*(4), 268–284.

Frey, N., & Fisher, D. (2010). Identifying instructional moves during guided learning. *The Reading Teacher, 64*, 84–95.

Frey, N., & Fisher, D. (2011). The first 20 days: Establishing productive group work in the classroom. *ILA E-ssentials*. Newark, DE: International Literacy Association. Retrieved from https://www.literacyworldwide.org/get-resources/ila-e-ssentials/8006

Ganske, K. (1999). The developmental spelling analysis: A measure of orthographic knowledge. *Educational Assessment, 6*(10), 41–70.

Ganske, K. (2000). *Word journeys: Assessment-guided phonics, spelling, and vocabulary instruction*. New York: Guilford Press.

Gansle, K. A., VanDerHeyden, A. M., Noell, G. H., Resetar, J. L., & Williams, K. L. (2006). The technical adequacy of curriculum-based and rating-based measures of written expression for elementary students. *School Psychology Review*, *35*, 435–450.

Gelzheiser, L. M., Scanlon, D., Vellutino, F., Hallgren-Flynn, L., & Schatschneider, C. (2011). Effects of the interactive strategies approach—extended: A responsive and comprehensive intervention for intermediate-grade struggling readers. *Elementary School Journal*, *112*(2), 280–306.

Gill, S. R. (1996). Shared book experience: Using poetry to teach word recognition strategies. *The State of Reading*, *3*(1), 27–30.

Goeke, J. L. (2008). *Explicit instruction: A framework for meaningful direct teaching*. Upper Saddle River, NJ: Pearson.

Graff, G., & Birkenstein, C. (2010). *They say/I say: The moves that matter in academic writing* (2nd ed.). New York: W. W. Norton.

Graham, S. (2006). Strategy instruction and the teaching of writing: A meta-analysis. In C. A. MacArthur, S. Graham, & J. Fitzgerald (Eds.), *Handbook of writing research* (pp. 187–207). New York: Guilford Press.

Graham, S., Berninger, V., Abbott, R., Abbott, S., & Whitaker, D. (1997). The role of mechanics in composing of elementary school students: A new methodological approach. *Journal of Educational Psychology*, *89*(1), 170–182.

Graham, S., Harris, K., & Hebert, M. (2011). *Improving writing: The benefits of formative assessment, A report from Carnegie Corporation of New York*. Retrieved from https://www.carnegie.org/media/filer_public/37/b8/37b87202–7138–4ff9–90c0–cd6c6f2335bf/ccny_report_2011_informing.pdf

Graham, S., & Hebert, M. (2010). *Writing to read: Evidence of how writing can improve reading*. Washington, DC: Alliance for Excellent Education.

Graham, S., Liu, X., Aitken, A., Ng, C., Bartlett, B., Harris, K., & Holzapfel, J. (2018). Effectiveness of literacy programs balancing reading and writing instruction: A meta-analysis. *Reading Research Quarterly*, *53*(3), 279–304.

Graves, M. F., & Fitzgerald, J. (2003). Scaffolding reading experiences for multilingual classrooms. In G. G. García (Ed.), *English learners: Reaching the highest level of English literacy* (pp. 96–124). Newark, DE: International Reading Association.

Guthrie, J. T., Hoa, A. L. W., Wigfield, A., Tonks, S. M., Humenick, N. M., & Littles, E. (2007). Reading motivation and reading comprehension growth in the later elementary years. *Contemporary Educational Psychology*, *32*(3), 282–313.

Guthrie, J. T., Wigfield, A., & Barbosa, P. (2004). Increasing reading comprehension and engagement through concept-oriented reading instruction. *Journal of Educational Psychology*, *96*(3), 403–423.

Harvey, V. S., & Chickie-Wolf, L. A. (2007). *Fostering independent learning: Practical strategies to promote student success*. New York: Guilford Press.

Hattie, J. (2012). *Visible learning for teachers: Maximizing impact on learning*. New York: Routledge.

Hattie, J. (2018). *Visible Learning Plus: 250+ influences on student achievement*. Retrieved from https://www.visiblelearningplus.com/content/research-john-hattie

Heckelman, R. G. (1969). A neurological-impress method of remedial-reading instruction. *Academic Therapy*, *4*, 277–282.

Henderson, E. H. (1990). *Teaching spelling* (2nd ed.). Boston: Houghton Mifflin.

Hiebert, E. H. (1994). Becoming literate through authentic tasks: Evidence and adaptations. In R. B. Ruddell, M. R. Ruddell, & H. Singer (Eds.), *Theoretical models and processes of reading* (4th ed., pp. 391–413). Newark, DE: International Reading Association.

Holmes, K. P. (2003). Show, don't tell: The importance of explicit prewriting instruction. *Clearing House*, *76*(5), 241–243.

Honig, W. (1996). *Teaching our children to read: The role of skills in a comprehensive reading program*. Thousand Oaks, CA: Corwin.

Hudson, A. (2016). Get them talking! Using student-led book talks in the primary grades. *The Reading Teacher*, *70*(2), 221–225.

Hughes, J., Cao, Q. C., West, S., Allee Smith, P., & Cerda, C. (2017). Effect of retention in elementary grades on dropping out of school early. *Journal of School Psychology, 65*, 11–27.

International Reading Association. (2000). *Providing books and other print materials for classroom and school libraries: A position statement of the International Reading Association.* Newark, DE: Author. Retrieved from https://www.literacyworldwide.org/docs/default–source/where–we–stand/providing–books–position–statement.pdf?sfvrsn=e44ea18e_6

Jago, C. (2002). *Cohesive writing: Why concept is not enough.* Portsmouth, NH: Heinemann.

Jenkins, S. (2002). *The top of the world: Climbing Mount Everest.* New York: HMH Books for Young Readers.

Jiyeon Lee, l., & So Yoon, Y. (2017). The effects of repeated reading on reading fluency for students with reading disabilities: A meta-analysis. *Journal of Learning Disabilities, 50*(2), 213–224.

Johnson, D. W., Johnson, R. T., & Holubec, E. J. (2008). *Cooperation in the classroom* (8th ed.). Edina, MN: Interaction.

Justice, L. M., Pence, K., & Bowles, R. B. (2006). An investigation of four hypotheses concerning the order by which 4-year-old children learn the alphabet letters. *Early Childhood Research Quarterly, 21*(3), 374–389.

Justice, L., Sofka, L., & Sofka, A. E. (2010). *Engaging children with print: Building early literacy skills through quality read-alouds.* New York: Guilford Press.

Kalman, B. (2000). *How and why do animals adapt.* New York: Crabtree.

Kasper-Ferguson, S., & Moxley, R. (2002). Developing a writing package with student graphing of fluency. *Education and Treatment of Children,* 25, 249–267.

Klein, P. D., Arcon, N., & Baker, S. (2017). Writing to learn. In C. A. MacArthur, S. Graham, & J. Fitzgerald (Eds.), *Handbook of writing research* (2nd ed., 243–256). New York: Guilford Press.

Kuhn, M. E., Schwanenflugel, P. J., & Meisinger, E. B. (2006). Aligning theory and assessment of reading fluency: Automaticity, prosody and definitions of fluency. *Reading Research Quarterly, 45*(2), 230–251.

Kuhn, M. R. (2005). A comparative study of small group fluency instruction. *Reading Psychology, 26*(2), 127–146.

LaBerge, D., & Samuels, S. J. (1974). Toward a theory of automatic information processing in reading. *Cognitive Psychology, 6*(2), 293–323.

Lamarche, J. (2000). *The raft.* New York: HarperCollins.

Langer, J. A., & Nicolich, M. (1981). Prior knowledge and its relationship to comprehension. *Journal of Reading Behavior, 13*(4), 373–79.

Lapp, D., Fisher, D., & Johnson, K. (2010). Text mapping plus: Improving comprehension through supported retellings. *Journal of Adolescent and Adult Literacy, 53*(5), 423–426.

Lassonade, C. A., & Richards, J. C. (2013). *Writing strategies for all primary students: Scaffolding independent writing with differentiated minilessons, grades K–3.* San Francisco: Jossey-Bass.

Leal, D., & Moss, B. (1999). Encounters with information text: Perceptions and insights from four gifted readers. *Reading Horizons, 40*(2), 81–101.

Lee, I. (2009). Ten mismatches between teachers' beliefs and written feedback practice. *ELT Journal, 63*(1), 13–22.

Lewison, W. C. (2002). *F is for flag.* New York: Grosset & Dunlap.

Limpo, T., Alves, R. A., & Fidalgo, R. (2014). Children's high-level writing skills: Development of planning and revising and their contribution to writing quality. *British Journal of Educational Psychology, 84*(2), 177–193.

Llewellyn, C. (2002). *Earthworms.* New York: Franklin Watts.

Lupo, S. M., Strong, J. Z., & Smith, K. C. (2019). Struggle is not a bad word: Misconceptions and recommendations about readers struggling with difficult texts. *Journal of Adolescent & Adult Literacy, 62*, 551–560.

MacArthur, C. A., Graham, S., & Harris, K. R. (2004). Insights from instructional research on revision with struggling writers. In L. Allal, L. Chanquoy, & P. Largy (Eds.), *Revision: Cognitive and instructional processes* (pp. 125–137). Amsterdam, the Netherlands: Kluwer.

MacLachlan, P. (1985). *Sarah, plain and tall.* New York, NY: HarperCollins.

Manzo, A. (1969). The ReQuest procedure. *Journal of Reading, 13*, 123–127.

Marchand-Martella, N. E., Slocum, T. A., & Martella, R. C. (Eds.). (2004). *Introduction to direct instruction.* Boston: Allyn & Bacon.

Marinak, B. A., & Gambrell, L. B. (2016). *No more reading for junk: Best practices for motivating readers.* Portsmouth, NH: Heinemann.

Marshall, J. (1986). *Wings: A tale of two chickens.* New York: Puffin.

Martinez, M., Roser, N., & Strecker, S. (1998). "I never thought I could be a star": A readers theatre ticket to fluency. *Reading Teacher, 52*(4), 326–334.

Matthews, M. W., & Kesner, J. (2003). Children learning with peers: The confluence of peer status and literacy competence within small-group literacy events. *Reading Research Quarterly, 38,* 208–234.

Mattick, L. (2015). *Finding Winnie: The true story of the world's most famous bear.* New York: Little, Brown.

McCarrier, A., Pinnell, G. S., & Fountas, I. C. (2000). *Interactive writing: How language and literacy come together, K–2.* Portsmouth, NH: Heinemann.

Medina, M. (2018). *Merci Suárez changes gears.* Somerville, MA: Candlewick.

Mesmer, H. A. E., & Griffith, P. L. (2005). Everybody's selling it—But just what is explicit, systematic phonics instruction? *The Reading Teacher, 59,* 366–376.

Michaels, S., O'Connor, C., & Resnick, L. B. (2008). Deliberative discourse idealized and realized: Accountable talk in the classroom and in civic life. *Studies in Philosophy and Education, 27*(4), 283–297.

Millay, E. (1917). Afternoon on a hill. In Milford, N. (Ed.). (2001). *The selected poetry of Edna St. Vincent Millay.* New York: Modern Library.

Moebius, W. (1986). Introduction to picturebook codes. *Word and Image: A Journal of Verbal/Visual Enquiry, 2*(2), 141–158.

Munsch, R. (1980). *The paper bag princess.* Buffalo, NY: Annick.

Munson, (2000). *Enemy pie.* San Francisco, CA: Chronicle.

Murray, J. (2018). *Technology in the classroom: Keyboarding 101.* Retrieved from http://www.teachhub.com/technology–classroom–keyboarding–101

Nagy, W. E., Anderson, R. C., & Herman, P. A. (1985). Learning words from context. *Reading Research Quarterly, 20*(2), 233–253.

Nagy, W. E., Anderson, R. C., & Herman, P. A. (1987). Learning word meanings from context during normal reading. *American Educational Research Journal, 24*(7), 237–270.

National Writing Project & Nagin, C. (2003). *Because writing matters: Improving student writing in our schools.* San Francisco: Jossey-Bass.

Neuman, S. (2017). The information book flood: Is additional exposure enough to support early literacy development? *The Elementary School Journal, 118*(1), 1–27.

Novak, B. J. (2015). *The book with no pictures.* New York: Penguin.

Oliver, E. (1995). The writing quality of seventh, ninth, and eleventh graders, and college freshmen: Does rhetorical specification in writing prompts make a difference? *Research in the Teaching of English, 29*(4), 422–450.

Osborne, W., & Osborne, M. P. (2005). *Sleeping Bobby.* New York: Atheneum.

Ouellette, G., & Beers, A. (2010). A not-so-simple view of reading: How oral vocabulary and visual-word recognition complicate the story. *Reading & Writing Quarterly: An Interdisciplinary Journal, 23,* 189–208.

Pak, S. S., & Weseley, A. J. (2012). The effect of mandatory reading logs on children's motivation to read. *Journal of Research in Education, 22*(1), 251–265.

Palincsar, A. S., & Brown, A. L. (1984). Reciprocal teaching of comprehension–fostering and comprehension–monitoring activities. *Cognition and Instruction, 1*(1), 117–175.

Paris, S. G. (2005). Reinterpreting the development of reading skills. *Reading Research Quarterly, 40*(2), 184–202.

Pearson, P. D., & Gallagher, G. (1983). The gradual release of responsibility model of instruction. *Contemporary Educational Psychology, 8,* 112–123.

Perenfein, D., & Morris, B. (2004). *Literature circles: The way to go and how to get there.* Westminster, CA: Teacher Created Resources.

Perfetti, C. A. (1997). The psycholinguistics of spelling and reading. In C. A. Perfetti & L. Rieben (Eds.), *Learning to spell: Research, theory, and practice across languages* (pp. 21–38). Mahwah, NJ: Lawrence Erlbaum.

Piazza, C., & Siebert, C. F. (2008). Development and validation of a writing dispositions scale for elementary and middle school students. *Journal of Educational Research, 101*(5), 275–286.

Porath, S. (2014). Talk less, listen more. *The Reading Teacher, 67*(8), 627–635.

Purcell, J. J., Turkeltaub, P. E., Eden, G. F., & Rapp. B. (2011). Examining the central and peripheral processes of written word production through meta-analysis. *Frontiers in Psychology, 2*, 239–245.

Raphael, T. E. (1982). Teaching children question-answering strategies. *The Reading Teacher, 36*, 186–191.

Raphael, T. E., & Au, K. H. (2005). QAR: Enhancing comprehension and test taking across grades and content areas. *The Reading Teacher, 59*(3), 206–221.

Rapp, B., & Lipka, K. (2011). The literate brain: The relationship between spelling and reading. *Journal of Cognitive Neurosciences, 23*(5), 1180–1197.

Rasinski, T. (2005a). *Daily word ladders 2–4*. New York: Scholastic.

Rasinski, T. (2005b). *Daily word ladders 4–6*. New York: Scholastic.

Rasinski, T. (2008). *Daily word ladders 1–2*. New York: Scholastic.

Rasinski, T. (2012). *Daily word ladders K–1*. New York: Scholastic.

Rasinski, T., & Padak, N. (2013). Fluency at the core of effective reading instruction. In T. Rasinski & N. Padak (Eds.), *From fluency to comprehension: Powerful instruction through authentic reading* (pp. 1–8). New York: Guilford Press.

Raskin, E. (1978). *The westing game*. New York: Puffin.

Rawls, W. (1961). *Where the red fern grows*. Garden City, NY: Doubleday.

Read, C. (1975). *Children's categorization of speech sounds in English*. Urbana, IL: National Council of Teachers of English.

Reagan, J. (2012). *How to babysit a grandpa*. New York, NY: Alfred A. Knopf.

Rodgers, E. (2017). Scaffolding word solving while reading: New research insights. *Reading Teacher, 70*(5), 525–532.

Rodgers, E., D'Agostino, J. V., Harmey, S. J., Kelly, R. H., & Brownfield, K. (2016). Examining the nature of scaffolding in an early literacy intervention. *Reading Research Quarterly, 57*(3), 345–360.

Rosenshine, B. (2008). *Five meanings of direct instruction*. Lincoln, IL: Center on Innovation & Improvement. Retrieved from http://www.centerii.org/search/Resources%5CFiveDirectInstruct.pdf

Roth, K., & Dabrowski, J. (2014). Extending interactive writing into grades 2–5. *The Reading Teacher, 68*(1), 33–44.

Rowling, J. K. (1997). *Harry Potter and the sorcerer's stone*. New York: Scholastic.

Rumelhart, D. E. (1980). *Schemata: The building blocks of cognition*. Hillsdale, NJ: Erlbaum.

Santa, C., & Havens, L. (1995). *Creating independence through student-owned strategies: Project CRISS*. Dubuque, IA: Kendall-Hunt.

Santangelo, T., & Graham, S. (2016). A comprehensive meta-analysis of handwriting instruction. *Educational Psychology Review, 28*(2), 225–265.

Saperstein Associates. (2012). *Handwriting in the 21st century? Research shows why handwriting belongs in today's classroom*. Retrieved from https://www.hw21summit.com/media/zb/hw21/files/H2948_HW_Summit_White_Paper_eVersion.pdf

Sapon-Shevin, M. (1998). *Because we can change the world: A practical guide to building cooperative, inclusive classroom communities*. Boston: Allyn & Bacon.

Scholastic. (2010). *What's the weather?* New York: Author.

Schunk, D. H., Meece, J. R., & Pintrich, P. R. (2013). *Motivation in education: Theory, research, and applications* (4th ed.). Boston: Pearson.

Scriven, M. (1991). *Evaluation thesaurus* (4th ed.). Thousand Oaks, CA: Sage.

Shanahan, T. (1977). Writing marathons and concept development. *Language Arts, 54*, 403–405.

Shanahan, T. (2019, February 9). Which texts for teaching reading: Decodable, predictable, or controlled vocabulary? [Blog post]. https://shanahanonliteracy.com/blog/which–texts–for–teaching–reading–decodable–predictable–or–controlled–vocabulary

Shanahan, T., Fisher, D., & Frey, N. (2012). The challenge of challenging text. *Educational Leadership, 69*(6), 58–63.

Sheets, W. (2013). *Developmental spelling stages* (handout for 2014 National Reading Recovery & K–6 Classroom Literacy Conference). Columbus: Literacy Collaborative, The Ohio State University.

Simmons, J. (2003). Responders are taught, not born. *Journal of Adolescent and Adult Literacy, 46*(8), 684–693.

Smith, J. (2004). *Bone: The complete cartoon epic in one volume.* Columbus, Ohio: Cartoon Books.

Spandel, V. (2005). *Creating writers through 6 trait writing: Assessment and instruction* (4th ed.). Upper Saddle River, NJ: Pearson.

Spandel, V. (2012). *Creating writers: 6 traits, process, workshop, and literature* (6th ed.). Upper Saddle River, NJ: Pearson.

Swick, K. J. (2009). Promoting school and life success through early childhood family literacy. *Early Childhood Education Journal, 36*(5), 403–406.

Tarchi, C. (2015). Fostering reading comprehension of expository texts through the activation of readers' prior knowledge and inference–making skills. *International Journal of Educational Research, 72*, 80–88.

Templeton, S. (2011). Teaching spelling in the English/language arts classroom. In D. Lapp & D. Fisher (Eds.), *Handbook of research on teaching the English language arts* (3rd ed., pp. 247–251). Mahwah, NJ: Lawrence Erlbaum.

Thomas, S. M. (1998). *Somewhere today: A book of peace.* New York: Albert.

Troia, G. A. (2013). Effective writing instruction in the 21st century. In B. M. Taylor & N. K. Duke (Eds.), *Handbook of effective literacy instruction: Research-based practices K–8* (pp. 298–345). New York: Guilford Press.

Truss, L. (2004). *Eats, shoots and leaves.* New York: Gotham.

Vellutino, F. R., Scanlon, D. M., Zhang, H., & Schatschneider, C. (2008). Using response to kindergarten and first grade intervention to identify children at-risk for long-term reading difficulties. *Reading & Writing, 21*(4), 437–480.

Videen, J., Deno, S. L., & Marston, D. (1982). *Correct word sequences: A valid indicator of proficiency in written expression* (Research Report No. 84). Minneapolis: University of Minnesota, Institute for Research on Learning Disabilities.

Vygotsky, L. S. (1978). *Mind in society.* Cambridge, MA: Harvard University Press.

Walpole, S., & McKenna, M. (2006). The role of informal reading inventories in assessing word recognition. *Reading Teacher, 59*(6), 592–594.

Wollenschläger, M., Hattie, J., Machts, N., Möller, J., & Harms, U. (2016). What makes rubrics effective in teacher-feedback? Transparency of learning goals is not enough. *Contemporary Educational Psychology, 44*, 1–11.

Wood, D. J., Bruner, J. S., & Ross, G. (1976). The role of tutoring in problem solving. *Journal of Child Psychiatry and Psychology, 17*(2), 89–100.

Wozniak, C. L. (2011). Reading and talking about books: A critical foundation for intervention. *Voices From the Middle, 19*(2), 17–21.

Wulffson, D. L. (2000). *Toys: Amazing stories behind some great inventions.* New York: Macmillan.

Yopp, H. K. (1995). A test for assessing phonemic awareness in young children. *The Reading Teacher, 49*, 20–29.

INDEX

CORWIN Fisher & Frey

" Every student deserves a great teacher, not by chance, but by design. "

Read more from Fisher & Frey

DOUGLAS FISHER, NANCY FREY, OLIVIA AMADOR, JOSEPH ASSOF

With crosscurricular examples, planning templates, professional learning questions, and a PLC guide, this is the most practical planner for designing and delivering highly effective instruction.

DOUGLAS FISHER, NANCY FREY, RUSSELL J. QUAGLIA, DOMINIQUE SMITH, LISA L. LANDE

Engagement by Design puts you in control of managing your classroom's success and increasing student learning, one motivated student at a time.

DOUGLAS FISHER, NANCY FREY, DIANE LAPP

In this edition of the best-selling *Text Complexity,* the renowned author team lays open the instructional routines that take students to new places as readers.

DOUGLAS FISHER, NANCY FREY

Nancy Frey and Douglas Fisher articulate an instructional plan for close reading so clearly, and so squarely built on research, that it's the only resource a teacher will need.

DOUGLAS FISHER, NANCY FREY

Newly revised and updated throughout, this new Texas Edition has been specially developed to align with the Texas Essential Knowledge and Skills standards.

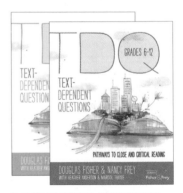

DOUGLAS FISHER, NANCY FREY, HEATHER ANDERSON, MARISOL THAYRE

The authors break down the process into four cognitive pathways that help teachers "organize the journey through a text" and frame an extended discussion around it.

To order your copies, visit corwin.com/FisherandFrey

A SAGE Publishing Company

Helping educators make the greatest impact

CORWIN HAS ONE MISSION: to enhance education through intentional professional learning.

We build long-term relationships with our authors, educators, clients, and associations who partner with us to develop and continuously improve the best evidence-based practices that establish and support lifelong learning.